# CIVIL LITIGATION.

by

## DELMAR KARLEN

*Tazewell Taylor Professor of Law*
*Marshall-Wythe School of Law*
*College of William and Mary*

THE BOBBS-MERRILL COMPANY, INC.
PUBLISHERS
INDIANAPOLIS • NEW YORK • CHARLOTTESVILLE, VIRGINIA

# PREFACE

This book bears a family resemblance to my Primer of Procedure published in 1950. Parts I and III cover the same ground as did the Primer, but in greater detail, supported by references (the Primer had none). Parts II and IV are wholly new.

While intended primarily for students in their first year or two of law school, it is my hope that the book will prove equally helpful to those embarking on careers as paraprofessionals. They are a new and welcome group in the legal fraternity. Their role is discussed briefly in Chapter 15.

My colleague, Professor Doug Rendleman of the Marshall-Wythe School of Law of the College of William and Mary, was kind enough to read the manuscript and make many valuable suggestions for its improvement. I am most grateful to him. I should also like to acknowledge with thanks the research help of Ms. Susan Gamble and Ms. Jane Kelly, both students at the University of Florida Law School and Ms. Linda Groome, Mr. James Cox and Mr. Kevin Huennekens, all students at Marshall-Wythe. Finally, my gratitude is due Mrs. Betty Abele of Marshall-Wythe for typing and retyping the "final" manuscript and then typing it again once or twice.

DELMAR KARLEN

Williamsburg, Virginia
September 1977

iii

# SUMMARY TABLE OF CONTENTS

# TABLE OF CONTENTS

TABLE OF CONTENTS

TABLE OF CONTENTS

# INTRODUCTION

Most of the time of a student embarking on the study of law is spent in reading the opinions of appellate courts. At the outset, however, he or she* probably does not know what an appellate court is or how it differs from any other kind of court; and probably does not have a very clear idea of what an opinion is, what its place in a lawsuit is, or what has preceded or will follow it. It is the purpose of this book to explain matters such as these as simply as possible.

Many beginners have a hard time understanding the process of litigation and consider procedure (another name for the process) dull. After they have been in practice a few years, they discover that their interest in the subject is growing, and that it commands the continuing attention of judges and lawyers. This is "lawyer's law" in which lawyers have a special concern, and in which all of them are expected to have a minimum competency. In other fields of law, laymen can talk on equal or almost equal terms with lawyers—the sociologist in the area of criminal law, the accountant in taxation, the politician in constitutional law, the businessman in contracts, leases and creditors' rights. The same is not true of procedure. The only persons expected to know anything about this field are lawyers, judges, and members of the emerging new paralegal profession, who increasingly are being called upon to perform some of the functions formerly performed only by licensed lawyers.

Why do beginning students of law and practitioners have different attitudes toward procedure? The chief reason probably is that the information about procedure that is traditionally presented to the beginner has little relation to his existing knowledge. Just as a piece of news about nuclear fission may be exciting to a physicist but unintelligible to a layman, so information about a branch of law may be in-

---

* Hereafter, solely to avoid awkward terminology and sentence structure, "he" will be used to include "she." This implies no disrespect toward women judges, lawyers, students, administrators, or litigants.

teresting or dull according to the previous experience and knowledge of the person to whom it is conveyed. This soil must be prepared to receive the seed; new knowledge must find some contact with old.

For most law subjects, beginners have enough background to make them receptive to the material they study. Who has not seen, or perhaps been involved in, an auto accident or a fist fight? Who has never made a promise or broken one? Who has never owned or sold or leased or bought or found or possessed property? Merely by reason of having grown to adulthood, the person entering upon the study of law has amassed enough knowledge to make him curious to learn more about such subjects as torts, contracts and property.

On the other hand, few beginning students of the law have enough acquaintance with life in or near the courthouse to make them curious to learn about jurisdiction, pleading, discovery, evidence, or trial or appellate practice. For most people, such knowledge as they have is likely to be fictionalized and distorted by television shows and mystery stories. A taste for understanding how courts really work has to be acquired.

Bearing in mind the beginner's problems, this book tries to get at the causes of them by looking at a lawsuit as a whole and in context.

Part I analyzes step-by-step in chronological order the most common and least difficult type of civil case—where a single plaintiff is suing a single defendant, both being residents of the same state, on a single claim based upon state law asserted in a local state court.

Part II delves into more complex litigation, where difficult problems are presented because of the dual system of state and federal courts or because of the presence of multiple parties or multiple claims.

The procedure described in both Parts I and II is based upon the Federal Rules of Civil Procedure. These apply of their own force only in federal courts, but they have been widely copied in the states. Although some states depart from the federal pattern, the departures are not so fundamental as to diminish the value of studying the federal rules for those intending to practice in states where divergent rules apply. If students understand the Federal Rules, they will have mastered the main concepts of procedure, so that they can readily grasp local variations and exceptions (the more important of which are noted in the text) and fit them into their proper places.

Part III sketches the background of modern procedure. This material, covering the forms of action at common law, the development of equity and the merger of law and equity, is directed toward an understanding of modern problems in the present court system.

Part IV deals with litigation in context, indicating what courts can and cannot do in relation to other institutions designed to prevent or resolve conflicts, and considering the personnel involved in the administration of justice.

The main purpose of the book has been sufficiently indicated. A subsidiary purpose, however, should be noted. That is to dispel the erroneous notion that procedure and substance are quite distinct, neither having much relation to the other. The fact is that these two great subdivisions of the law are but different sides of a single coin. There never was and never will be a case involving only substantive law or one involving only procedural law. Every case involves both, and both are equally vital. Rights and duties—the subject matter of substantive law—have little practical significance except insofar as there exist means for realizing and enforcing them—the subject matter of procedural law. The reason for distinguishing between substantive law and procedure, and for that matter between subdivisions of these subdivisions, is only to help in analyzing, clarifying and learning about the problems that confront lawyers and judges.

# Part I

# ANALYSIS OF A BASIC LAWSUIT

---

## Chapter 1

## THE SUMMONS

A law suit is officially launched by issuance of a summons. Many events have preceded this step, but we shall touch them here only briefly. First, the raw facts have happened—one person has injured or annoyed another, as by reneging on a contract, trespassing on property, negligently causing an automobile accident or the like. Second, the aggrieved person has consulted a lawyer and recounted his version of what happened. The lawyer, either on the basis of his existing knowledge or a study of the law books, has ascertained what rights his client has, how they may be enforced, and what the probabilities of success are; and he has drafted a complaint (to be considered in the next chapter) outlining his client's grievance. Finally, efforts toward amicable adjustment out of court, involving correspondence and talks of settlement, probably have been made. They have not succeeded, which is why a lawsuit becomes necessary.[1] "Self-help"—by way of beating up the other person or taking his property, or even one's own if it happens to be in his possession—is prohibited except in very special and unusual circumstances.

What is the summons? How is it issued and served? What function does it perform?

### The Document and What It Means

The summons is a brief document which, upon being delivered to the defendant, notifies him that suit has been started and in what court. It contains at the top the name of the court in which the action is brought; then in a box on the left hand side, the name of the person suing, who is called the "plaintiff," and the name of the person being sued, who is called the "defendant"; and finally language indicating that the next step is up to the defendant if he wishes to contest the action. Here is what it looks like:[2]

............ Court of the State of ............;

............ County

Civil Action, File Number ......

A.B., Plaintiff ⎫
      v.     ⎬   Summons
C.D., Defendant ⎭

To the above-named Defendant:

You are hereby summoned and required to serve upon ........., plaintiff's attorney, whose address is .........., an answer to the complaint which is herewith served upon you, within 20 days after service of this summons upon you, exclusive of the day of service. If you fail to do so, judgment by default will be taken against you for the relief demanded in the complaint.

........................
               Clerk of Court

[Seal of the Court]

Dated ............

The form of the summons is fixed, being the same no matter what kind of a law suit is being prosecuted, whether assault and battery or breach of contract or whatnot.

In states that follow the federal pattern of procedure, the summons is issued by the clerk of the court where the action is brought. But his role is purely clerical; he cannot refuse if a complaint (to be considered in the next chapter) has been filed, and this step normally is taken by a private lawyer acting for the plaintiff. Any individual is privileged to sue or defend "pro se"—that is, for himself,[3] but most litigants who have substantial money or property at stake retain professional help.[4] A prospective litigant cannot go to court and ask the judge or clerk to begin proceedings. He either fends

2

for himself or hires a private lawyer. That lawyer is authorized by law to start a suit without obtaining permission or clearance from any official. Indeed in some states, including New York, the private lawyer himself is authorized to issue the summons. Once the summons has been issued and handed to the defendant,[5] the lawsuit is on its way. Should the defendant disregard it, he will find the judicial machinery of the state, supported by the executive branch of the government, ordinarily personified in the sheriff, arrayed against him, ready to enter judgment and take his property in payment.

The role of the plaintiff's lawyer is only suggested, rather than spelled out, in the language of the summons. Also implicit is the role of the defendant's lawyer. The defendant is called upon to serve an "answer" within 20 days if he wishes to defend the case. This is a formal document, and as we shall see in Chapter 3, its preparation involves legal work, including an analysis of the plaintiff's complaint, a study of the facts and an examination of the applicable law, both substantive and procedural.

Thus we encounter for the first but not the last time, a fundamental characteristic of Anglo-American procedure: that private lawyers occupy as important a position as judges and other officials in the administration of justice. Without private lawyers, our system would be unworkable. They determine what cases are to be brought to court, what issues are to be determined, what facts are to be produced, and to a very large extent, what law will be called to the attention of the judges and hence applied. There are few rights a client has that cannot be waived or lost by his lawyer. And whether it is thought desirable or not, the analogy which compares a judge to a referee at a sporting contest is not far from the truth. Indeed, the analogy overstates the judge's role. Unlike the football referee who is present when the action he judges takes place and who actively watches for infractions of the rules of the game and makes rulings on them immediately, the judge rarely can or will act on his own initiative. He is not present to observe the events to be judged. Normally, he acts only when one of the parties (ordinarily acting through his lawyer) asks him to do so.

Ours is an "adversary," as distinguished from an "inquisitorial," system of procedure. Courts have no resources for independently inquiring into the facts underlying the disputes presented to them, and very limited resources even for independently investigating the applicable law. They rely upon the parties, acting through their lawyers, to conduct the necessary investigations and present their conflicting versions of the facts and the law for decision. Out of this clash of self-interest we assume that the truth will emerge and justice will be done. The assumption turns out to be at odds with reality when one party is represented by counsel and the other party is not, or when counsel for one side is highly competent and counsel for the other side is incompetent. Nevertheless, we proceed on that assumption, attempting meanwhile to make it realistic by providing, so far as possible, high quality legal representation for all litigants (see Chapter 15).

## The Problem of Jurisdiction

Not only does the plaintiff's lawyer determine whether and when a lawsuit shall be brought; he also determines the court in which it shall be prosecuted. Often he has a choice, as between different courts operating under the authority of the state, or as between a state court and a federal court. No official guides him in making the decision. He makes it on the basis of his knowledge of the powers of the various courts and his views as to the strategical advantages of proceeding in one rather than another. His minimum task is to pick a court which has "jurisdiction"—the power to decide.

Jurisdiction is made up of two elements: (1) power to handle the type of case brought (sometimes called "jurisdiction over the subject matter"); and (2) power over the defendant ("jurisdiction over the person").

### Jurisdiction over Subject Matter

To understand jurisdiction over the subject matter, it is necessary to have a picture of the courts. Each state, by

4

constitutional or statutory provisions or both, divides its judicial power among several courts. The resulting structure roughly resembles a pyramid.

At the bottom of the pyramid are a large number of courts of limited authority, empowered to try civil cases involving small sums of money, such as bill collections and (though not of concern in this book) minor criminal cases carrying light penalties, such as traffic offenses. In rural areas, the judges are sometimes part-time officials without formal legal training.[6] In urban areas, they are usually full-time professionals. In both rural "justice of the peace" courts, as they are commonly called, and in urban "municipal" or "county" courts, as many of them are called, the procedure is so informal, the interests at stake so small and the number of contests so few that many litigants handle their own cases without the help of lawyers. For this reason, the operations of such courts are not described in detail in this volume.

Above these so-called "inferior"[7] courts are trial courts of more ample jurisdiction, empowered to handle larger civil cases involving substantial sums of money or substantial property interests. These are the focus of discussion in most of Part I of this book. In order to distinguish them from appellate tribunals, they are sometimes called "lower" courts, but they are better described as "trial" courts or courts of "first instance" or courts of "original jurisdiction." Here cases are initiated, juries sit, witnesses are heard and trials are conducted. Such courts are far fewer in number than the courts below them, not being found in every town, village and city. Usually they are organized on a single county or multi-county basis. In a metropolitan area, several judges may serve on a single court for a single county; in a less densely populated area, a single judge may serve several adjoining counties, travelling between them "on circuit." This explains the name "circuit court," used in many states. Other names, however, are not uncommon: "Superior" Court, for example in California and New Jersey; "District" or "County" court in other states; and, most confusingly, "Supreme" court in New York. In some states, the kind of court under discussion, whatever its name, is empowered to handle all types of major cases—civil, criminal, matrimonial, juvenile and so forth.[8] If so, it is properly described as a court of general jurisdiction. In other states, jurisdiction is fragmented among several coordinate courts, one handling civil cases, another criminal cases, another cases involving the administration of estates, etc.[9] Usually the one handling larger civil cases is colloquially, though inaccurately, described as the court of general jurisdiction.

At the top of the judicial pyramid in every state is a single appellate court, usually called the "Supreme Court," but sometimes the "Court of Appeals" or some other name. Several judges compose the court, not a single judge as in a trial court. They do not preside over juries, hear evidence or "try" cases. Their function is to review the proceedings that took place in lower courts to see whether errors occurred of such nature as to require a new trial or reversal or modification of the judgment rendered below. In the more populous states, where the volume of trials is too great to allow review by a single tribunal, there are "intermediate" appellate courts sandwiched in between the highest court and the trial courts. We are not immediately concerned with appellate events, intermediate or final. Their nature and functions will be described in Chapter 7.

In addition to state courts, there are federal courts, but discussion of them will be postponed to Part II of this volume. For the present, we are concerned with the "basic" lawsuit, uncomplicated by nonresident parties or the law of other jurisdictions, state or federal.

Unless a court is authorized by constitution or statutory provisions to handle a particular type of case, the consent of the parties cannot confer jurisdiction. Lack of jurisdiction over the subject matter is a fatal defect. Federal Rule of Civil Procedure (hereafter "F.R.C.P.") 12 (h) (2) expresses the general principle, applicable to state as well as federal courts, in these words:

> Whenever it appears by suggestion of the parties or otherwise that the court lacks jurisdiction of the subject matter, the court shall dismiss the action.

6

Thus if a plaintiff attempted to initiate a civil action seeking $20,000 in an appellate court or in a justice of the peace type court or in a court possessing only criminal jurisdiction, it would have to be dismissed regardless of the willingness of both parties to have the court proceed with the case.

## Jurisdiction over the Person

The second element of jurisdiction requires that the court possess power to render a judgment which will be binding on both parties. As to the plaintiff, there is no problem because, by bringing suit, he acknowledges the court's authority and thus submits himself to its power.[10] The problem is to acquire power to bind the defendant. Normally this is accomplished by "serving" the summons upon him, notifying him that the lawsuit has been started and giving him an opportunity to defend.

## Service upon the Defendant

It is not enough that the defendant be notified of the suit in any simple and direct manner that may occur to the plaintiff's attorney—as by telephone, or mail or wire. A prescribed ritual must be followed, which involves specified methods of conveying the news to the defendant. Personal delivery or delivery to someone of "suitable age and discretion" at the defendant's home is usually required. The most common method of service is personal delivery to the defendant within the state where the court designated in the summons is located.[11] Such service authorizes the court to render any kind of a judgment against the defendant which the facts of the case and the applicable law justify.[12] In the absence of this or another authorized type of service, the court has no power whatever.[13]

Actually handing the summons to the defendant may not be as easy as it sounds—particularly if the defendant is on guard. The job is usually done by a deputy sheriff, marshal, constable or other court official[14] but, in some states any person except the plaintiff himself can do it.[15] In the larger cities of such states persons calling themselves "process servers" (for a summons is also called a "process") make a

7

livelihood out of the job. With practice, some of them become highly skilled at flushing reluctant defendants into the open so that they can be handed a summons.[16]

A summons, subject to certain exceptions which need not concern us immediately (they will be considered in Chapter 9), is ineffective outside of the state in which it is issued. The defendant, therefore, has to be sued in a state where he can be served. When he is a resident of the state in which the suit is brought (our assumption in Part I of this book), service of the summons seldom presents much difficulty. However, if an improper method of service is employed, the defendant is entitled to assert that the court lacks jurisdiction over him and on that basis have the action dismissed.[17] Such dismissal would be without prejudice to the plaintiff's right to initiate service again before the running of the applicable Statute of Limitations (in every state, there are statutes limiting the time within which various actions must be commenced).[18] For this reason, the defendant might not consider it worth his while to challenge improper service. In that case, he would enter a "general appearance," meaning that he would acknowledge the court's authority to proceed and concentrate on trying to defeat the action on the merits. He might inadvertently bring about the same result by defending the action on the merits without raising the question of jurisdiction. If so, he would be deemed to have waived any objection to lack of jurisdiction over him.[19] In this important respect, lack of jurisdiction over the person differs from lack of jurisdiction over subject matter, which, as we have noted, is not subject to waiver.

Once the defendant has been served, a record of that fact is made. If the service was effected by a private individual, the record takes the form of an affidavit; if by a court official, it takes the form of a certificate. Both are statements as to the fact of service at a certain time and place, the only difference being that the one made by a private individual (the affidavit) is made under oath before a notary public, whereas this formality is dispensed with in the case of the one made by the court official (the certificate).

Whether certificate or affidavit, the primary purpose of the record is to lay the foundation for a judgment against the defendant in the event that he does nothing within the twenty days given him. If that happens, he is in "default" which means that the court in which the action is brought can enter judgment against him for the relief demanded by the plaintiff without any proof that the facts alleged in the complaint have actually happened. But since the court is powerless to enter judgment unless service has been made, it requires proof of that fact before it will act. The affidavit or certificate furnishes such proof.[20] If judgment is entered on default in this manner, it will be the first and probably the last contact that the court has with the case. If the defendant does not pay up or convince the court that there is good cause to relieve him from the consequences of his neglect in answering, the sheriff will seize and sell his property in an attempt to raise enough money to discharge the judgment.[21]

## Venue

Closely related to the concept of jurisdiction is that of "venue," which defines the proper place for the trial of a given action within the state court system. Venue rules usually provide that suit may be brought in the county where the defendant resides or does business, but sometimes that it may or must be brought where the claim arose, where property involved in the action is located, where the plaintiff resides or where other factors, often arbitrarily determined, are present.[22] Such provisions, varying widely from state to state, impose additional geographical restraints upon the plaintiff's choice of a court beyond those imposed by the rules governing jurisdiction over the defendant. The summons of a court of general jurisdiction can be served anywhere within the state where the court is located, but this does not help if venue is improper and the defendant objects.

Improper venue, like lack of jurisdiction over the person but unlike lack of jurisdiction over subject matter, can be waived by the defendant's failure to object.[23] Unless so waived, the action must either be dismissed or transferred to a proper place for trial.

## Chapter 2

## THE COMPLAINT

Attached to the summons and served with it is another paper—or sheaf of papers—called the "complaint" or in earlier times, the "declaration" or "bill." It has the same title and caption as the summons, but there the similarity ends.

The summons tells the defendant nothing about the kind of action brought against him, or what facts the plaintiff is relying on. The complaint informs him. It is the plaintiff's story of what happened, the first "pleading" in the case, normally drafted and filed in court before the summons can be issued.

Unlike the summons, the complaint has no set form of words. Official forms and unofficial form books help, but they should not be relied upon too heavily. There can be no fixed formula, because every occurrence is unique, the facts of every lawsuit being different at least as to dates and places and often as to more substantial matters.

### A Sample Complaint

The complaint in a common situation involving the running down of a pedestrian by an automobile might read like this:

. . . . . . . . . . . . Court of the State of . . . . . . . . . . . . ;

. . . . . . . . . . . . County

Civil Action, File Number . . . . . . . . .

William Smith, Plaintiff ⎫
           v.    ⎬    Complaint
Mary Jones, Defendant ⎭

    1. On June 1, 1977, in a public highway called Elm Street in the City of . . . . . . . . . . , State of . . . . . . . . . . , defendant negligently drove a motor vehicle against plaintiff, a pedestrian who was then crossing said highway.

2. As a result, plaintiff was thrown down and had his leg broken and was otherwise injured, was prevented from transacting his business, suffered great pain of body and mind, and incurred expenses for medical expenses and hospitalization in the sum of one thousand dollars.

Wherefore the plaintiff demands judgment against defendant in the sum of ten thousand dollars and costs.

Signed:

Address:   John Olsen,
Attorney for Plaintiff
123 Main Street.

. . . . . . . . . ., . . . . . . . .

This complaint is adapted from one of the official forms accompanying the Federal Rules of Civil Procedure.[1] Numbered paragraphs 1. and 2. state briefly and in generalized terms the plaintiff's version of what happened between him and the defendant to give rise to the lawsuit. They are not unlike the lead paragraph of a newspaper story, omitting details and concentrating on the salient facts comprised in the traditional "five W's": who—the parties; when—the date; where—the highway; what—the accident; and why—the defendant's negligence. The facts are selected on the basis of their relevancy in justifying the legal remedy the plaintiff seeks, namely damages. The remedy asked is indicated in the final unnumbered paragraph, which is customarily described as the "prayer for relief." At the end is the signature of the plaintiff's lawyer, constituting his certificate that he has read the document and that "to the best of his knowledge, information and belief there is good ground to support it."[2] Under the signature of the plaintiff's lawyer is his address, signifying that henceforth documents in the case and dealings with respect to it are normally to be directed to him rather than personally to his client.

### The Function of Pleadings

Why do we need such a document? And why should a similar responsive document (the answer, to be considered in the next chapter) be required of the defendant? Why

12

should not both parties simply appear in court ready to proceed with the trial?

The traditional answer to such questions was given by an English Commission in 1851:[3]

> Some persons, irritated by the mischiefs which have followed from the abuse of technical rules, have proposed that parties should come into Court without any previous authentic information as to the complaint or answer. From this we wholly dissent. Such a mode of or rather want of, procedure, may answer the purpose in a rude state of society or in matters of very trifling moment, in which from the nature of the case the parties know beforehand the precise matter in dispute; but in a highly civilized state, where commercial transactions are numerous and complicated, it would lead to intolerable fraud, oppression, and expense; and we believe that it has never existed in the code of any civilized nation. Dishonest plaintiffs would make unfounded claims, the nature of which could not be ascertained by previous inquiry. The party summoned must either come prepared with all the witnesses who could depose to anything that had ever passed between him and the plaintiff, or must hear the complaint, and then be entitled to an adjournment to bring his witnesses at a future day. In the former case, great unnecessary expense would be incurred, and frequently incurred with a view to oppression. In the latter case there would, in truth, be a notice given by word of mouth before the Judge, which had much better have been previously given. In many cases, an adjournment would be necessary for the purpose of justice, but dishonest defendants would equally claim it, and every case would be something like twice tried, each party being at the expense and trouble of twice attending with witnesses.

Despite the persuasiveness of this reasoning, there remain lingering doubts as to whether the time and effort spent on written pleadings justify the results achieved. Formal pleadings are dispensed with in courts dealing with small claims; in criminal courts—even in major cases so far as the defendant is concerned; in many administrative agencies; and in arbitration tribunals; and yet these institutions seem able to function with reasonable efficiency and to as great a degree of public satisfaction as is bestowed upon civil courts of general jurisdiction. Nevertheless, the requirement of written pleadings in civil cases involving substantial money or property is deeply rooted. Each side is thought to need advance notice of the other side's contentions; and it is further believed—with some justification as we shall see in the next chapter—that if the parties are forced to reduce their contentions to writing, some cases may be disposed of without trial either through settlement or judicial rulings on the legal sufficiency of their respective contentions. While members of the legal profession are today willing to de-emphasize the importance of written pleadings, they are far from willing to eliminate them completely.

## Drafting the Complaint

How does a lawyer draft a complaint? Very briefly, by learning the facts of the case and the law applicable to them, and then stating the facts in such a manner that a court will be able to see that under the law the plaintiff, if able to prove those facts, is entitled to the relief he seeks.

Stating the job in a single sentence is misleading, however. It is as if one were to describe the duties of the President of the United States by saying that he is the head of the executive branch of the federal government. True enough, but so brief as to be almost meaningless. Neither the President's job nor the job of the lawyer in drafting a complaint can be described so quickly. Far from being simple, drafting a complaint can be one of the most difficult tasks a lawyer has. It requires a high degree of skill and knowledge.

The lawyer's first problem is to get the facts. Normally he gets them through an interview or series of interviews with his client, supplemented by interviews with other people as well and the examination of correspondence and various types of records, public and private.[4] In order to do the job intelligently, the lawyer needs to know the substantive law which determines what rights and duties arise out of the fact situation at hand. If ever he needs to go to the law

14

books—statutes, treatises, indices, etc.—it is at this stage of the case. Later may be too late.

Whatever the substantive law is (it may not fit into the traditional law school classification of torts, contracts, etc., or it may overlap several of the traditional lines), it determines which facts are important and which are unimportant. Perhaps the client in telling his story has omitted some legally crucial fact, or else deluged the lawyer with a hundred details which seem important to the client but have no legal significance. The lawyer's task is to screen the facts, taking only those which are legally important and rejecting (at least for the time being) the rest. In doing this, his guide is the governing substantive law. To take a simple example: A wants to sue X for failing to live up to a contract and places great stress on the fact that X is Jewish or Catholic or Moslem or Protestant, but says nothing about whether X received anything by way of promise or otherwise in return for his promise. The law of contracts makes it clear that X's religion is irrelevant, while "consideration" (the giving of something in return) is crucial.

It may be that the lawyer first hearing his client's story, does not know which branch of substantive law governs. If so, he must find out and then reconsider the facts. Or possibly he knows the branch of law that governs, but not enough about it to appreciate the exact significance of the factual situation presented to him. If so, he must go to the books and then return again to dig at the facts.

The process of finding the applicable law is not as esoteric as it may first appear. Rules of law are nothing more than statements of the consequences which courts attach to various factual situations. They must be and they are indexed according to the facts to which they refer. If a person can find his way around in a dictionary or encyclopedia, there is no reason why he cannot do the same with law books. Just as a knowledge of the law points to the facts that are relevant, so a knowledge of the facts leads to the applicable law.

15

The checking of law against facts and facts against law may go on for a considerable time in a complicated case. But regardless of how simple a case may be, the lawyer must consider facts and law together before drafting his complaint. A study of the facts alone apart from their legal significance will not accomplish the lawyer's job.

Having the facts and their legal significance well in mind, the lawyer is now ready to draft the complaint. Here he runs into a strange obstacle: the rule that he is required to separate the law from the facts, and state in the complaint only the facts.[5] This is a rule of procedure, having nothing to do with the rights and duties arising out of a given fact situation, but dealing only with the way in which lawyers and judges proceed in handling a lawsuit.

The reason the lawyer must say nothing in the complaint about the law or why the facts are legally important—even though he has picked them on that basis—must be sought mainly in history. In the system of law which prevailed in the United States and England in about the year 1800, pleading was highly artificial and technical. The facts upon which the plaintiff relied were obscured, if not concealed, by verbiage which only lawyers could understand. There was no effort to tell a plain and concise story of what happened.[6] This situation was irksome to laymen and to some lawyers, and strenuous efforts at reform were made in the first half of the nineteenth century. The men who drafted a new Code of Civil Procedure for the state of New York that went into effect in 1848 decided to do away with the technical and legalistic language which had prevailed in the past. Their formula was to require that the complaint should contain "a statement of the facts constituting the cause of action, in ordinary and concise language, without repetition, and in such a manner as to enable a person of common understanding to know what is intended."[7] This seemed like a fine solution at the time, and it was copied, with minor variations, in other states. Judges interpreted the command to plead "facts" as a prohibition against pleading "law."

Little did the reformers realize, however, how slippery were the words they used. What are "facts"? What is a "cause of action"? American courts spent about a century working at these concepts and evolved the not too helpful explanation that facts lay somewhere between "evidence" on the one hand and "conclusions" on the other;[8] and the not very much more helpful explanation that a "cause of action" consisted of a statement of those "ultimate facts" which showed that the plaintiff was entitled to a remedy.[9]

There was little agreement between various courts as to the proper form of allegations in a complaint, and little recognition that the problem of pleading facts was simply a question of the degree of detail required. Some courts held that in pleading consideration in a contract case, it was sufficient to allege that the defendant's promise was made "for a valuable consideration"; others held that the pleader had to specify what the consideration was. Some courts held that in pleading negligence in a tort case, it was sufficient to characterize the defendant's actions as "negligent"; others held that the pleader had to spell out in detail what the negligence was.[10]

Because of such difficulties, the legal profession gradually became aware of the unsatisfactory character of the prevailing formula. A fresh start became feasible in 1934 when Congress authorized the Supreme Court of the United States to promulgate rules of pleading and practice for the federal courts,[11] which until then had been laboring under even more unsatisfactory procedural rules than prevailed in most state courts. The Supreme Court appointed an Advisory Committee of judges, lawyers and law professors to draft the new rules. After a careful study of the deficiencies of the "ultimate facts—cause of action" formula, they came up with a new formula: the complaint should contain "a short and plain statement of the claim showing that the pleader is entitled to relief" and "a demand for judgment for the relief to which he believes himself entitled."[12] Gone were the troublesome words "fact" and "cause of action," and with them the occasion for much fruitless metaphysical haggling over the degree of detail required or permitted. More clearly exposed than theretofore was the relationship between the plaintiff's statement of what had happened, his prayer for relief and the underlying substantive law.

Fully as important as the substitution of one general formula for another was the drafting by the Advisory Committee of official forms. Originally "intended to indicate the simplicity and brevity of statement which the rules contemplate" these forms were later[13] declared "sufficient under the rules." Now a pleader, finding an appropriate form that fits his fact situation, can safely rely on the language suggested, filling in only names, dates, places, amounts, etc. The forms cover most common types of litigation, including auto accident cases, claims on promissory notes and the like, thus relieving lawyers of most of the burdens of draftmanship for recurring fact patterns. In addition to the new general formula and the forms, the Advisory Committee helped pleaders by providing highly specific rules for alleging certain situations which recur in a variety of cases—the capacity of a party to sue or be sued; fraud, mistake or condition of mind; the performance of conditions precedent; official documents, acts or judgments and the like.[14]

In 1938, the Supreme Court, adopting the work of the Advisory Committee, promulgated the Federal Rules of Civil Procedure, radically simplifying pleading in the federal courts. The rules have been amended and improved several times since their original promulgation; and, equally important, they have been widely copied for state courts.[15] It is fair to say that in the many states that now follow the federal pattern, the difficulty of achieving the desired degree of detail in pleading has all but disappeared. In states that still cling to the "facts—cause of action" formula, the difficulty persists. Pleaders working under that formula have little to guide them beyond "precedent and analogy,"[16] supplemented by such unofficial form books as are at hand.

Is there any modern justification for the idea that only facts, not law, should be stated in a complaint? One thought comes to mind: judges are supposed to know the law without being told, whereas they are not expected to know anything about the particular facts of the cases brought before them. If so, it seems unnecessary to say anything about the law in a complaint. But is it true that judges can be relied on to know the law?[17] Yes, in the sense that every judge knows enough about the law to examine some complaints and, without going to the law books or getting outside help, decide whether or not the facts stated are sufficient to justify the remedy asked. But no judge knows enough about the law to do the same with every complaint. In some cases he will need help beyond what his own memory can furnish. Since the plaintiff's lawyer has already been through the process of checking the facts against the law, there is no valid reason why his research should not be made available to the judge and the opposing party.

Such help can be made available, but not through the complaint. It must come, if at all, through oral arguments or written arguments called "briefs" or "legal memoranda," showing how the opposing lawyers believe that the judge should interpret the law and apply it to the facts of the case. Such arguments come at a later stage of the case, if and when the defendant's lawyer challenges the legal foundation of the complaint.

## Allocating the Burdens of Pleading

Another problem that the draftsman of a complaint faces is how completely he should attempt to state his client's case. In traditional terms, he should not "anticipate defenses" but restrict himself to alleging only those facts necessary to make out a "prima facie case."[18] These vague terms offer little guidance. Equally unilluminating is the prescription that the plaintiff is required to plead whatever he must prove at trial. The illusory character of this "rule" becomes apparent when it is placed alongside of its companion "rule" that the plaintiff must prove whatever he has pleaded[19]—a perfect example of circular reasoning which leads nowhere. In truth, the burdens of pleading and proof do not always go together, though usually they do; and there is no general principle to determine in all kinds of cases the extent of the plaintiff's burden of pleading.[20] That he must start the process of issue formulation by pleading enough facts to invoke a rule of substantive law that will entitle him to some remedy is clear; but what if anything, must he say about other facts which, under substantive law, may defeat the remedy he seeks? Any lawsuit can become the focal point of many different rules of substantive law, some favoring the plaintiff and others favoring the defendant but all equally determinative of whether a remedy shall be granted or withheld. Consider for example, an auto accident case. The basic rule on which the plaintiff relies is that one who negligently injures another is liable to that person for the damage caused.[21] Another equally important rule, which prevails in many, though not all states, is that the plaintiff cannot recover if he was contributorily negligent—if, in other words, his own fault was partially responsible for the damage.[22] Must the plaintiff plead in his complaint that he was free from contributory negligence, or is it up to the defendant to allege that the plaintiff was guilty of contributory negligence? Some courts have placed the burden of pleading as to contributory negligence on the plaintiff, but others have reached the opposite conclusion.[23] Or consider a contract case where the plaintiff is seeking to collect a bill for goods sold to the defendant. Clearly the plaintiff must allege an express or implied promise on the part of the defendant to pay, supported by consideration, for these are among the essential elements of his claim under substantive law. But an equally essential element for recovery under substantive law is that the debt has not already been discharged by payment.[24] Must the plaintiff allege that no payment has been made, or is it up to the defendant to allege that payment has been made? Most courts confronted with this problem have placed the burden of pleading payment on the defendant, presumably on the theory that it is easier for him to prove payment—as by producing a receipt or cancelled check—than for the plaintiff to prove nonpayment.[25]

As these examples (among many others that could be cited) show, the burdens of pleading are not imposed exclusively upon either the plaintiff or the defendant, but divided between them. How they are divided in various types of cases is determined by precedent and analogy, in default of more specific guidance by statute or general rule.[26] For practitioners in federal courts and in state courts that follow the federal pattern, such guidance is provided in Federal Rule 8(c) and its state counterparts, reading as follows:

> Affirmative Defenses. In pleading to a preceding pleading, a party shall set forth affirmatively accord and satisfaction, arbitration and award, assumption of risk, contributory negligence, discharge in bankruptcy, duress, estoppel, failure of consideration, fraud, illegality, injury by fellow servant, laches, license, payment, release, res judicata, statute of frauds, statute of limitations, waiver, and any other matter constituting an avoidance or affirmative defense.

This rule by its express terms only specifies the factual situations that must be dealt with by the defendant in his answer, but by implication it also guides the plaintiff. He is not required to make any allegations with respect to matters that are to be dealt with, if at all, in the defendant's answer. Most troublesome problems as to allocating the respective burdens of pleading between the two parties are solved by this rule, leaving only unusual fact situations to be solved by precedent, analogy or more or less arbitrary judicial choice as to which side ought to bear the burden of pleading.

## The Distinction Between Allegations and Proof

The statements in a complaint are not facts, but only "allegations" of fact. Their purpose is not to convince the judge or jury, but rather to state the plaintiff's contentions as a first step in defining the issues between him and the defendant. Later, if issues of fact have developed and there is a trial to resolve them, the plaintiff may tell his story again, as a witness; but if he does, his statements will have to be much more specific and detailed. He will be allowed to tell only what he himself perceived or experienced, not what he learned from others; and his story will be subject to cross-examination by the defendant's lawyer. Very likely other persons will have to be called to the witness stand to testify what they have personally perceived in order to sustain the plaintiff's allegations.

It is important to grasp this difference between allegations and proof. Allegations are made at the outset of the case by the plaintiff in the complaint and by the defendant in the answer (to be considered in the next chapter) ; and they have the limited purpose of disclosing the areas of dispute between the parties. Proof, on the other hand, comes during the trial; its purpose is to resolve issues of fact which have been framed by the pleadings; and it is hedged about by various guaranties of trustworthiness embodied in the rules of evidence.

In view of the distinction between allegations and proof, it may strike one as strange that in some jurisdictions a "verification" is included at the end of the complaint.[27] This is a sworn statement by the plaintiff (or, if he is not readily available, his attorney) that the allegations in the complaint are true to the best of his knowledge and belief. Why should an oath be required if the complaint proves nothing but merely helps to formulate issues? A brief answer is that trials are expensive and the public should not be burdened with their cost unless there is a genuine dispute between the parties. The verification of pleadings is designed only to eliminate the necessity of litigating false issues. If a plaintiff does not himself believe what he alleges in his complaint, he is not entitled to a trial. If a defendant does not believe his own answer, he is not entitled to a trial. Requiring the verification of pleadings is supposed to have a healthy psychological effect, especially in view of the fact that the person who signs the verification is subject to the possibility of criminal prosecution if he knowingly swears falsely. Perhaps verifications are ineffective and ought to be dispensed with, but whether effective or not, they do not even purport to eliminate the necessity for a trial when there is an honest dispute between the parties.

In the federal courts, and in state courts following the federal pattern, verification, except in a few specialized situations,[28] has given way to "certification." As we have seen in the sample complaint above, the plaintiff's lawyer, rather than his client, merely signs the complaint without having taken an oath. His signature is a representation by him he has read the pleading and that there is good ground to support it.[29] Thus primary responsibility is shifted from the client to the lawyer, as it should be in view of the fact that the lawyer has prepared the document. For a willful violation of his obligation, the lawyer may be subjected to disciplinary action—reprimand, suspension from practice, conceivably even disbarment, or if the client is the one responsible by reason of having misled the lawyer on the facts, his complaint may be stricken out as sham.[30] Such sanctions, though seldom used, are thought to be more effective than relying on the cumbersome and even more rarely invoked procedure of criminal prosecution for false verification.

## Remedies

In the last paragraph of the complaint proper (the prayer for relief) the plaintiff is no longer telling his story; he is making a demand for some remedy to which his lawyer thinks he is entitled. This is what he is after in the lawsuit —help from the court—and the pivot around which the action revolves.

Needless to say, a court will not redress every grievance. Nor can a court accomplish miracles. It cannot restore a life wrongfully cut short, or mend a broken body, or give back an unsullied reputation. Usually the most that can be done is to attempt to provide some substitute for whatever loss the plaintiff has suffered. Hence we should expect to find, as we do, that legal remedies are limited.

The most common remedy is a judgment for "damages," meaning a determination that the defendant owes money to the plaintiff (how it will be collected we shall see in Chapter 6). The purpose of granting this or any other civil remedy is not to punish the defendant (although that may be an incidental result),[31] but rather to make the plaintiff whole, as nearly as possible. Punishment is left almost exclusively to criminal proceedings. It may be that the defendant has committed an assault and battery or done some other act which will subject him to criminal punishment as well as civil liability, but if so, two separate lawsuits will be necessary: one, a criminal proceeding brought against him by the state, and the other, a civil action brought against him by the person injured.

A judgment for money damages is sometimes inadequate because the damages are too hard to measure, or because the defendant will persist in his misconduct even if he has to pay, or because damages, for some other reason, are unequal to the situation. If so, other remedies may be available.

Suppose that the defendant persists in dumping garbage on the plaintiff's lawn. Here the remedy would be an order of the court that he stop. Such a remedy is called an "injunction" and is enforced if the defendant refuses to obey it by putting him in jail until he is willing to comply.

Suppose that the defendant agrees to sell a certain house and lot to the plaintiff, but then goes back on his bargain. The remedy would be an order, called a "decree for specific performance," requiring the defendant to do what he promised. Compliance with the order would be enforced if need be by jail; or the court's judgment could effectively convey the property.

Suppose the defendant occupies a piece of real estate belonging to the plaintiff. The remedy is "ejectment," accomplished by the sheriff putting the defendant off the property if he refuses to leave peaceably.

Suppose, instead of real property, that it is an automobile of the plaintiff's that the defendant is keeping. The remedy is "replevin," meaning that the sheriff will seize the car and return it to the plaintiff.

Suppose the defendant has tricked the plaintiff into making an unconscionable contract. Here the remedy would be "rescission" or "reformation," meaning that the contract would be cancelled or amended.

Suppose the controversy between plaintiff and defendant is not such that any coercive relief is needed. Here a declaratory judgment, merely defining the rights of the parties, will be enough. Such judgments are allowed in a wide variety of situations by modern statutes. Prior to these statutes, such relief was allowed only in special situations, as in actions to "quiet title" to real estate.

We have mentioned the principal, though by no means all, of the remedies available: damages, injunctions, specific performance, ejectment, replevin, reformation, recission, and a declaration of rights; and we shall mention others as our discussion proceeds (particularly in Chapters 11 and 12). How does the plaintiff's lawyer determine which of these his client should have? Does he appeal to the judge's discretion in choosing the one most appropriate to the situation? No. Again he refers to the applicable substantive law. That determines which remedy, if any, is available in a given fact situation. Indeed, from the point of view of a lawyer drafting a complaint, the rules of substantive law are nothing more than statements of the factual conditions for the granting of particular remedies. Hence the research which is a necessary preliminary to drafting the complaint will take care not only of the allegations as to what happened but also of the prayer for relief. The two are inextricably bound together, and the tying force is substantive law. If the substantive law provides that a remedy will be granted upon proof of the facts alleged, the plaintiff has succeeded in stating a "cause of action" or, to use the modern federal terminology, a "claim showing that the pleader is entitled to relief."[32]

The fact that the plaintiff may seek a remedy to which he is not entitled is not fatal to his case under modern rules of procedure. If, suing for breach of contract, he mistakenly asks for specific performance when he is only entitled to damages, he is not turned out of court, as was formerly the case (see Part III). His complaint is good so long as the facts stated entitle him to some remedy.[33]

## New Situations and New Ideas

Thus far we have been considering actions where the governing substantive law is settled. In some situations, how-

25

ever, it is not settled.[34] Perhaps a unique kind of fact pattern, never before adjudicated, is presented. If so, the lawyer drafting the complaint is in effect asking the court to make law. Whichever way the case is ultimately decided, whether the remedy sought is granted or denied, a precedent will have been established to govern future cases of similar nature.[35] Perhaps a common fact pattern is presented, but at a time when the pleader believes that the familiar rules for dealing with it have become discredited or obsolete. If so, he must contend that the familiar rules should be changed in favor of new ones, governing not only the case at hand but also the cases of like nature.[36]

In either of the cases supposed, the lawyer states the facts as he sees them and, if the complaint is challenged (in the manner to be described in the next chapter), he supports it not on the basis of the law as it is, but on the basis of the law as he contends it ought to be. He may not succeed at the trial court level, but he will at least have laid the foundation for an appeal at which his viewpoint may prevail. Law is made not only by legislatures, but also by courts as a by-product of deciding cases. The doctrine of precedent, or to use its Latin name "stare decisis," commands that, absent exceptional circumstances, what is done in one case must be done in other cases of like nature and that persons similarly situated will be similarly treated, so that the ideal of equal justice under law will be realized.[37] But the common law—another name for judge-made law—is never static. It is constantly evolving to meet new situations and changing to deal with old situations in new ways. The changes are finalized in the written opinions of appellate courts, but they are initiated by lawyers, often in the course of drafting or attacking pleadings in the initial phases of litigation.

## Chapter 3

## THE DEFENDANT'S RESPONSE

After the complaint and summons have been served on the defendant, the next move is up to him.

If he does nothing, a default judgment will be entered against him, to be enforced in the same manner as a judgment entered after a contest.[1] What can he do if he hopes to defeat the plaintiff's claim?

Basically, there are two avenues open to him—one, he can dispute the plaintiff's version of what happened, and two, he can dispute the implied contention that the plaintiff is entitled to a remedy from the court. These two fundamental problems are present in every lawsuit—first, what happened? and second, what ought to be done about it?

If the defendant succeeds on either issue, he will win the case. That does not mean, however, that he must choose between them. He may be in a position to contest both issues. Suppose, for example, the claim is that the defendant promised to give the plaintiff an automobile worth $5,000 but then refused to deliver it. The defendant may honestly believe that this version of the facts is incorrect—that he never made any such promise. He may also believe that even if he had made such a promise, it is not legally binding because it was not supported by consideration. In this situation he would want to and would be allowed to contest both issues. Just how does one go about contesting issues of fact or issues of law, or both, and in what order?

### The Motion to Dismiss

Logically it would seem that one who had to decide both what happened and what ought to be done about it should attack the problem of what happened first, and the other problem second. Why worry about what ought to be done about a situation which may have never existed?

In law, however, the process is frequently, indeed normally, reversed. That is because the problem of what ought to be done, being a question of law, can be decided by studying the law books; whereas the problem of what happened, being a question of fact, can be determined only after receiving evidence. The determination of a question of fact always involves people besides the judge and the lawyers, and usually involves more time and expense than the determination of a question of law.

The possibility of disposing of a case on the law in advance of trial is one of the justifications for requiring a written complaint. By examining the complaint, the judge will not know what happened, but at least will know what the plaintiff claims happened; and assuming the plaintiff can prove his story to be true, the judge can determine whether the plaintiff will be entitled to a legal remedy. If the plaintiff would be entitled to no remedy even if his story were true, there is no point in wasting time and expense in a trial to determine what happened.

The traditional weapon for challenging the legal sufficiency of a complaint is a "demurrer," used at common law[2] and still used in some states. In the federal pattern of procedure a different name is used, namely, "motion to dismiss,"[3] but the device is fundamentally the same. By such a motion the defendant says in effect, "So what? Even if what the plaintiff says is true, he still is entitled to no remedy against me."

The defendant does not have to challenge the complaint in advance of trial, but he may. Whether he decides in favor of the move or against it depends primarily upon whether or not his lawyer's view of the applicable law coincides with that of the plaintiff's lawyer. By "applicable" law is meant, of course, the law governing the facts alleged in the complaint. So the first step in deciding whether a motion to dismiss should be made is to study the complaint.

The complaint, as we have noted, contains no statement of the law relied on. Implicit in it, however, is the plaintiff's lawyer's view either of existing law or law as he contends it ought to be. His assertion that such and such facts happened

28

coupled with his demand for a certain remedy is like the statement of an incomplete chain of reasoning in logic: "Rover is a dog; therefore Rover is vicious." The conclusion is there, and so is the minor premise, but the major premise is missing. Though unexpressed, we can discover what it is without much difficulty. It is the proposition: "All dogs are vicious." If this premise is rejected, the conclusion fails.

So with the complaint. The unexpressed major premise is the rule of law relied on or contended for; the minor premise is the statement of facts; and the conclusion is the prayer for relief. A successful attack against the major premise (which is the purpose of the motion to dismiss) will destroy the conclusion as surely as would a successful attack against the minor premise (by way of a trial on the facts).

The defendant's lawyer can study the law applicable to the facts alleged as well as the plaintiff's lawyer. If upon such study, he concludes that the legal underpinnings of the complaint are not sufficient to support it, he will probably move to dismiss. Probably, we say, because he need not take this step. He may, for reasons of strategy, decide to wait and raise the question later. Most questions call for prompt action upon the part of the lawyers, who if they do not take appropriate steps as soon as possible, will waive whatever rights their clients may have. But not so with a question as to the legal sufficiency of a complaint. This, like jurisdiction over subject matter, is one of the very few questions that can be raised at a later stage of the lawsuit.[4]

The longer a lawyer delays in raising the question, however, the less likely he is to succeed. This is for two reasons: (1) judges are prone to interpret complaints more leniently in later stages of a case than in earlier stages; and (2) there is a doctrine that a complaint may be "aided" by subsequent proceedings, meaning that imperfect or missing allegations can be cured or supplied by allegations in the defendant's answer, by evidence adduced at the trial, by the jury's verdict, or by the court's judgment.[5] The question of the legal sufficiency of the complaint is such a fundamental one that courts are willing to listen to arguments on it at any time.

If the defendant's lawyer decides not to make a motion to dismiss either because he is satisfied that it would be futile or because he decides to postpone the question until later, the lawsuit will proceed on the assumption that the complaint is legally sufficient—that it states a claim showing that the pleader is entitled to relief, or to use the older terminology, "a cause of action." The judge on his own initiative will not examine the complaint to determine its legal sufficiency. He is likely to be too busy with other cases where the parties are calling upon him for rulings. Here again we see the adversary nature of litigation.

If the defendant's lawyer decides to make a motion to dismiss, he does so by serving on the lawyer for the plaintiff (not the plaintiff himself, for personal service on a party is not necessary except at the commencement of the action)[6] a paper in standard form substantially as follows:[7]

............ Court of the State of ............;

............ County

Civil Action File Number ........

| | |
|---|---|
| A.B., Plaintiff<br>v.<br>C.D., Defendant | Motion to Dismiss |

Defendant moves the court to dismiss the action because the complaint fails to state a claim upon which relief can be granted.

Signed:  Alice Attorney
Address: 130 Elm Street
...... City, ......

To: Leonard Lawyer
Attorney for Plaintiff

Please take notice that the undersigned will bring the above motion on for hearing before the Court at Room ......, County Court House, ...... on the 20th day of September 1977 at 10:00 o'clock in the forenoon of that day or as soon thereafter as counsel can be heard.

Signed:  Alice Attorney
Address: 130 Elm Street
...... City, ......

This paper is served several days (in the federal courts 5 days,[8] but local practice varies) before the date set aside by the court for the hearing of such motions, at which time it and the complaint against which it is directed will be brought to the attention of the judge. This normally will be his first look at the case. Both lawyers will appear to present legal or written arguments or both, depending upon local custom and the complexity of the problem presented.

In discharging his responsibility, the judge goes through substantially the same process as the defendant's lawyer did in deciding whether to challenge it. That is, he assumes the facts stated in the complaint to be true, and looks at them in the light of substantive law to determine whether or not the plaintiff is entitled to a remedy.[9] He should consider not only the rule of substantive law relied on by the plaintiff, but also any other rule which might justify a remedy. Sometimes a plaintiff suing on one theory of law (*e.g.*, negligence) recovers on another (*e.g.*, breach of warranty). The judge's task is not limited to determining whether the plaintiff is entitled to the exact remedy he asks on the exact legal theory he invokes, but rather the broader one of determining whether the plaintiff is entitled to any legal remedy on the basis of any rule of law.[10]

The motion to dismiss normally reaches only defects which appear on the face of the complaint. If the defendant disputes the truth of what the plaintiff has alleged, or if he wishes to call to the court's attention facts not stated in the complaint, the proper device for him to use is an answer, soon to be considered, or a motion for summary judgment, to be considered in Chapter 4. The judge, in ruling upon a motion to dismiss, ordinarily treats all of the plaintiff's allegations as true, and also assumes that they tell the complete story—that there are no other facts relevant to the controversy.[11] In states that still use the demurrer, it is an inflexible rule that a "speaking" demurrer, meaning one that supplies facts not stated in the complaint, is prohibited.[12] In states that follow the federal pattern, there is less emphasis on this procedural nicety: if facts outside of the complaint are stated by the defendant *and not excluded* by the court, the motion to dismiss is treated as one for summary judgment.[13] If the facts are beyond the realm of reasonable dispute and if they, together with the complaint, show that the defendant is entitled to judgment as a matter of law, such judgment may be entered forthwith.[14] Nevertheless, the normal function of a motion to dismiss is not to present new facts, but like the demurrer, to test the legal sufficiency of the complaint on the assumption that it correctly states all the relevant facts.

Another distinction between the modern motion to dismiss and the traditional demurrer is timing. The demurrer is said to "admit" the facts properly pleaded in the complaint. On that assumption, it would be inconsistent to allow the defendant simultaneously to deny the facts in the complaint. The obstacle, however, is purely semantic. Any "admission" made by the demurrer is temporary, lasting only until the court makes its ruling on the legal sufficiency of the complaint. If the judge overrules the demurrer, the defendant is then free to answer, denying the very allegations he has previously "admitted."[15] Recognizing the temporary and hypothetical nature of the "admission" made by the defendant, the federal rules allow him simultaneously to challenge the sufficiency of the complaint and deny its allegations. Both types of defense may be stated in the answer.[16] Nevertheless, the normal procedure in courts that follow the federal pattern is for the defendant who wishes to challenge the legal sufficiency of the complaint to do so by motion prior to answering.

A hypothetical case may help to illustrate the normal function of a motion to dismiss as distinguished from that of an answer. Suppose the plaintiff is suing for breach of promise of marriage. If it is the defendant's contention that he made no such promise as alleged, or that he has settled with the plaintiff and secured a release of liability, he proceeds by way of answer, not a motion to dismiss (or demurrer). These defects in the plaintiff's case do not appear on the face of the complaint. They ordinarily must be developed through the defendant's answer and evidence in support of it. On the other hand, if it appears in the complaint that the events in the relationship between plaintiff and defendant took place in the state of New York, a different situation is presented. That is because New York has a statute providing as follows:

> The rights of action heretofore existing to recover sums of money as damages for the alienation of affections, criminal conversation, seduction, or breach of promise to marry are hereby abolished.[17]

The law of New York is not stated in the complaint, but implicit in it is the assertion that the facts stated give rise to liability under the applicable law (in this case, New York's). Consequently, the fatal weakness of the plaintiff's case appears "on the face of the complaint" in the sense that a person reading it and knowing the applicable law will realize that the plaintiff is not entitled to recover. No facts other than those stated in the complaint are needed to reach that conclusion. In such a case, a motion to dismiss or demurrer will succeed. Such a motion attacks the unexpressed major premise of the complaint—the rule of substantive law relied on by the plaintiff. That is its main function.

On what basis does the judge make his ruling? Does he know all the law to begin with, so that all he needs to do is think about the problem, extracting the law from his memory and applying it, or is something more involved? A little reflection will indicate that no judge knows or can know all the law. He knows some law, of course. Presumably that is one of the reasons he was elected or appointed. But he cannot know all of the law even for a single jurisdiction. In any state there are thousands of pages of statutes, hundreds of volumes of reported cases, each volume probably averaging 800 or 900 pages; and in addition, many more volumes containing ordinances, treatises, digests, etc. Obviously no judge could be expected to carry all this in his head. Besides, judges as we shall see in Part II often have to apply federal law, or the laws of other states or other nations.

33

In view of the fact that no case will be presented unless it has been screened by the plaintiff's lawyer, and no complaint will be attacked unless the defendant's lawyer insists, there is every reason for making the researches of the lawyers available to the judge, as they are through written and oral arguments. If a case is well presented and argued by both sides, little, if any, study will be called for by the judge. On the other hand, if the lawyers have done their jobs poorly, the judge may have to do independent research if he is to decide correctly. So great is our reliance on private lawyers, however, that a judge often is exonerated from criticism and even insulated from reversal on appeal for failing to apply the correct law if he has not been aided by proper briefs and arguments.[18]

When the judge reaches his decision, he embodies it in an "order." This is the name given any judicial determination short of final judgment disposing of the entire case.

If the judge decides that the plaintiff is not entitled under substantive law to any remedy on the facts he has alleged, the order will state that the defendant's motion to dismiss is granted. This means that the complaint is invalidated, but not necessarily that the plaintiff loses the case for good. He may have mistakenly omitted from his complaint some essential fact; or he may have stated his version of the facts so verbosely, so laconically or otherwise in so defective a form that it is impossible to tell whether he really has a "cause of action" or claim upon which relief can be granted. If so, the plaintiff is allowed an opportunity to amend his complaint; it would not be fair to enter final judgment against him.[19] On the other hand, if he has told his whole story in proper form, then granting the motion to dismiss means that he is really through. Even if he were given the privilege of submitting an amended complaint, it would do him no good, because his second complaint would be challenged just as the first was, and the court would rule the same way.[20]

The consequence of denying a motion to dismiss (or overruling a demurrer) is that the plaintiff's complaint is held legally sufficient. This does not mean that the court has decided that what he has alleged is true. His whole claim may be a fraud, or at least some of the statements in the complaint may be false. The defendant has had no chance to be heard on the truth of the plaintiff's version of the facts. Consequently, the denial of a motion to dismiss is not followed by judgment against the defendant, but rather by an opportunity for him to answer the complaint and have a trial on the issue of what happened.[21]

## The Answer

If the defendant does not wish to challenge the complaint, or if having challenged it, he has been unsuccessful, his next move is to answer the complaint. By doing so, he creates one or more issues of fact as distinguished from issues of law. Instead of saying "So what?" he says in effect that the plaintiff's story is untrue, or, if not untrue, incomplete.

As might be expected from the fact that the complaint is in writing and either verified or certified, there is a requirement that the "answer" be in writing too, and similarly verified or certified.[22] It is the defendant's pleading—his version of what happened, prepared by his attorney and served on the opposing attorney.

Drafting an answer involves a different technique for the lawyer than challenging the complaint. In deciding whether to challenge the complaint, the lawyer needs little or no help from his client. He finds out by studying his law books, using as the basis for study the facts stated in the complaint. Answering the complaint, on the other hand is quite a different matter. Here the lawyer must rely on his client, for it is the client's story that is to be told. The lawyer must ask the defendant not only whether the plaintiff's version of the facts is correct, but also whether there are any other facts which may bear on the lawsuit. The technique of the defendant's lawyer at this stage is substantially the same as that of the plaintiff's lawyer when drafting the complaint.

Two different approaches are possible in an answer. One is to deny all or part of the plaintiff's version of the facts.

The other is to avoid their effect by stating additional facts which exonerate the defendant from liability.

## Denials

Let us look first at denials. They relate not to the legal effect of the plaintiff's allegations, for that is the province of the motion to dismiss, but to the allegations themselves. The plaintiff says the defendant hit him with a brick; the defendant denies it. The plaintiff claims that the defendant made a certain promise; the defendant denies that he did. It is as if the defendant wrote "Not so" across the face of the complaint or some portion of it and sent it back to the plaintiff. An issue of fact is created—to be resolved by a trial, where the judge or judge and jury (depending upon the type of case) may hear the plaintiff, the defendant, and other witnesses who have knowledge which can throw light on their dispute.

The defendant need not and normally should not deny every allegation in the plaintiff's complaint. Some allegations are probably true and should be admitted. It is enough if the defendant denies a single material allegation making up the plaintiff's claim. If the denial succeeds—that is, if the trier of fact finds that the challenged allegation is untrue— the whole cause of action will fall, like a house of cards when a single card is removed.

Any allegation which the defendant does not deny is deemed admitted, relieving the plaintiff from the necessity of proving it at trial.[23] The defendant cannot legally "put the plaintiff to his proof" by a blanket repudiation of the complaint. A general denial is theoretically possible, but would be appropriate only in the very rare case where the plaintiff sued the wrong person. Denials should be specific, responding to the complaint paragraph by paragraph, sentence by sentence, even clause by clause. In the language of Federal Rule 8 (b): "Denials shall fairly meet the substance of the averments denied. When a pleader intends in good faith to deny only a part or a qualification of an averment, he shall specify so much of it as is true and material and shall deny only the remainder." Denials should also be unambiguous. If the defendant, instead of responding to the plaintiff's allegations point by point, tells his own variant version of what happened (this is called an "argumentative denial"),[24] the issues are likely to remain fuzzy. If he simply repeats the exact language of some allegation in the complaint, preceded by the words "Defendant denies that . . ." (this is called a "negative pregnant")[25] it will not be clear whether he is denying main facts alleged or only some relatively unimportant qualification such as time or place.

At common law and under traditional codes, judges dealt harshly with ambiguous denials, treating them as if they were admissions of all or some of the allegations to which they were directed. Judges operating under the modern federal pattern are prone to be more lenient, giving the defendant the benefit of the doubt, at least to the point of allowing him to amend his answer in such a way as to phrase his denials in proper form.[26]

In the event that a defendant is honestly in doubt as to whether to admit or deny, he is not without protection. He may deny "knowledge or information sufficient to form a belief" as to any allegation not within his personal knowledge or readily discoverable in public records.[27] Thus a defendant would not ordinarily be permitted to deny knowledge or information as to whether he assaulted the plaintiff, but he would be permitted to deny knowledge or information as to the extent of the plaintiff's injuries. Such a denial has the same effect as a flat denial, requiring the plaintiff to prove his allegation at trial.[28] Substantially the same type of qualification is permitted with respect to affirmative allegations. The plaintiff in his complaint or the defendant in an affirmative defense may preface an allegation with the words "on information and belief."[29] This indicates that he is not relying upon personal knowledge, but upon information received from others.

## Affirmative Defenses

The other type of approach in an answer is called an "affirmative defense" or, in the more colorful language of old common

37

law, a "plea in confession and avoidance."[30] By it, the defendant says in effect: "That is not the whole story. Other things happened which exempt me from liability and bar the plaintiff from remedy he seeks." We might characterize this as the "yes but—" approach to distinguish it from the "So what?" and "Not so" approaches considered earlier. A couple of examples may help. Suppose the defendant, driving his car, negligently runs over the plaintiff, a pedestrian. Later the defendant visits the plaintiff in a hospital and gives him $1000, which the plaintiff accepts in full satisfaction of his claim for damages, signing a "release" which exonerates the defendant from liability. Nevertheless, the plaintiff, becoming dissatisfied with his bargain, sues the defendant, alleging the accident, the defendant's negligence, and the injuries sustained. These allegations are true, but they do not cover all of the facts. The defendant, therefore, will prepare an answer which alleges the payment made by him and the release given by the plaintiff in return. Or suppose that the defendant borrows $100 from the plaintiff and repays it. Nevertheless, for some reason, possibly bad bookkeeping, the plaintiff sues the defendant, setting forth in his complaint only the original transaction. What he says is true, but again it does not tell the whole story. Hence, the defendant should set up an affirmative defense of payment in his answer.

The considerations which apply to the drafting of a complaint also apply to the drafting of an affirmative defense. The lawyer for the defendant screens the facts through substantive law to determine which of them are important and which are unimportant in defeating the plaintiff's claim. The substantive law on which he relies will not appear on the face of his pleading but will form its implicit foundation.[31]

The same rules as to form also apply. The same degree of detail in stating the facts is required in an affirmative defense as is required in a complaint.[32] Thus if the plaintiff is allowed to plead negligence in general terms, the defendant is allowed to plead contributory negligence in equally general terms; but if the plaintiff is required to spell out the details of negligence, so also is the defendant required to spell out the details of contributory negligence. Practitioners operating under the federal pattern of procedure are again greatly aided by the official forms of pleading provided for their guidance.

Finally, as indicated in the preceding chapter, the burdens of pleading that have to be carried by the defendant are determined by the same rules that define the burdens of pleading to be carried by the plaintiff. The guiding principle is that the defendant must allege as an affirmative defense any fact which does not tend to disprove any allegation of the complaint, but which will as a matter of substantive law defeat the plaintiff's claim.[33]

Unlike a denial, an affirmative defense does not in itself create an issue of fact. It does not involve any contradiction between the parties, for the defendant is not denying what the plaintiff has alleged, and the plaintiff has not yet had an opportunity to deny what the defendant alleges. Before the pleading reforms which took place about a century ago, this meant that further pleadings were necessary. The plaintiff had to deny or demur to the allegations in the affirmative defense. A denial would have created an issue of fact; a demurrer, an issue of law. If, instead of doing either, the plaintiff had admitted the allegations in the affirmative defense and countered with more "new matter," there still would be no issue. The process could go on almost indefinitely through "replications," "rejoinders," "surrejoinders," "rebutters," and "surrebutters" until an issue was finally framed.[34]

Today, issue formulation has been vastly simplified by a rule to the effect that any affirmative defense is "deemed" to be "controverted" by the plaintiff.[35] This means that the plaintiff, without further pleading, can use at the trial any evidence tending to disprove the affirmative defense, or to prove any "new matter" which will avoid the effect of the affirmative defense. For example, if the plaintiff is suing for damages sustained by him in an auto accident through negligence of the defendant, and if the defendant pleads a release as an affirmative defense, the plaintiff without further pleading on his part is permitted to introduce evidence either (1) that he did not give a release or (2) that the release was procured from him by fraud. The result is that pleadings almost invariably end with the answer (unless the defendant interposes a counterclaim, to be considered in Part II). A reply to an affirmative defense can be compelled by court order,[36] but this is seldom done.

Although denials and affirmative defenses are different, they are not necessarily inconsistent. The allegations in the complaint may be untrue, but in addition there may be other facts which will defeat the claim anyway. Suppose, for example, in an auto accident case, that the defendant was not guilty of the slightest negligence, but that out of sympathy and a desire to avoid the bother of fighting a groundless claim he gave the injured person $1,000, extracting a general release in return. If such were the facts as the defendant saw them, he would be justified in denying negligence, and also alleging the release as an affirmative defense. Modern practice permits such an answer. Indeed, the defendant can even assert defenses which are actually inconsistent with each other in the same answer if they are separately stated and if the pleader's obligation of good faith is observed.[37]

### Motions Addressed to the Pleadings

If an affirmative defense is legally insufficient, the plaintiff is privileged to attack it much in the same way that the defendant is allowed to attack the legal foundation of the complaint. Instead of a motion to dismiss, a motion for judgment on the pleadings is used,[38] but the two are fundamentally alike. Again substantive law determines whether the pleading attacked is legally sufficient: do the facts stated in the affirmative defense, assuming they can be proved at trial, defeat the plaintiff's claim? The main difference between a motion for judgment on the pleadings and a motion to dismiss the complaint is that the former "searches the record."[39] This means that the judge in considering such a motion will look first at the complaint to see whether it is legally sufficient. If not, the defendant will prevail. On the other hand, if the judge determines that the complaint is legally sufficient, then and only then will he go on to consider whether the answer is legally sufficient. The motion for judgment on the pleadings, normally intended for use by the plaintiff, can be made by either party after all the pleadings are in. The defendant, therefore, would use it only after submitting his answer.

Still other motions addressed to the pleadings alone, as distinguished from the motion for summary judgment (to be considered in Chapter 4), are possible. One is the motion to strike certain allegations in the complaint or answer rather than the entire document.[40] It is granted only if the matter challenged is "redundant, immaterial, impertinent or scandalous" and if retaining it in the pleading would prejudice the other side.[41] Since prejudice rarely results from including too much detail in a pleading, the motion is seldom made or granted. Another is the motion to make a pleading more definite and certain, used where one side thinks the other has provided too little detail. This also is a disfavored motion, and under the federal pattern a judge should grant it only when the complaining party is required to file a responsive pleading and is unable to do so because the pleading to which he must respond is excessively vague or ambiguous.[42] Ordinarily the only responsive pleading required is the defendant's answer to the complaint (because a reply from the plaintiff is seldom permitted or required) and ordinarily therefore only the defendant can make the motion. It is not likely to be granted, however, because any further information the defendant needs to prepare for trial (which is why he probably seeks more detail) can be secured through discovery,[43] to be considered in Chapter 4. In states which follow the Code pattern of pleading rather than the federal pattern, an equivalent (and almost indistinguishable) motion is for a "bill of particulars," elucidating and expanding the material furnished in the pleadings.[44] Such states require more detailed pleading than is required under the federal pattern.

## Motions in General and How They Are Made

As already indicated and as will become more clear in subsequent chapters, a variety of motions are possible in the course of litigation. In general, a motion may be defined as an application to the court for a ruling. The ruling can embody any determination which the court is capable of making under the rules of substantive or procedural law. Normally, it will take the form of an "order," but occasionally that of a judgment. An order differs from a judgment in that it does not finally dispose of the entire controversy between the parties, but merely settles some problem in the course of the litigation. A special type of order, not to be confused with an ordinary order granted after hearing both sides, is an "order to show cause." It will be discussed further in a moment.

Motions are extremely flexible devices. They are used whenever no other specific procedural device is provided. That is to say, a lawyer need not find specific authorization in the statutes or rules for a particular type of motion. If he thinks that he is entitled to some judicial determination in his favor, he can use a motion to ask for it, regardless of whether his motion has a particular name or has ever been heard of before. The only limitation is that where some other device is provided for the purpose—like an "objection" to evidence—it should be used.

Motions can be made before, during and after trial. Those during trial, some of which will be considered in subsequent chapters, are made orally. Those made before and after trial are in writing, and are brought on for hearing either by "notice of motion" or by "order to show cause."

The distinction between a notice of motion and an order to show cause creates some difficulty. Perhaps the matter can be made clear by looking at a couple of hypothetical examples.

Suppose that the defendant is asking dismissal of the complaint. He wants an order from the court and he seeks it by motion. Normally he uses a notice of motion for this purpose, of the type reproduced earlier in this chapter, to indicate when and where a judicial hearing will be held on whether to grant or deny the motion. It must be served on the other side a certain number of days (specified by statute or rule) in advance of the date so set. Upon the return date, the judge hears both lawyers. If he decides that the complaint is legally insufficient, he embodies his determination in an order granting the motion. If he decides the other way, his order denies the motion.

In some situations, however, a notice of motion takes too long. Suppose the plaintiff claims a piece of real estate, and the defendant also claims it. The defendant proposes to build a house on it, and plans to start cutting trees and excavating tomorrow. The plaintiff sues to enjoin the defendant from building. However, it may be months before the case can come to trial. The plaintiff therefore will move for a temporary injunction ordering the defendant not to proceed while the action is pending. However, even a temporary injunction takes time if sought by means of an ordinary notice of motion. Immediate restraint is imperative. The cutting of the trees must be stopped before tomorrow. The plaintiff therefore applies for his temporary injunction by means of an order to show cause, or, as it is sometimes called, a "temporary restraining order." By the insertion of a few appropriate words, the order can be made to accomplish the restraint needed while at the same time fixing an early date for a hearing.

The order to show cause in such a case might read as follows:

> Upon reading and filing the annexed affidavit of John Doe, plaintiff, and upon all pleadings and proceedings heretofore had, served and filed in this action,

> IT IS ORDERED

> That the defendant show cause, if any he has, before the court at Room ......, County Court House, 15th day of September 1977 at 10:00 o'clock in the forenoon of that day or as soon thereafter as counsel can be heard, why a temporary injunction should not be granted restraining the defendant and his agents or servants from cutting trees, excavating or otherwise committing waste upon the premises involved in this action pending the final determination of the action; and

IT IS FURTHER ORDERED that pending determination of plaintiff's motion for a temporary injunction, defendant and his agents and servants be and they hereby are restrained from cutting trees, excavating or otherwise committing waste upon the premises involved in this action; and

IT IS FURTHER ORDERED that a copy of this order to show cause and the accompanying affidavit be served upon the defendant at least 24 hours before the return time of this order to show cause.
Dated September 12, 1977

By the Court
William Justice
Circuit Judge

An order to show cause, it will be noted, is signed by the judge, although prepared in draft form by the lawyer for the moving party. The judge's signature is required for either or both of these reasons: (1) The order to show cause may shorten the time normally required by statute for the hearing of a motion; (2) It may temporarily restrain the party against whom the motion is made from some activity. An order to show cause is granted *ex parte*—that is, on application of one side without notice to the other. The judge has discretion to refuse it if he believes that an ordinary notice of motion will be adequate in the circumstances. That is why an affidavit is required: to show the judge why the normal procedure of notice of motion should be dispensed with. If the time element is crucial or if preservation of the *status quo* between the parties is justified for the few days which will elapse before both of them can be heard, the order to show cause should be granted. If neither of these reasons is present, the judge should refuse to sign the order to show cause, and thus force the motion to be brought on for hearing by an ordinary notice of motion.

The order to show cause does not grant the basic motion. It calls upon the party against whom it is directed to show cause why the motion should not be granted. A hearing is necessary, just as where an ordinary notice of motion is

44

used, at which time the judge will hear both lawyers on the question of whether or not the motion should be granted. An order granting or denying the motion is still necessary.

If in the case supposed the judge at the hearing should find that no interference with the defendant's activities was warranted—for example, because the plaintiff did not show any likelihood of winning the case—the temporary restraint effected by the order to show cause would be lifted. If he should find the other way, the restraint already in effect would be continued in the form of a temporary injunction. This would last until the trial was concluded and a final determination made. If at the end of the case the plaintiff prevailed, a final injunction would be granted. If the defendant prevailed, the temporary injunction would be dissolved, and the defendant would be free to commence his building.

Having now considered three different types of defense that may be asserted, it may be helpful to examine an answer containing all three:

. . . . . . . . . . . Court of the State of . . . . . . . . . . . ;

. . . . . . . . . . . County

Civil Action File No . . . . . .

A.B., Plaintiff
     v.          ANSWER
C.D., Defendant

### First defense

The complaint fails to state a claim against defendant upon which relief may be granted.

### Second defense

Defendant admits the allegations contained in paragraph 1 of the complaint; alleges that he is without knowledge or information sufficient to form a belief as to the allegation contained in paragraphs 3 and 4 of the complaint; and denies each and every other allegation contained in the complaint.

45

*Third defense*

After the surgical operation described in paragraph 2 of the complaint, defendant paid plaintiff $10,000 in consideration of plaintiff's release of defendant from all liability.

Signed: Lillian Lawyer
Attorney for Defendant
Address: 135 Elm Street
City of ......, ....... [45]

## The Effect of Pleadings upon Proof

After all the pleadings are in, one can, by studying them, reading the complaint against the answer, determine the points where the parties are in dispute. These are the issues which will require a trial, and it is to them only that the parties will address their evidence. Thus the effect of the pleadings is to limit proof at the trial. The plaintiff is not permitted to prove any facts which will entitle him to a remedy, but only those which are alleged in his complaint. The defendant is not permitted to prove any facts which will defeat a remedy for the plaintiff, but only such as will disprove the plaintiff's allegations that the defendant has denied, or prove the affirmative defenses pleaded by the defendant. If there are such defenses in the case, the plaintiff may introduce any evidence which will tend to disprove them or to prove facts in avoidance of them. Thus we encounter the most fundamental of all rules of evidence: the rule of "relevancy." Nothing which is not logically relevant to the issues formed by the pleadings is admissible; and, subject to the other rules of evidence, whatever is logically relevant is admissible. [46]

## Amended and Supplemental Pleadings

The rules governing pleading discussed in this and the preceding chapter are less rigid than might first appear. This is because pleadings can be amended to correct errors and oversights. Mention has already been made of the fact that a successful attack on a complaint or answer does not necessarily terminate the case. The party whose pleading has been held defective in form or substance is allowed to try again, perhaps several times, to correct the defects in an amended pleading.[47] If they are corrected, the case proceeds as though a proper pleading had been submitted in the first place.

Even where the original pleading is not defective, it may be incomplete. Perhaps the plaintiff has failed to allege some item of damage suffered, or perhaps the defendant has inadvertently admitted something he should have denied, or forgotten to allege a valid affirmative defense. If so, an amended pleading can be allowed, even after the case has gone to trial.[48]

The court's permission is required for any amendment except one which takes place very early in the proceedings, but permission is freely granted in the belief that cases ought to be decided on their merits, not on the basis of the mistakes of lawyers. When allowed, an amendment relates back to the time of filing the original pleading, thus obviating any difficulties which otherwise might be caused by statutes of limitation.[49]

It sometimes happens at trial that evidence not properly admissible under any issue framed by the pleadings is admitted without objection. For example, the defendant, sued for a debt, might have failed to allege in his answer that he had made a partial payment. If he offered evidence of the payment and if the plaintiff did not object to such evidence, the pleadings would be "deemed" amended to conform with the proof.[50] This avoids injustice while at the same time eliminating costly and unnecessary retrials.

A supplemental pleading is designed not to correct errors, but to allege facts that have occurred since the filing of the original pleading. The plaintiff, for example, suing to collect one installment of rent, might find that another installment has become due before the case reaches trial. If so he would be allowed to submit a supplemental complaint stating the facts with respect to the second installment.[51] Supplemental pleadings, like amended pleadings, are freely allowed in the interest of avoiding a multiplicity of lawsuits, absent bad faith or undue delay on the part of the party seeking to interject the new facts.[52]

# Chapter 4

## PROCEDURE BEFORE TRIAL

Pleadings and motions directed to them, discussed in the preceding two chapters, are not the only tools for getting a case into shape for trial or earlier disposition. Three other procedural devices, the subject of the present chapter, are today of at least equal importance: discovery, the motion for summary judgment, and the pretrial conference. They are not used in all cases or in any fixed chronological order. In combination they account for the disposition of many cases without trial and for eliminating minor issues and clarifying major issues in other cases which do go to trial.

### Discovery

The main purpose of discovery[1] is to enable either party, backed by judicial sanctions but under minimal judicial supervision, to explore in advance of trial the evidence needed to sustain his own contentions and to rebut those of the other side. The goal is to make the lawsuit less of a "sporting contest" than it would be if the parties went to trial with no more information than is furnished by the pleadings and their own private, unofficial inquiries. An additional important purpose is to preserve evidence which otherwise might be lost before trial through the death or disappearance of key witnesses.

### *Oral Depositions*

The most commonly used discovery procedure is an oral deposition. Here is how it works. Any person believed to possess information relevant to the lawsuit—whether a party to the action or a third person—can be questioned under oath by either or both sides. The questioning takes place outside of court, usually in the office of the lawyer initiating the procedure, and without securing advance permission from any judge. That lawyer secures the attendance of the "deponent" (the person to be examined) by "subpoena," which is a

49

command to the deponent to appear for examination, issued routinely by the clerk of court upon proof that the lawyer has served notice on the other side that the deposition is to be taken at a certain time and place.[2] At the time and place fixed, the deponent is sworn to tell "the truth, the whole truth and nothing but the truth" by a person authorized to administer oaths. Normally this is a notary public, and not infrequently the same person who stenographically records the proceeding.[3] The lawyer who initiated the procedure questions the deponent just as if he were on the witness stand in court. After this "direct examination" is completed, the lawyer for the other side "cross-examines" the deponent, again as if the proceeding were taking place in court. The usual rules of evidence apply, prohibiting hearsay, opinion and so forth,[4] but since no judge is present, any rulings on the propriety of the questions posed are normally postponed until an attempt is made to use the deposition at trial.[5] The scope of questioning is broad, limited only by the requirements that (1) the information sought must be relevant, (2) not privileged, and (3) not the "work product" of opposing counsel. Information is considered relevant if it throws light upon any issue framed by the pleadings or if it might lead to relevant evidence, as by disclosing the names and addresses of other persons who were present at the incident involved in the lawsuit.[6] Information is privileged only if the rules of evidence in effect in the state protect it from disclosure because of some extrinsic consideration of social policy, such as the belief that no person should be compelled to incriminate himself or that certain confidential relationships, as between lawyer and client, doctor and patient, or husband and wife would be imperiled by the forced disclosure of communications between them.[7] The lawyer's work product consists of material prepared by him or for him in anticipation of trial—notes of private interviews with potential witnesses, mental impressions, memoranda concerning tests made by experts and the like.[8]

If the deponent should fail to appear for examination or refuse to testify or balk at answering a particular question, the lawyer seeking his testimony can schedule a hearing before a judge of the court where the action is pending. If the judge finds that deponent was not justified in failing to cooperate, he orders the witness to respond.[9] If the witness refuses, the judge can hold him in contempt of court and imprison him until he complies. Should the deponent be a party to the lawsuit, additional sanctions can be imposed— striking out his pleading, precluding him from offering proof at the trial or accepting without proof the other side's version of the facts.[10]

The questions posed by the lawyers and the answers given by the deponent are taken down in shorthand. After the conclusion of the examination, the stenographer makes a written transcript, which is submitted to the deponent for checking as to its accuracy. If he agrees that it is accurate, he is asked to sign it. If he claims that it is inaccurate in some respect, the changes he wishes made are noted at the end of the transcript. If he refuses to sign the transcript, the person who administered the oath and before whom the deposition was taken signs it,[11] and it is filed in the court where the action is pending for possible later use at the trial.

Whether the deposition can be used at the trial, and if so how, depends upon whether or not the deponent is a party to the action. If a party, the other side can introduce his deposition into evidence regardless of whether he is available to testify.[12] If the deponent is not a party, his deposition can be introduced only if at the time of trial he is dead, out of the jurisdiction or otherwise unavailable to testify.[13] If he is available, he must be put on the witness stand and examined and cross-examined in the presence of the judge and jury, so that they can appraise his credibility in the light of his demeanor—his tone of voice, facial expressions, etc.[14] If the deponent, whether a party or an ordinary witness, does testify, his deposition may be used to "impeach" (contradict) him by showing that his testimony in court is inconsistent with prior statements made by him.[15]

*Written Depositions and Interrogatories*

Written as well as oral depositions are possible.[16] Taking a deposition in written form is less expensive because it does not require the presence of lawyers. But it is also less satisfactory because each question they ask must be formulated in advance, without knowledge of how the deponent will have responded to previous questions. If the lawyers for both sides cannot agree on the propriety of the questions they wish to ask, they submit their differences to the judge for decision. The questions are then sent to an official authorized to administer oaths. He calls in the person to be examined, reads the questions to him and takes down the answers in writing. The scope of examination is the same as on an oral deposition, so are the sanctions available for one who is unwilling to cooperate, and so are the rules regulating the use of the deposition at trial.

Although a party as well as an ordinary witness can be requested to give a written deposition, an even simpler procedure is available against an adverse party in the form of "interrogatories."[17] The other side simply formulates the questions to be asked of the adverse party (not a third person) and submits them to him. They must be answered under oath within a prescribed period of time unless upon application the court relieves the party of the duty of responding to them.

*Inspections*

When the information sought is not in the minds of individuals but in the form of documents or physical things, another type of discovery is available: inspection of those things or documents with the right to make copies, tests, etc.[18] A request for inspection can be directed only to a party to the lawsuit, who is obliged to make the documents or things available, unless upon application to the court he is relieved of that necessity. Again the procedure is designed to work without prior judicial permission; a judge's ruling becomes necessary only if objection is made to the procedure invoked.[19]

*Physical and Mental Examinations*

When the physical or mental condition of any party is in controversy, the judge may require him to submit to a physical or mental examination.[20] This procedure, like the request for an inspection of documents or objects, is available only against a party to the lawsuit, but unlike inspection and the other procedures discussed thus far, it requires a court order in advance, entered upon a showing of good cause. In the ordinary personal injury claim where this procedure is most frequently invoked, good cause is easy to demonstrate because the nature of the injuries suffered by the plaintiff is likely to be a central issue. Indeed, physical examination in such a case is ordinarily arranged by agreement of the lawyers, obviating the necessity for a court order.[21] Should a court order be necessary, however, and should the party to be examined refuse to submit to examination, the judge can impose sanctions against him which would effectively destroy his right to recover. He cannot be held in contempt of court and imprisoned, but his pleading can be stricken or he can be precluded from offering evidence as to his condition.[22]

## The Notice to Admit

Also classified as a discovery device is the "notice to admit," used where one party already knows certain facts that need to be established, but desires to avoid the trouble, expense and delay of proving them at trial. If the other party can be forced in advance of trial to admit matters that are not reasonably subject to dispute, the trial will be speeded up and streamlined, saving unnecessary expense to the public and both litigants. A party taking advantage of this procedure serves on the other side a document specifying in detail the matters as to which admissions are sought. That side then has a limited number of days (30 under the Federal Rules) to respond. If he fails to respond within the time allowed, he is deemed to have made the admissions sought; the facts specified are established and need not be proved at the trial.[23] If, on the other hand, he denies the facts specified, they must be proved at the trial in the usual manner, but the cost of such proof can be imposed on him if his denial was unjustified —motivated, for example, solely by a desire to delay the proceedings and cause trouble for the opposing party.[24]

Thus, if a plaintiff were suing to collect on a promissory note, he might ask the defendant to admit the genuineness of his own signature on the document. If the defendant refused, the plaintiff might be forced to call a handwriting expert to testify that the document was authentic. Should the court find that the signature was genuine and that the defendant's refusal to admit that fact was unreasonable, he could require the defendant to pay the fees of the handwriting expert and the fees of the plaintiff's lawyer in preparing, introducing and supporting the evidence. Ordinarily the losing party is not required to pay the expenses of the other side in litigation, but only fairly nominal "costs."[25] The notice to admit procedure represents a partial exception to this general rule.

Generally speaking, discovery procedures are operated by the lawyers without judicial help or supervision. The judge's role is relatively passive: only to rule on disputes arising during the course of discovery. If neither lawyer initiates discovery, none will take place. If discovery takes place and no dispute arises, no judge will be aware of it unless and until an attempt is made to use the information gained thereby at trial.

### Summary Judgment

A motion for summary judgment is often, but not always, based upon information secured through discovery.[26] Equally well, it can be based upon affidavits (sworn statements under oath) containing information possessed by a party prior to the commencement of litigation or acquired through private, unofficial investigation thereafter.[27] Its essence is that it is based upon data not appearing on the face of the pleadings. In this vital respect, it differs from the motions discussed in the preceding chapter. The motion to dismiss, the motion to strike and the motion for judgment on the pleadings are addressed to the face of the pleadings. They assume that the allegations in the pleadings are true and raise only a question of law—whether the facts stated justify a remedy under substantive law. They do not go behind the pleadings to the underlying facts.[28]

The motion for summary judgment is different. It looks behind (or "pierces") the pleadings to see if the statements made in them are true. It raises questions of fact that would ordinarily have to be resolved by a trial at which witnesses would testify and documentary evidence would be introduced. If prior to trial the facts are so clear that reasonable persons could not disagree about them, there is no need for a trial.[29]

A hypothetical case will reveal the limitations of motions addressed to the face of the pleadings and the need for the motion now under consideration. Suppose the actual facts are as follows: The defendant has bought an automobile from the plaintiff, giving a promissory note for the purchase price, and payment is not made when due. The plaintiff sues, alleging the purchase, the giving of the note and the defendant's failure to pay. The defendant in his answer denies all allegations of the complaint. This denial, while legally sufficient on its face and therefor presumptively enough to force the plaintiff to trial where he would have to prove his allegations, is false in fact. It is interposed only in the hope of frustrating the plaintiff and delaying collection of the debt. If the plaintiff moved to strike the answer or for judgment on the pleadings, he would not succeed, for the denials would be taken at face value until their falsity could be established by evidence.

If, on the other hand, the plaintiff moved for summary judgment, he would submit to the court documentary proof in support of his motion. One such item of proof would be the note signed by the defendant. Another might be the affidavit of the plaintiff setting forth the dealings between the parties and the fact that the note was never paid; or alternatively, if discovery had been used, admissions of the defendant obtained thereby as to the purchase, the giving of the note and his failure to pay. An affidavit must be made by one who has personal knowledge of the facts and who would be competent to testify as to them if the case were on trial. His statements must be as specific and detailed as if he were giving evidence before the judge and jury. He cannot indulge in the type of broad, conclusory statements that are allowed in pleadings.[30] The defendant would be given the opportunity of submitting contradictory proof in similar documentary form—his affidavit for example. But in the factual situation supposed, he could not truthfully submit a counter affidavit. He might have been willing to sign a false verification of the generalized legal verbiage of his answer or to allow his lawyer to sign a false certification, but he would probably balk at signing an affidavit in which he affirmatively told specific lies under oath and the threat of possible criminal prosecution for perjury or false swearing. Assuming that the defendant submitted no affidavit in opposition or that he merely asserted that he stood on his answer and demanded trial[31] or that he submitted an affidavit which did not fairly meet the substance of the plaintiff's affidavit, the trial judge would have little difficulty in concluding that a trial was not warranted. He would grant the plaintiff's motion for summary judgment and this would have the same effect as a judgment entered at the end of a full dress trial. If, on the other hand, the defendant were willing to submit a deliberately false affidavit and so risk the possibility of a criminal prosecution, the judge would be powerless to dispose of the case summarily. A trial would be necessary, for as we shall see in Chapter 5, the credibility of the parties cannot be determined by simply comparing their contradictory affidavits.

Changing the facts of our hypothetical case, let us suppose that the promissory note was in fact fully paid. In this situation, the defendant would move for summary judgment, attaching to his affidavit either his cancelled check endorsed by the plaintiff or the plaintiff's receipt for payment in full. The plaintiff, although privileged to submit contradictory proof, would probably not attempt to do so, and summary judgment would be entered for the defendant. Either party, in other words, can move for and be granted summary judgment in an appropriate case.[32] Furthermore, there is no restriction on the type of case in which summary judgment can be used—whether for breach of contract, to recover property, to collect damages for a tort or whatever.[33]

If the judge cannot dispose of the entire case by summary judgment, he can grant a partial summary judgment on particular issues, leaving the remaining issues for trial.[34] Thus, in a given case the question of whether the defendant was liable might be crystal clear, but the amount of damages suffered by the plaintiff might be hotly contested. If so, the court could enter summary judgment as to liability, leaving damages to be determined at trial in the usual manner. It goes without saying that any dispute which would justify trial must not only be genuine but must concern a material issue—one which under substantive law would affect the grant or denial of a remedy.[35] If in either of the hypotheticals just discussed, the defendant asserted that he was poor and the plaintiff rich and the plaintiff disagreed, this controversy would be immaterial and so would not justify trial or prevent the granting of the motion for summary judgment.

If there is a genuine dispute between the parties on a material issue of fact, a trial is necessary to resolve it. Summary judgment is not meant to be used except in very clear cases.[36] If it were used too freely, litigants would be deprived of their day in court, and judges would usurp the function of juries in violation of constitutional guarantees.[37] When a judge rules on a motion for summary judgment, he is not in theory deciding any question of fact, but rather whether there is a genuine dispute as to any material issue of fact. If the facts are undisputed, a jury decision is not constitutionally necessary. Historically, judges have long exercised the power to direct verdicts in cases tried before juries.[38] If the evidence is so clear that reasonable people could reach only one conclusion, the judge decides the case himself by granting a motion for a directed verdict. Essentially the same judicial power is exercised on a motion for summary judgment, the only difference being that the exercise of the power is moved forward in point of time.[39] Instead of waiting the months or years needed to reach trial and imposing on the parties and the public the trouble and expense of formally introducing evidence, the process of disposing of very clear cases is expedited and telescoped into the motion for summary judgment.

The foregoing discussion has emphasized the difference between the motion for summary judgment and motions

57

addressed to the face of the pleadings. The difference is fundamental and deserves emphasis. Nevertheless, lawyers sometimes fail to grasp the distinction and use a motion to dismiss or to strike or for judgment on the pleadings when they ought instead to use a motion for summary judgment. When this happens, judges are likely to view the mistake leniently. If the party making a motion normally addressed only to the face of the pleadings submits in support of it documentary material outside of the pleadings and if the judge is willing to accept and consider such material, the motion is converted into one for summary judgment and decided accordingly.[40] This is poor practice on the part of the lawyer, but since courts today are reluctant to visit the sins of the lawyer on his client and anxious to come to grips with problems of substance rather than form, the error is frequently overlooked.

Motions for summary judgment, like proceedings for discovery, are the responsibility of the lawyers, to be used or not as they see fit. Under the adversary system of procedure, we must remind ourselves, judges have no independent responsibility to develop facts, to formulate issues or to dispose of cases in the most efficient and expeditious manner possible.

### The Pretrial Conference

Whereas discovery procedures and summary judgment rely upon the initiative of lawyers, the pretrial conference depends upon judicial initiative. It is exactly what the name suggests —a meeting between the lawyers and the judge to discuss the case before trial. Judges possess broad discretion as to whether they will hold such conferences at all, and if so, in what kinds of cases they will be used.[41] They have broad discretion also as to when they will be held (whether on the eve of trial or shortly after the pleadings are filed), where (whether in the courtroom with a court reporter present or more informally in the judge's chambers) and how (whether the emphasis should be on settlement or on clarifying the issues in anticipation of trial).[42] Not surprisingly, great variations are found from jurisdiction to jurisdiction, and within a single jurisdiction even from one judge to another. The only common thread is the idea that if the judge and the lawyers can get together to talk about a case before it reaches trial, settlement may result, or if not, the issues may be more clearly formulated and some of them eliminated.

All of the procedures considered earlier in this book are formalized and governed by rules of general application. The pretrial conference is unstructured except insofar as a judge formulates his own rules as to how he will proceed. At least this is true for the federal courts and the courts of most states. In a few places, however, either state-wide or local rules may have been formulated to guide and control individual judges.[43] Nevertheless, even in such places the keynote of the pretrial conference is individual flexibility—a characteristic which follows almost inevitably from the nature of this procedure.

A judge has little power in a pretrial conference. He cannot try the case or dispose of it summarily or decide issues of law or fact. All he can force the lawyers to do is attend the conference,[44] and possibly prepare for it.[45] Unless they are willing to cooperate, the judge is powerless, for his only function in the pretrial conference as such is to try to persuade them to reach agreement. He may, of course, schedule the hearing of motions previously made for the decision at the pretrial conference, but his power of decision is derived from the rules governing such motions, not from the pretrial conference itself. And he may in the course of the conference suggest additional formal steps to be taken by the lawyers, which might result in judicial rulings—discovery for example —but again, the judge's power of decision would be derived from the rules governing those steps rather than from his role in the pretrial conference.[46] So far as the pretrial conference itself is concerned, uncomplicated by motions previously made or procedures which may take place subsequently, the judge's only job is to try to induce the parties to agree.

Both sides are asked to state in a relatively informal fashion their respective positions as to the law and the facts. The lawyers' perceptions of the issues are probably different —or at least more mature—than they were at the time their pleadings were filed because of additional knowledge gained from discovery, private investigations and other procedural steps that have taken place in the meantime. The judge, listening to and questioning the lawyers, tries to define the areas of agreement between them and the points of difference, the areas of doubt and the areas where the result is predictable. If he is a skillful negotiator, he may convince both sides that it is in their interest to settle the case. When this happens, the litigation is ended. When settlement cannot be reached, the lawyers may nevertheless agree on some matters, restricting their dispute to issues that appear critical. In that case, the judge may enter what is called a "pretrial order,"[47] summarizing the agreements reached at the conference. This order supersedes the pleadings and provides a blueprint for trial.[48] Not all judges take the trouble to draft a pretrial order, however, for here again each judge exercises his own individual discretion. If the judge disdains the role of conciliator, seeing himself as one whose only job is to preside in Olympian fashion at a formal trial, little good is likely to come out of the pretrial conference—except what may result from inducing the lawyers to meet face to face, thereby "breaking the ice" for talk of settlement without causing either lawyer to lose face by approaching his opponent.

Many cases are settled during or shortly after pretrial conferences; always, of course, with the consent of both clients.[49] This has led a not inconsiderable number of judges and lawyers to praise the procedure extravagantly for what they see is its primary role in disposing of litigation and helping courts keep abreast of their heavy caseloads. The relationship of cause and effect seems obvious. Nevertheless, a note of skepticism must be sounded, based upon empirical study.[50] Probably the cases would have been settled without pretrial conferences, simply because trial was imminent. If so, the time spent in conducting pretrial conferences is wasted and could better be devoted to trying as many cases as possible in the usual way. Other cases would then be settled "on the courthouse steps" on the eve of trial in accordance with long standing habits of the legal profession.

## Chapter 5

## THE TRIAL

Relatively few cases reach trial. The vast majority of them—about 90 percent—are disposed of in the pleading and pretrial stages of litigation. Most are settled, and some are eliminated when plaintiffs voluntarily discontinue, defendants default, or the judges rule on pretrial motions.[1]

From one point of view, the trial is the heart of litigation. All the earlier stages of a case are pointed toward and predicated on the assumption that trial will be necessary. Quantitatively, however, the trial stage of litigation merits less attention than the pretrial stages. Wise practitioners, aware of the relatively small number of trials, put great effort into the pretrial stages of a case in an attempt to achieve a satisfactory disposition without the cost, uncertainty and delay of a trial.

### Issues

The purpose of a trial is to resolve disputed issues of fact —that is, to determine what happened between the parties. If only issues of law are disputed, the judge can decide the case on a motion to dismiss or some other motion addressed to the face of the pleadings, without hearing witnesses and solely upon the basis of the pleadings and legal arguments submitted by the attorneys.

This is not to imply that no issues of law are involved when a case goes to trial. There are always questions pertaining to the admissibility of evidence, the competency of witnesses to testify, the legal significance of facts found and the like. But these legal issues are dependent upon and revolve around the issues of fact. Without issues of fact, there would be no need for trial.

The issues of fact involved in a particular case ordinarily are determined by the pleadings. The rule that only relevant evidence will be admitted at the trial means simply that evidence must be logically connected to the issues previously formulated.[2] If not so connected, it has no place in the case. Thus in an assault case, if the plaintiff alleged in his complaint that the defendant struck him, and the defendant in his answer set forth no defense except a denial, the only issue of fact for trial would be whether the striking took place. There would be no issue as to whether the striking, if established, was justified; and, subject to what is said below, no evidence bearing on that problem would be admissible. If, on the other hand, the defendant had admitted striking the plaintiff but alleged justification, there would be no issue as to the striking, but only as to whether the blow was justified.

Issues of fact as originally framed by the pleadings may be modified before trial by a variety of pretrial procedures discussed in the preceding chapters. A pretrial conference may be held, at which denials previously made are withdrawn; or a motion may be addressed to the pleadings, resulting in the elimination of certain allegations or even a whole claim or defense; or there may be a successful motion for partial summary judgment; or the parties may, with the permission of the court, amend the pleadings so as to eliminate some issues or add others; or they may, with less formality, stipulate to the same effect.

Issues also may be modified without any formality or motion by the conduct of the parties during the trial. Thus, in an auto accident case, the defendant in his answer may have denied the plaintiff's allegations as to the extent of the injuries suffered, and such denial may have survived all of the pretrial maneuvers mentioned above. Yet at the trial itself, the defendant may concede without contest the injuries claimed and concentrate exclusively on the question of liability.

Less often, but still frequently enough to merit mention, the parties may by their express or implied consent add issues to those formulated in the pleadings. If one side offers evidence unrelated to the formal issues of the case, and the other side does not object or offers contradictory proof, the latter is deemed to consent to such evidence being received and considered for whatever bearing it may have on the controversy. In such a case, the pleadings are deemed amended to conform to the proof.[3] In a slander case, for example, the only issue formulated by the pleadings and related pretrial procedures may be whether the defendant spoke the slanderous words. There may be no formal issue as to the truth of the words spoken. Yet in the course of the trial, the defendant may adduce evidence tending to establish that the words were true and the plaintiff, instead of objecting, may counter with evidence tending to prove that the words were false. In this way, the parties may interject a wholly new issue beyond those appearing in the pleadings.

One final technique of modifying the issues at trial rests in the discretion of the trial judge. A single trial may involve a large number of issues framed by the pleadings and pretrial procedures, relating either to a single claim or to a number of claims. If a multiplicity of issues threatens to become confusing or prejudicial to one of the parties, the judge in his discretion may order separate trials of one or more of the issues.[4] Thus if the plaintiff in a single case were suing the defendant for injuries received in an automobile accident and for an entirely unrelated breach of contract, the court could, and, if requested, probably would order two separate trials. Usually such is not the situation. In the average case, all the issues are likely to be interrelated so that the determination of one tends to clarify rather than confuse the determination of the others.

## Bringing a Case on for Trial

When a case is ripe for trial, the court must be set in motion to decide it. Procedures for placing a case on the trial calendar vary from one jurisdiction to another, but are of two main types. The first requires the parties to take the initiative in requesting or demanding trial. The second provides for an automatic placing of cases on the trial calendar.

The first method is illustrated by the practice in New York, where either party may serve upon the other and the court what is called a "note of issue" or "notice of trial." This paper, which briefly indicates the nature of the action and whether a jury is demanded, does nothing more than tell the clerk to place the case on the proper calendar for trial. Normally the note of issue is served as soon as the pleadings are complete, when the issues have been initially formulated.[5] If it is not served by the plaintiff within a specified period from that time, the court, upon motion of the defendant may dismiss the complaint for failure to prosecute.[6] The second and simpler method of bringing a case to trial is to require the clerk of the court, without prodding by the parties, to place each case in line for trial as soon as the pleadings are complete.[7]

Placing a case on a trial calendar does not insure its immediate or even prompt trial. Adjournments are frequently granted, sometimes for good cause such as conflicting engagements of counsel, but sometimes simply because the lawyers have neglected to properly prepare their cases.

Furthermore, it is a national scandal that many courts, particularly those in large metropolitan cities, are far behind in their work. Delays as long as three or four years between the placing of a case on the calendar and its trial are not uncommon.[8]

This situation calls for a classification of pending cases so that those which require prompt decision are preferred over less urgent cases. All cases ought to be tried promptly, for "justice delayed is justice denied." But sometimes this is impossible and choices must be made. One common device is to use one calendar for criminal cases, which clearly require prompt disposition, and another for civil cases, where the need for speed is not usually as great. Further subdivision and classification, separating jury cases from non-jury cases, contract cases from tort cases, equity cases from common law cases are not unusual.[9] Sometimes the system of classification is predicated solely upon the criterion indicated above —the need for prompt disposition. Sometimes, however, a court's classification system is predicated upon other, more arbitrary bases, such as the desire of judges to discourage jury trials, or to prevent potential commercial litigation from finding its way to arbitration, or to control the flow of cases between courts of overlapping jurisdiction. Whatever motive or method is used, some system of classification is necessary unless a court is completely current and waiting for business.

In addition to classifying cases by type, preferences sometimes must be given to individual cases within a group. Special situations may justify special treatment, as where the plaintiff is destitute, or where a crucial witness is so aged or ill that he might die before the case in which he is to testify is reached in regular order. Such situations may be handled informally by the judge granting particular preferences, or governed by rules of more or less general application.[10]

Crowded calendars delay not only trials, but also pretrial dispositions. Many lawyers are reluctant to settle cases except on the courthouse steps. If they know that a given case may not reach trial for three or four years, they may devote little attention to it in the early stages of litigation, neglecting motions which might dispose of it, participating halfheartedly in pretrial conferences, and refusing to talk settlement seriously. Hence, even cases which ultimately are destined to be settled drag their way for years until trial becomes imminent. The entire course of litigation and disposition is slowed down, and calendars become more and more congested. On the other hand, once trial calendars are cleared, pending cases are likely to disappear like snow on a warm spring day, for they are disposed of not only by trial, but also by settlement, default or discontinuance on the way toward trial.[11]

### Voluntary Discontinuance

Instead of bringing a case on for trial, the plaintiff may wish to discontinue it voluntarily. At common law, this right was absolute; until about 1400, the plaintiff could discontinue his case even after an adverse verdict without prejudicing his right to bring another action on the same claim. In that year, the right was abridged to the extent of prohibiting him from discontinuing after verdict, but he was still privileged to discontinue without prejudice at any time up to the submission of the case to the jury.[12]

Today, the right is generally much more limited. A growing number of jurisdictions make discontinuance a matter within the discretion of the trial court.[13] The good sense of such a rule is obvious. The defendant may have a claim against the plaintiff which ought to be tried regardless of the plaintiff's desires; or he may have incurred substantial expense in preparing to defend the case; or he may have a legitimate interest in the final disposition of the controversy so that his reputation will be cleared, his credit bolstered, or his title to property made secure.

The trial judge may insist that a final disposition be made, or permit a discontinuance only upon the payment by the plaintiff of expenses incurred by the defendant, or he may sever from the rest of the case an independent counterclaim, leaving it to be adjudicated even though the rest of the action is discontinued.[14]

## Constitutional Guarantees of Trial by Jury

A threshold question to be determined before the trial proceeds is whether the issues of fact are to be decided by judge or jury. More accurately, the alternatives are a judge alone or a judge with a jury, for a jury never sits alone. It is always presided over by a judge, who, as we shall see, has important duties and a large measure of control.

To understand why some cases are tried by jury and others without a jury, we must look to relevant constitutional provisions and interpret them in the light of history.

The right to trial by jury in civil cases is protected, so far as the federal courts are concerned, by the Seventh Amendment to the United States Constitution, reading as follows:

> In suits at common law, where the value in controversy shall exceed twenty dollars, the right of trial by jury shall be preserved, and no fact tried by a jury, shall be otherwise re-examined in any Court of the United States, than according to the rules of the common law.

So far as state courts are concerned, the right to trial by jury is protected by similar, but not identical, provisions in the constitutions of the various states. Representative of these is the guarantee found in the Alaska Constitution, as follows:

> In civil cases where the amount in controversy exceeds $250, the right of trial by a jury of twelve is preserved to the same extent as it existed at common law. The legislature may make provision for a verdict by not less than three-fourths of the jury and, in courts not of record, may provide for a jury of not less than six or more than twelve.[15]

The Supreme Court of the United States thus far has not held that the federal provision is incorporated into the due process clause of the Fourteenth Amendment and so made binding upon the states.[16] This is so despite the fact that the Court has extended a parallel guarantee of jury trial in criminal cases, (found in the Sixth Amendment to the Constitution) to the states via the Fourteenth Amendment, holding that trial by jury in serious criminal cases was so "fundamental" that state as well as federal courts were required to accord the right to accused persons.[17]

The fact that there is no federal constitutional guarantee of the right to trial by jury in civil cases in state courts is explained in part by a pervasive feeling in the legal profession and the public at large that the interests at stake in criminal cases—life and liberty—deserve greater protection than the interests at stake in civil cases—money and property—and that such protection is worth the sacrifice of some of the efficiency, economy and speed which characterize trials before a judge alone. People who believe passionately in the virtues of juries in criminal cases are less certain about their virtues in civil cases.[18]

Although the states are free to dispense with trial by jury in civil cases, most have not done so. Except in Louisiana, state constitutions contain guarantees of the right to trial by jury in civil as well as criminal cases. What many states have done, however, is to alter the characteristics of the traditional trial by jury, as by reducing the size of the jury from twelve to six, or dispensing with the requirement of unanimous verdicts.[19]

The right to trial by jury in civil cases, whether guaranteed by federal or state constitutional provisions, is not as extensive as is commonly believed. Not all civil cases are covered, but only those in which juries historically had been empaneled to determine issues of fact. The constitutional guarantees, promulgated for the most part in the last quarter of the 18th and in the 19th centuries reflect the long standing ambivalence toward civil juries mentioned earlier. These provisions did not undertake to extend the right as it then existed in England and the colonies, but only to hold the line against diminution of the right. At that time, the "courts of common law" were separate from the Court of Chancery, or as it was often called "equity." Certain actions could be brought only in the common law courts, where the method of trial was by jury. In general, these were cases where the plaintiff was seeking a money judgment, or to recover land or chattels. Other cases could be brought only in equity, where trial was by the judge alone. In these, the plaintiff normally was seeking a decree which would compel the defendant to do or refrain from doing some act. We shall have more to say of the jurisdiction of the two types of courts in Part III. For the present, this distinction is enough.

We imported the English system into this country, but before long in most states the two types of courts were merged into one, which could handle all kinds of cases, whether formerly triable by jury or by judge alone. Also, thinking the right to trial by jury an important element of our form of government, we guaranteed the right by constitutional provisions of the type quoted above. These took account of the distinction between the modes of trial that had prevailed in the two kinds of tribunals by providing that the right to trial by jury should be "preserved" or "remain inviolate" or be available only in actions "at common law." These phrases meant, as their language suggests, that the right to trial by jury was preserved in those types of cases where it had been enjoyed before, but not that it was extended to all types of cases. Today, therefore, in order to determine how a particular case is to be tried, we look to see whether it would have been tried with or without a jury prior to the adoption of the governing constitutional provision.

In an action seeking damages for a past tort, the parties are entitled to a jury trial because that type of action formerly would have been tried in a common law court. In an action seeking an injunction against a future wrong, the parties are not entitled to a jury trial because that type of action formerly would have been tried in a court of equity. In short, the distinction between law and equity is embalmed in the constitutional provisions guaranteeing trial by jury. For that reason, the present extent of the right to trial by jury cannot be defined in the abstract, but only in terms of history. In Part III, we shall trace the development of the common law, the growth of equity and their ultimate merger. With that background we shall be better able to understand the extent of the right to trial by jury in modern cases involving multiple claims and defenses, some of which are historically traceable to the common law, others to equity.[20]

Not all modern controversies fit comfortably into legal and equitable categories. Some concern new rights and remedies created by legislative action. In such cases, the legislature is free to choose the mode of trial—whether with or without a jury. For example, if the legislature should substitute a system of workmen's compensation for traditional tort liability in industrial accidents, an injured workman could not insist upon the right to trial by jury because "new rights" and "new remedies" would be involved.[21] But, if the legislature should merely abolish the defense of contributory negligence, the change probably would not be regarded as sufficiently radical to amount to the creation of a new right and remedy.[22] In cases containing issues of substantially similar nature to those tried at common law the right to trial by jury is preserved.

Although the constitutional right to trial by jury is preserved only for common law actions, a judge may in his discretion empanel an "advisory" jury in other cases. If he does, the responsibility for decision still rests on him. He may accept the jury's advice, but he is not bound by the verdict.[23]

## Characteristics of Juries

The common law jury had well defined characteristics. It consisted of 12 persons, no more, no less. Those persons were all males. They had to reach a verdict by unanimous agreement. They possessed specified powers and a specified relationship to the judge presiding at trial.[24]

Today's juries are more diverse in character, varying from state to state. Often they consist of six persons, of whom many are likely to be women. Instead of operating by unanimous agreement, they may be empowered to reach a verdict by a three-fourths or five-sixths vote. Their powers and their relationships to judges also vary, not only from the common law pattern, but also from one state to another.

Such changes as have occurred have come about in large part because of the fact that there is no uniform, nation-wide requirement of jury trial in civil cases. Free of compulsion from the federal constitution, the states have been free to experiment. One of the innovations introduced by state practice has even seeped into most, but not all, federal courts: the use of six person juries in civil cases.[25]

## Waiver of Jury Trial

Although a case is one in which the right to trial by jury is constitutionally guaranteed, the parties may waive that right. But both sides must be willing, for if either insists, a jury will be empaneled. If neither party insists, a judge alone may determine the issues of fact as well as the issues of law. If one party demands trial by jury and the other claims that the case is not one where the constitutional right to that mode of trial exists, the judge decides this dispute between them in advance of trial.[26]

Waiver may be explicit, as where the parties agree in open court or stipulate in writing to proceed before a judge alone; or implicit, as where they fail to take necessary steps to insist upon trial by jury. In the federal courts, for example, a party desiring trial by jury must make a written demand during the pleading stage of the case. If he fails to do so, he waives his right.[27]

### Selection of a Jury

Lawyers are directly involved only in the final stage of the selection of a jury, when a determination is made as to the fitness of prospective jurors to serve in a particular case. Preceding this stage, however, are other steps in the process, whereby citizens are screened as to their eligibility and availability to serve as jurors in any type of case. These steps take place outside of court, well in advance of the time that any of the persons being screened will serve, and without reference to specific cases. While lawyers are not directly involved, they should be alert that the procedures followed do not depart from the statutory scheme of jury selection or from constitutional norms.

Each state is free, within constitutional limits, to devise its own method of jury selection.[28] It may prescribe by statute the "qualifications" of jurors—that they must be citizens residing in a certain locality within a certain age range, not suffering from physical or mental disability, capable of understanding the English language, not felons, etc. The statutes may go beyond such relatively objective criteria to other worthy but more subjective criteria, requiring persons of "intelligence," or "sound judgment" or "good character." The danger of using such criteria is that when officials charged with jury selection are given a free hand in determining what persons are eligible to serve, they may consciously or subconsciously abuse their powers, consistently failing to select members of minorities, such as blacks, or women or members of ethnic, economic or religious groups. While the Fourteenth Amendment does not require a jury trial in civil cases in state courts, it requires a fair trial. If a jury is used, it must be selected in such a way that persons who otherwise meet legitimate standards for jury service are not systematically and intentionally excluded on illegiti-

71

mate grounds such as sex, race, color or creed.[29] The tendency today is to draft statutes on jury selection so as to eliminate hand picking and subjective standards in favor of a system of minimal objective standards and random choice, with the hope of qualifying for jury duty a fair cross section of the community.[30]

Statutes on jury selection, in addition to prescribing qualifications, also define "exemptions." A person who is exempt is given the right to refuse to serve. If he waives the right or fails to claim the exemption and is otherwise qualified for jury service, he is eligible to serve. Some exemptions are justified, as when they are extended to firemen, policemen, members of the armed forces or others in critical occupations who cannot normally be spared from their daily jobs. Others are constitutionally forbidden, as where all women are exempt[31] or at least questionable, as where particular pressure groups such as chiropodists, linotype operators or school teachers have prevailed on the legislature to relieve them from one of the normal obligations of citizenship. The evil of such exemptions is not only in the special treatment involved, but also in depleting the reservoir of capable people from which jurors can be drawn, thus imperilling the ideal of juries which represent a fair cross section of the community.

A person who is neither disqualified nor exempt may nevertheless be "excused." This is done by the judge on an individual basis and should be (but is not always) predicated on special hardship or inconvenience, as in the case of the owner of a one-man shop or a woman who has infant children and no one at home to care for them.

Any substantial departure from the statutory scheme of jury selection in its initial phases, or from the constitutional norms just discussed, as when blacks are systematically excluded from jury service, may be the subject of a "challenge to the array." If granted, the whole process of jury selection must be undertaken again in accordance with constitutional and statutory requirements.[32]

When a particular case is called for trial, the final phase of jury selection takes place. Prospective jurors are questioned under oath on "voir dire," an examination to determine their fitness to serve. The questioning may be done by the judge, by the lawyers for the parties, or by a combination of judge and lawyers. In the federal courts, judges tend to do most of the questioning themselves, but permit lawyers to suggest questions and sometimes to directly supplement the judge's questions.[33] In some state courts the same practice is followed, but in others lawyers do most, if not all, of the questioning themselves. Sometimes questioning by counsel gets out of hand, being prolonged for weeks or months at a time, "brain-washing" prospective jurors and subjecting them to unnecessarily intimate inquiries into their thoughts, backgrounds, associations and lifestyles.[34]

Based on the voir dire questioning, a juror is subject to a "challenge for cause" by either side. This calls for a judicial ruling as to his fitness to sit in a particular case. If it appears that he is related to one of the parties or interested in the outcome, or that he has formed a fixed opinion about the case as a result of pretrial publicity,[35] or that he is disqualified for any other reason,[36] he is (or should be) excused. There is no limit to the number of challenges for cause that may be made or granted.

In addition to challenges for cause, each side is allowed "peremptory" challenges, usually three in number. These allow the lawyers to eliminate prospective jurors for any or no reason. No reason need be stated, and no judicial ruling is required.[37]

When the requisite numbers of jurors have been "accepted" by not being successfully challenged either for cause or peremptorily, they are sworn to try the case impartially and the trial is under way.

## Orientation of the Jury

Jurors start their work ignorant of the facts of the case they are to decide, but with much generalized knowledge drawn from their combined life experiences. Without this

73

knowledge, trials would be impossible. The jurors could not understand what was going on in front of them or make sense out of the sounds issuing from the mouths of witnesses. If a witness said that the defendant's automobile ran over the plaintiff's leg, it would mean nothing to them, for they would not understand what a leg or an automobile was. Trying a case to such a jury would be as futile as trying it before a newborn infant, or for that matter a blank wall.

On the other hand, too much knowledge on the part of the jurors is equally bad. We have long since discarded the notion that prevailed in early common law that jurors ought to be "neighbor witnesses," relying on their own knowledge.[38] Our present system of jury selection is designed to eliminate persons having firsthand knowledge of the controversy. We operate on the belief that they must learn the facts of the case while the trial is in progress and under the watchful eyes of the judge and the opposing lawyers.

At the outset, jurors need some frame of reference both with respect to the case they are about to hear and also with respect to their general duties. As to their general duties, they may receive some help from a juror's handbook distributed to them at the beginning of their service or from generalized oral instructions given by the judge at that time.[39]

As to the case they are about to hear, they already may have learned a little about it during the voir dire examination, but they need a fuller and more coherent exposition. This is provided not by the judge—who may know no more about the case than the jurors—but by the opening statements of counsel, who have studied the evidence and prepared their presentations. Their statements are intended to provide an outline into which the jurors will fit the evidence as it is received piecemeal from a variety of witnesses, no one of whom may be able to tell the whole story about to be unfolded. Opening statements bear about the same relationship to evidence that the picture on a jigsaw puzzle box bears to the pieces inside.

The plaintiff's lawyer speaks first, stating his client's claim and indicating in a general way what he expects to prove. Then the defendant's lawyer speaks, indicating what he disputes in the statement made by his opponent and what affirmative evidence he plans to offer. The object at this stage is not to persuade, but only to prepare the jurors for the evidence they are about to hear.[40]

Controversies about opening statements seldom arise. Usually each lawyer is content to let his opponent talk without interruption, confident that if he overstates his case, promising to prove more than the evidence will show, the jurors will remember or be reminded of that fact and hold it against him. If, however, a lawyer talks about something clearly outside the issues of the case or about something that obviously cannot be admitted into evidence, his opponent can object and the court may sustain the objection, confining counsel to the permissible boundaries of opening statements.[41]

### Presentation of the Plaintiff's Evidence

Opening statements having been completed, the time has come to hear evidence. It is not the judge who produces evidence, but the lawyers. Courts have no facilities to discover the facts for themselves. They must rely on the lawyers. If the lawyers fail to produce needed evidence, the case proceeds on the assumption that such evidence does not exist.

The first witness is called. He may be one of the parties to the action or a person having no interest in the outcome of the case.[42] The only requirement is that he have some knowledge to contribute toward the determination of the issues. He may have appeared in court voluntarily or been brought in by "subpoena," a written order to appear under penalty of fine or imprisonment.

After taking an oath to tell "the truth, the whole truth and nothing but the truth," he is seated in the witness stand and the plaintiff's lawyer begins questioning him. The first few questions are related to the witness' identity—what his name is, where he lives, etc. After these preliminary questions, he is asked to tell what he knows about the facts in issue. The questions are not in such general form, however, but considerably more specific: "Where were you on the night of January 5, 1977? Did you see the defendant on that occasion? Describe what you saw," etc.

We are now in a position to complete our formulation of the distinction between evidence and allegations, between pleading and proof. Evidence is normally oral and detailed, whereas allegations are written and general. Evidence may be given by any person, whether a party to the action or not, whereas allegations are found only in the pleadings of the parties. Evidence is offered as proof for the purpose of persuasion, rather than as mere assertion for the purpose of framing issues. Evidence is addressed primarily to the jury, whereas a pleading is addressed to the judge and the opposing lawyer.

When the plaintiff's attorney has completed his questions, the defendant's attorney cross-examines the witness. Cross-examination is a safeguard designed to protect against the dangers of the jurors having to rely upon the testimony of others rather than their own knowledge. Used by all of us in every day affairs (for the most part without conscious effort), cross-examination is developed to a high degree of skill in the courtroom. In capable hands, it can go far toward demonstrating whether the testimony against which it is directed is trustworthy or the reverse.[43]

Here is how it works: The defendant's lawyer asks the witness questions that the plaintiff's lawyer did not ask. "Isn't it true that the witness is the brother-in-law of the plaintiff? Doesn't the witness owe the plaintiff $1,000 which is overdue? Was the previous testimony given by the witness based in part upon what X had told him? Wasn't the night too dark to identify the person running away? Is it possible that the witness forgot a few little details and guessed as to them? What did the witness mean by a certain word used in his earlier testimony?" And so on. "Leading questions," meaning those which suggest to the witness the answer desired by the questioner, are permitted on cross-examination, but not on direct examination (unless the witness is "adverse").[44]

When the defendant's lawyer has finished his questioning, the plaintiff's lawyer gets another chance at the witness in the form of a "redirect examination." Leading questions are prohibited (again unless the witness is "adverse"), but otherwise the technique is much the same as on cross-examination. The purpose of redirect examination, of course, is to bolster the witness' earlier testimony and establish its trustworthiness. Thus full opportunity is afforded both sides to probe into what the witness saw, what he remembers, what he means by his testimony and whether he is lying or speaking honestly.

After the first witness has been examined, cross-examined and perhaps examined again on "redirect," the plaintiff's lawyer calls his next witness, and the same process is repeated. This goes on until the lawyer has called enough witnesses (though one may be enough) to substantiate all allegations of the complaint that have been denied by the defendant. (Matters not denied, it will be recalled, are deemed admitted.) There may be only one such allegation or many. Other facts may be in dispute, raised by affirmative allegations in the defendant's answer, but if so, the plaintiff need not attempt to prove them in his original presentation. He is required at this point only to introduce evidence on those matters on which he has the burden of proof. Since a party who alleges a fact usually has to prove it, the plaintiff need not at this time attempt to disprove any of the defendant's allegations. In practice, however, the plaintiff's lawyer is likely to put on all the evidence he has, whether or not it pertains to issues on which he has the burden of proof. Why disturb an orderly presentation by one of his witnesses merely because parts of his testimony may relate to issues on which the defendant has the burden of proof?

In addition to testimony of witnesses, other evidence may be offered—documents and physical objects where relevant. If evidence has been taken through discovery proceedings in advance of trial, that too must be introduced at the trial and is subject to the special rules which govern the use at trial of discovery materials.[45]

When the plaintiff's attorney has called and introduced all the evidence he thinks he needs, he states to the judge that he "rests." This indicates his belief that enough evidence has been produced for his side to enable the jury to find in his favor, and that it is now the defendant's turn.

## The Directed Verdict

The defendant's attorney may at this point begin putting on his own witnesses; or he may feel that the plaintiff's case is so weak that production of evidence by the defendant is unnecessary. If so, he will ask the judge to decide in his favor without hearing further evidence and without submitting the case to the jury. He does this by an oral motion for a "directed verdict."[46] (The name "directed verdict" is misleading, for modern practice does not require the judge to actually direct the jury to bring in a certain verdict. The clerk merely makes an appropriate entry in the court records, upon which judgment will be entered.[47])

The test for granting or denying such a motion is whether reasonable persons could find in the plaintiff's favor. In order to apply it, the judge will have to analyze the plaintiff's evidence—first, to determine whether there is some evidence on every essential issue raised by the plaintiff's pleading; second, to determine as to each issue whether there is enough evidence to justify a jury finding in the plaintiff's favor. The judge looks at the evidence in the light most favorable to the plaintiff and draws from it all inferences which it reasonably will support. If he decides that the plaintiff has produced enough evidence, he will deny the motion and the case will go on. But if he decides to grant the motion, the case is over: the plaintiff loses.

Is not the judge, then, deciding questions of fact? Certainly, although he might not admit it. The conventional theory (which must be taken with several grains of salt) is that the judge is not deciding the actual issues, but only what reasonable persons could find as to them. For a long time judges have been exercising the power of dismissing lawsuits at the end of the plaintiff's case without submitting the issues to the jury. We shall discuss later in this chapter and in more detail the judge's power to determine issues of fact in connection with the motion for a directed verdict at the end of all the evidence.

## Presentation of the Defendant's Evidence

If a motion for a directed verdict made at the end of the plaintiff's case has been denied, it means that the judge believes there is enough evidence to justify the jury in finding in the plaintiff's favor. It does not mean that the jury must find in his favor, or even that the judge himself would so find if he were on the jury. Even though the defendant puts on evidence of his own, he may still win if the jury disbelieves the plaintiff's evidence.[48] On the other hand, the plaintiff's evidence might well be so convincing that the jury would find in his favor; or it might even be so strong, standing alone, that reasonable persons would have to find in his favor, with the consequence that the judge would direct a verdict in his favor if no contrary evidence were produced. Hence it is dangerous for the defendant to refrain from putting in any evidence.

The burden of producing evidence has shifted to the defendant. If he decides to put in evidence, and almost always he will if he has any, he does exactly what the plaintiff did: he calls his own witnesses, examines them directly, allows them to be cross-examined by the attorney for the plaintiff and possibly reexamines them himself on redirect. Again there may be only one witness, or many, depending upon what the defendant is trying to prove or disprove. The testimony may be directed solely toward disproof of the plaintiff's evidence, or it may be in support of the defendant's affirmative defenses and thus on issues on which the plaintiff may have introduced no evidence. The defendant's burden of producing evidence is not as onerous as the plaintiff's. He might win without producing any evidence at all, or by merely producing enough to disprove one of the plaintiff's allegations or by producing enough to prove one of his own affirmative defenses. But since the defendant has no way of knowing how the jurors will respond to the plaintiff's presentation, he normally will produce all the evidence he has.

When the defendant's presentation has been completed, he "rests" too. Now the plaintiff has an opportunity to call additional witnesses to rebut any evidence which may have been offered by the defendant. The same procedure is followed as before: direct examination of witnesses, followed by cross-examination, followed by redirect examination.

## The Rules of Evidence

All questions asked of any witness are subject to objection by the other side and screened by the judge through the rules of evidence. These numerous and complicated rules are the subject of an advanced law school course. Here we can only describe them in very broad terms.

We have already mentioned two of the rules: that excluding irrelevant material[49] and that protecting privileged information.[50] Now we shall note briefly three additional rules, which exclude even relevant evidence on the ground that it may be untrustworthy. These are: (1) the hearsay rule; (2) the opinion rule; and (3) the best evidence rule. As usual they come into play only upon objection by counsel, with no independent responsibility imposed on the judge to screen the evidence offered.

The hearsay rule prohibits proof of a fact by showing that someone outside of court said that it was a fact.[51] For example, if John Doe sees an auto accident and tells a policeman about it, the policeman is not permitted to testify to what Doe told him. Doe himself will have to be called to the stand, where he can be cross-examined. The fundamental reason for excluding Doe's out-of-court statement is that unless opposing counsel has had an opportunity to cross-examine Doe, we have little or no assurance that his account is accurate or complete.[52]

Some statements out-of-court, however, are made under such circumstances that the courts believe them to be reasonably trustworthy even though not subjected to cross-examination. When that is so, we usually find some exception to the hearsay rule which will let the statements in. There are many such exceptions. For example, a witness may testify to another's statement relating to a startling event made under the stress of excitement caused by that event on the theory that the speaker had no time or opportunity for conscious fabrication;[53] and out-of-court admissions by a party are received on the theory that a person does not go around telling lies which can be used against him.[54]

There is nothing evil or inherently unreliable about hearsay. Outside of court it is relied on extensively, and often regarded as more trustworthy than direct evidence. Almost all of our education is hearsay, as is our knowledge of when and where we were born and who our parents were. Practically everything we do is guided by hearsay. Many members of the legal profession believe that courts should get in step, and relax the arbitrary rules which now prevail.[55] A total abolition of the hearsay rule is unlikely, but it is consoling to realize that more hearsay is admitted by virtue of oversight or through one of the many exceptions to the rule than is excluded in the name of the basic rule itself, and further, that major reforms in the hearsay rule are being made.[56]

The opinion rule is designed to force a witness to tell what he has seen and heard rather than what he thinks. The jury, rather than the witness, is supposed to make the inferences and draw the conclusions.[57] Thus the judge would forbid a witness in an auto accident case from testifying that the defendant was driving "negligently" or "carefully." He would be required to describe the driving more specifically. How fast was the defendant travelling? Was he on the wrong side of the road? Did he sound his horn? Did he go through a stop light? On the basis of answers to questions such as these, the jury can decide for itself whether the defendant was negligent.

The trouble with the rule is that it tongue-ties many witnesses, forcing them into a pattern of speech that is alien to them. A witness ought to be allowed some latitude in telling his story in his own way. It is impossible to screen out all opinion from what a witness says. Every sentence that is uttered contains some opinion, for pure perception cannot be conveyed in words. Consequently, there is a good deal of fruitless wrangling in the courts about whether a given statement should be excluded as "opinion," or admitted as a "shorthand rendition of fact." A simpler solution, being used increasingly by skilled trial judges, is to allow the witness to tell his story in his own words, and then rely upon cross-examination to probe into the details of what the witness saw and heard as to the basis for any conclusions he may have expressed.[58]

One type of opinion evidence is universally recognized as proper—that coming from experts. If the matter under investigation requires highly specialized knowledge for its understanding, the jury, composed as it is of laymen, is incapable of drawing the necessary inferences.[59] It needs help. For example, in an accident case, it may be necessary to decide whether a certain injury is permanent. Though the injury may be described in the minutest possible detail, the jury still will be unable to decide unless it has the benefit of the opinion of a doctor, based upon his special knowledge and experience. Of course, if there are two doctors, one on each side, contradicting each other, the jury is not much better off than it was before.[60] The only way out of this quandary would be to allow the court to appoint expert witnesses of its own, and thus cease relying so heavily upon the "expert advocates" called by the parties. This solution, however, has not been widely adopted.[61]

The best evidence rule is not as broad as its name indicates. There is no general requirement that the best possible evidence must be produced on every issue or even that such evidence will be admitted, but only a very limited rule with respect to proof of the contents of a writing. The document itself must be offered in evidence unless failure to produce it can be satisfactorily explained.[62] Thus, if a party wants to prove what was said in a certain letter, he normally must offer in evidence the original letter itself. If it has been lost, a copy may be used. If no copy is available, oral testimony as to the contents may be given. The reason for the rule is obvious: it makes for accuracy in the information presented to the jury.

By screening all proof offered through the rules of evidence, and by subjecting that which gets through to cross-examination, we arrive at evidence whose trustworthiness, if not established, has at least been investigated. But we have not yet arrived at a decision. All we have is raw material, which requires further working.

## The Motion for a Directed Verdict
## At the End of All the Evidence

With all the evidence in, the time would seem to be ripe for decision by the jury. But first there is a hurdle—that of getting to the jury. The judge may be called upon by a motion for a directed verdict, interposed by either side, to decide whether the evidence is such that reasonable persons could disagree as to the conclusion to be drawn from it. The only cases which are allowed to go to a jury are those in which there is sufficient doubt so that reasonable persons could disagree.[63] Where the case is "perfectly clear," it may be decided by the judge.

Here again we see the same type of judicial control as is involved on a motion for directed verdict at the end of the plaintiff's case. But with this difference: if the motion is made at the end of the plaintiff's case and denied, the case proceeds to the defendant's evidence; if made at the end of the whole case and denied, there is no further evidence to hear and the case goes immediately to the jury. If a motion for a directed verdict, whenever made, is granted, it results in a final disposition which can be upset only on appeal.

The practice of directing verdicts leads us to consider in some detail the issues involved. If the plaintiff moves for a directed verdict, he can succeed only if the judge finds that he has proved every disputed allegation of his own complaint so conclusively that reasonable persons could not disagree, and also that he has disproved any evidence adduced by the defendant in support of affirmative defenses in the answer to an equal certainty. This is so difficult a job that a directed

83

verdict in favor of the plaintiff is a rarity. On the other hand, a directed verdict in favor of the defendant is not so uncommon, for, in order to succeed on such a motion, the defendant has merely to disprove to such a certainty that reasonable persons could not disagree any one of the essential elements of the plaintiff's case, or to prove any one of the affirmative defenses relied upon by the defendant.

Assume that the plaintiff is suing for injuries received in an auto accident, and the defendant is defending on the ground that the accident did not happen in the manner claimed by the plaintiff and on the further ground, set forth in an affirmative defense, that the defendant paid the plaintiff for his injuries and received a release. Upon the trial of the case it would be necessary for the plaintiff to prove at least these facts: (1) that he was injured; (2) that the defendant was negligent in some respect; and (3) that such negligence was the cause of the plaintiff's injuries. Also, if the defendant had produced evidence relating to the alleged release, it would be necessary for the plaintiff to disprove that he executed the release or to prove that the release was invalid because of fraud, duress or the like. As to each of these matters, his proof would have to be so strong that reasonable persons could not find against him if he hoped for a directed verdict. On the other hand, if the defendant succeeded in disproving any of the matters relied upon by the plaintiff, he would be entitled to win, or if he succeeded in proving a valid release, he would win, regardless of how weak or nonexistent his proof might have been with respect to the essential elements of the plaintiff's claim. If the defendant's proof on any of these issues reached such a degree of certainty that reasonable persons could not disagree, he would be entitled to a directed verdict.

The power to determine when reasonable persons may disagree gives the judge an opportunity to invade the province supposedly reserved for the jury. In theory, the jury alone has the right to determine which witnesses to believe, to weigh the evidence and to decide what inferences and conclusions to draw from it.[64] In practice, however, some judges, even those sitting on appellate courts, occasionally arrogate these powers to themselves. The extent to which they do so is beyond the scope of this introductory treatment. It is enough for us to develop some skepticism about judicial clichés in this field, and to realize that the test of what reasonable persons can believe is, by its nature, a vague and subjective one. In general, it can be said that a verdict should not be directed if one witness directly contradicts another on a material issue[65] or if the direct testimony of a witness is opposed by circumstantial evidence[66] or if on an issue wholly dependent on circumstantial evidence, conflicting inferences can be drawn from it.[67] A directed verdict is justified only in the rare case where there is a total absence of proof, either direct or circumstantial, on some material issue or where testimony is conclusively shown to be false by "physical facts" that are not in dispute.[68]

A verdict may be directed not only when the judge believes that reasonable persons could not differ as to what happened between the parties, but also when he believes that they could not differ as to the legal standards to be applied to the parties' conduct—for example, in determining whether either or both of the parties were "negligent." The two problems are essentially different, as we shall see in discussing the verdict, but the same test is applied. At least it is formulated verbally in the same terms. Precisely how the concept of "reasonableness" is applied to "mixed questions" of law and fact, involving ethical, legal judgments, is never satisfactorily explained. Nevertheless, judges frequently use the formula when they take a case from the jury on the ground that the standard of conduct to be applied is clear.[69] Perhaps what they really mean is that they feel so strongly as to what consequences should follow from the facts proved that they do not need and will not tolerate the jury's opinion.[70]

The power to determine when reasonable persons may disagree enables judges to prevent jurors from acting irrationally or taking the law into their own hands. However, if judges exercise the power of directing verdicts too freely, they are invading the power historically and constitutionally reserved for the jury.

## Submitting the Case to the Jury

If no motion for a directed verdict is made, or if made, it is denied, the case will be submitted to the jury. How is this accomplished?

First come arguments by the lawyers, called "summations." Each lawyer, addressing the jury, analyzes the evidence, discussing its weight and trustworthiness, comments upon the credibility of witnesses, and points out inferences which he thinks ought to be drawn.[71] In the ordinary case, the plaintiff's lawyer talks first; then the defendant's lawyer; and finally the plaintiff's lawyer has a chance at rebuttal.[72] The object of each lawyer is to persuade the jury to reach a conclusion in his client's favor. In addition to arguing the facts, the lawyers also discuss the application to the facts of rules of law to be formally enunciated by the judge. They know what the judge is going to say, because they have submitted requests for instructions to him and he has notified them of his rulings on their requests.[73] By means of these summations, the jury is given the benefit of skilled, albeit partisan, analysis.

After the lawyers have concluded their arguments, the judge takes over. He gives the jury a "charge," consisting of instructions as to how they are to proceed. For the most part the instructions deal with the applicable rules of law, but to some extent, also with matters of fact. In most jurisdictions, the judge is not supposed to express his opinion on the evidence,[74] but he is allowed to tell the jury how to weigh and assess various types of evidence which have been introduced.[75] Also, he may summarize the evidence.[76] In some jurisdictions the judge can go further and actually express his opinion, but even so he may not go too far.[77] He must speak fairly and impartially.[78]

In giving instructions, the judge does not rely entirely upon his own initiative or his own knowledge. In general, he is required to give only such instructions as properly have been requested by the attorneys in the case. They submit to him in advance various requests for instructions, from which he can choose in making up the charge to be delivered.

For example, in a case dealing with gross negligence in operating a car, the lawyer may submit the following instruction:

> If you believe from the preponderance of the evidence that the defendant in the operation of his automobile at the time of and immediately prior to the accident, exhibited such an entire absence of care for the safety of others, including the plaintiff, as amounted to a conscious indifference to the consequences of his conduct, you may conclude that his misconduct was willful and wanton.[79]

Here again we see private lawyers bearing a heavy responsibility for the proper administration of justice.

## The Verdict

The jury determination will be expressed in the form of a verdict. There are two main types—special and general. In the general verdict, the jury is asked only to say who wins and by how much—for example, "We, the jury, find for the plaintiff in the amount of $10,000" or "We, the jury, find for the defendant." In the special verdict, the jury is not asked to decide who wins but to answer a series of specific questions relating to the central issues of the case—for example, "1. Was the defendant negligent? 2. If so, was his negligence the proximate cause of the plaintiff's injuries? 3. Was the plaintiff negligent? 4. If so, did such negligence contribute to his injuries? 5. At what sum do you assess the plaintiff's loss?"

The general verdict is the traditional type. The other is relatively uncommon and not available in all jurisdictions. Where available, its use may be either discretionary with the trial judge,[80] or mandatory upon timely request by either party.[81] The claimed advantages of the special verdict are: (1) it forces the jury to a detailed consideration of specific issues; (2) it minimizes the jury's concern over who shall win and thus tends to diminish the importance of extraneous facts such as the wealth of the parties, their appearance, their religion, whether insurance is involved, etc.; and (3) it takes from the jury and gives to the judge the job of understanding and applying the law to the facts found.[82] Whether these are really advantages or not depends upon one's view as to the proper province of a jury, especially in the matter of determining questions as to the standard of conduct.[83] Where a special verdict is used, the judge's instructions tend to be less voluminous than where a general verdict is used. Many, though not all, questions of law are withdrawn entirely from the consideration of the jury by use of the special verdict. For example, the jury still has to determine in a tort case whether the defendant was negligent and whether the plaintiff was also negligent but not the legal consequence of finding them both negligent. In other words it does not have to wrestle with the concept of "contributory negligence."

Still a third type of verdict is possible—a "general verdict with interrogatories."[84] It requires the jury not only to decide who wins, but also to answer specific questions on the key issues. It has the merits as well as the disadvantages of both the general verdict and the special verdict. It requires the same full instructions as are required with any general verdict.

It may be that the case is one which should go to the jury, but that particular issues in it are so clear that reasonable men could not disagree as to them. A directed verdict is impossible because of other issues where the evidence is not so clear. In such a case, the judge submits to the jury only those issues on which reasonable doubt exists, deciding the others for himself. He does this by means of instructions, or by drafting a special verdict so as to eliminate questions which might otherwise be in it.[85] The questions thus reserved for the judge may relate either to matters of "pure" fact—i.e., what happened, or to the standard of conduct to be applied—i.e., what ought to be done.

In general the issues submitted are those framed by the pleadings, but this is not invariably the case. Issues may be eliminated during the course of a trial by one side's failing to produce any evidence at all on a given issue, or by express agreement (called a "stipulation") eliminating one or more issues from the area of dispute. In the other direction, new issues may be added during the course of the trial. This would happen if the pleadings were amended during trial, or if evidence were received without objection on a matter not covered by the pleadings. A wholly new issue might be interjected in that fashion, and it would require the same treatment as an issue properly framed by the original pleadings.

When the judge has given his instructions and submitted the form of verdict to be rendered to the jury, that body retires behind closed doors to deliberate. We must recognize that scientific truth is beyond grasp in the courtroom. Jurors are not dealing with situations capable of experimental repetition, but with human events of the past, which can never be reproduced exactly, and which were not subject to observation under ideal conditions in the first place. Moreover, jurors do not have the time that a scientist has to devote to his researches, waiting until he is sure, and until his conclusions have been checked and rechecked by other scientists. They are engaged in an intensely practical affair—that of settling disputes between busy people who have other jobs to do besides attend court. Sometimes it is more important that a dispute be settled than that it be settled right.

Consider an auto accident. It happens in a split second, probably at night. There may be no witnesses who survive the accident, or if there are, their attention may have been directed elsewhere at the time, or they may have been so affected by shock and excitement that they failed to notice the little that was open to their observation. Yet months later, perhaps years later, a jury must attempt to decide what actually happened after hearing what these witnesses remember of what they saw. It is unlikely that any two of them will tell the same story. The evidence is unsatisfactory; nobody can find out what really happened; and yet the dispute must be decided one way or the other. Society cannot afford to permit the plaintiff and the defendant to carry on a feud.

In view of the fact that evidence on crucial issues is often unsatisfactory, or wholly lacking, we should not be surprised that lawsuits sometimes reach wrong results—that in criminal cases innocent men may be convicted and guilty men set free, or that, in civil cases, negligence or other misconduct may be fastened on the wrong party. The very nature of the fact-finding process in law courts is such that truth is often unattainable. We do our best, but our best may be none too good.

To decide what happened, it is necessary to do more than merely listen to witnesses; other mental processes are involved, which call into play all of the knowledge possessed by the jurors collectively. The evidence must be sifted to extract the truth from it, or the nearest approximation to the truth that is possible.

Sometimes there is no direct proof on a particular issue, but only circumstantial evidence. Suppose, for example, that an insurance company is being sued on a policy which provides double indemnity in the event of accidental death, but nothing in the event of suicide. The defense is that the insured met his death by suicide. No one saw him die. Nevertheless, his body was discovered in a gas-filled apartment. All burners of the kitchen stove were turned on full. A note in the deceased's handwriting found near his body said, "Goodbye, all is lost." The day before his death, he had admitted to his employer the embezzlement of $100,000, and to his wife the fact that the money had gone to support a mistress. From these facts we reach the conclusion that suicide was the cause of death. We do so by applying to the facts our pre-existing knowledge, consisting of generalizations like these: (1) gas is a convenient and painless method of death; (2) while one burner of a kitchen stove may be turned on accidentally, all of them are not likely to be turned on at the same time except by design; (3) a suicide note does not get written by itself; (4) a person overwhelmed by disgrace and remorse may prefer to take his own life rather than face the consequences of his misconduct. This method of proceeding from a known fact or group of facts to a hitherto unknown fact is a logical process called "inference." It comes naturally from our psychological habits, and depends, as we

THE TRIAL

have seen, upon the use of previously acquired knowledge. Circumstantial evidence may be used not only where direct evidence is lacking, but also in addition to or in contradiction of such evidence. It is not necessarily either weaker or stronger than direct evidence. Its weight in each case is ordinarily for the jury.[86]

Sometimes evidence is conflicting and the jury must choose between witnesses who contradict each other. Mere nose-counting is not enough, for it is possible that a single witness may be more worthy of belief than three or four who contradict him. How is the choice to be made? Again by the jury applying to the testimony in question its preexisting knowledge, supplemented by insights gained from watching and hearing the witness on the stand. Is this witness' testimony consistent with undisputed circumstantial evidence in the case? Did he have an opportunity to observe what he reports? Was he capable of accurate observation? Did he take the trouble to make exact measurements? Is his memory to be trusted? Was his manner in testifying that of a sincere man or one trying to conceal and obscure the truth? Is he impartial or interested in the outcome of the action? Questions such as these call upon all the understanding which the 12 jurors possess about human nature. By putting their heads together, the jurors determine, rightly or wrongly, which witnesses are to be believed.

### Presumptions and the Burdens of Proof

Even after the jury has done its best to analyze and weigh the evidence, to resolve conflicts and to draw reasonable inferences, it may be in doubt as to what happened. When that happens, the law steps in to force a finding of the "facts" nevertheless. It does so by allocating the burdens of proof and by creating "presumptions."

On each issue of fact one party or the other has the burden of proof: that is, he will fail and the decision will be against him unless he convinces the jury that the facts on that issue are as he has alleged them to be. If the testimony leaves the jury in doubt what those facts are, the jury's verdict

91

as to them will not be "we can't decide" or "there is not enough evidence," but "no." The party who makes an allegation in his pleading normally bears the burden of persuading the jury as to its truth. Should the jury be unable to make up its mind, the issue must be decided against him. If the burden rested on the other party, the result would be exactly opposite. A classic statement on the burden of proof was made by an English judge in a case involving the question of whether a man who had died in England was domiciled there so that his property could be subject to death duties:

> I must admit that I have regarded the whole history of Mr. Winans' life differently at different stages of the argument, and the conclusion I have come to is that I cannot say that I can come to a satisfactory conclusion either way; but then the law relieves me from the embarrassment which would otherwise condemn me to the solution of an insoluble problem, because it directs me in my present state of mind to consider upon whom is the burden of proof. Undoubtedly it is upon the Crown, and, as I cannot bring myself to a conclusion, either way, whether Mr. Winans did or did not intend to change his domicile, his domicile of origin must remain, . . .[87]

On some issues, in some circumstances, the party having the burden of proof is aided in meeting it by a "presumption."[88] A presumption is an inference compelled by law rather than logic. It works like this: if a certain fact is shown to exist, the jury must assume, in the absence of evidence to the contrary, that a certain other fact also exists. This is so whether there is any logical connection between the facts or not. Suppose that a husband and wife die in a shipwreck. It is impossible to discover who died first, and yet the heirs of the husband are squabbling with the heirs of the wife as to which group shall inherit a bank account owned by the husband during his lifetime. The case cannot end in a stalemate, so in many jurisdictions we find a presumption to resolve it. If from proof of the disaster, a presumption arises that the husband died first, ownership of the bank account is considered to have passed to the wife, and from her it goes to her heirs. If the presumption runs the other way, then the wife is considered to have died first, and ownership of the bank account passes to the husband's heirs. Either presumption is arbitrary, but both have the advantage of settling the dispute and letting at least one set of heirs get back to work. Perhaps the presumption is that the husband and wife died simultaneously—a most unlikely happening. In that case, the heirs of the husband will inherit what belonged to him (including the bank account), and the heirs of the wife what belonged to her. Again the dispute will be settled arbitrarily, but in accordance with a common notion as to what the result ought to be in such a situation. Perhaps there is no presumption at all. If so, the decision will depend upon which group of heirs bears the burden of proof. That in turn probably depends upon which group institutes the action. Arbitrary again? Yes, but at least the controversy is not allowed to smolder on and on, unresolved.

The term "presumption" is a slippery one, with many meanings beyond the one given here. Sometimes it is used as a left-handed description of a rule of substantive law (like the "irrebuttable presumption" that every man knows the law, meaning really that it makes no difference whether he does or not, since he will be held responsible for his conduct regardless); sometimes it is used as a synonym for what we have described as a mere logical inference (like the "presumption" that when an unmarried man and woman are found together in a hotel room in their night clothes, they are not there to say their prayers). With such meanings of the term, or with the widely varying reasons for the creation of different presumptions, we are not concerned here, leaving further development of the concept to the study of evidence. Our only interest in presumptions is to show how they help the party bearing the burden of proof to meet it.

Allocating the burdens of proof, though effective in resolving most close cases, is not invariably a solution. While a single judge is always enabled to reach a decision by applying the concept, the same is not true of a jury. The persons composing it may disagree among themselves as to whether the burden of proof on a particular issue has been met or not. Some of them may be convinced that the plaintiff has carried his burden of proof, and others that he has not. When that happens, there is a "hung jury"—meaning one that has reached an impasse in the sense that the required number of jurors are unable to agree upon a verdict. The sequel is a new trial before another jury.

The hung jury, however, is exceptional. Most juries, by applying their combined previous knowledge and reasoning powers to the evidence, and when these fail, by using the rules as to presumptions and burden of proof, will agree upon a finding as to what happened. That is, they reach the truth insofar as it can be reached in a lawsuit.

But still something further is often (though not always) necessary before a case can be disposed of—agreement on which side wins.

### Deciding Who Wins

Every lawsuit involves another question beyond that of what happened. The other question is: what should be done about it? This can be described as a question of law, but sometimes, indeed often, it is left up to the jury. The generalization that a jury's function is to determine the facts while a judge's function is to determine the law is useful, but not entirely accurate. As we have seen, the judge sometimes determines questions of fact, and, as we shall see now, juries often determine questions of law.

The legislature cannot anticipate every factual situation that will occur in the future. Neither can the judges writing appellate court opinions. Consequently, the details of some rules of law must be filled in with reference to specific cases. This job normally is left to the jury. Very often, as in most tort cases, the only rule which applies to a given case is phrased in terms of the standard of conduct of a reasonable person in the circumstances shown to exist in the particular case. The judge, of course, will instruct the jury that the standard of conduct to be applied is that of a reasonable person, but normally it is not for him to say whether or not the actual conduct involved measures up to the abstract standard. That is the jury's task. The question is often said to be one of "mixed law and fact," although this label is not always helpful.

When the jury applies the general standard to a particular case, it does so by way of an ethical rather than a factual judgment. What it is really doing is determining whether the conduct under consideration is or is not blameworthy, and the purpose of the determination is to decide what legal consequences ought to attend the conduct. In other words, the jury is deciding what ought to be done. This is quite a different question from that involved in determining what happened. Again the jury's general knowledge and experience come into play, but this time to aid it in its capacity as a law giver rather than in its capacity as a truth seeker.

The jury's function in deciding legal consequences is well illustrated in automobile accident cases. In them, the jury decides not only such questions as how fast the defendant was going and whether he passed through a stop light, but also the very different question of whether or not he was negligent. This involves a value judgment: was the defendant at fault? Implicit is the ultimate question of what ought to be done: who should be required to bear the loss— the plaintiff or the defendant?

Some lawyers and judges are reluctant to acknowledge this function of the jury. Others assert that it is the chief justification for the jury's continued existence.[89] As for the jurors themselves, whatever uncertainties they may have as to their specific duties, they seem to have little doubt that their main job is to decide who wins and thus "do justice." Not infrequently their determination of what happened is colored by their conclusion as to the result which they want to reach.

Indeed, it is probably no great exaggeration to say that, in the field of auto accidents, juries have virtually repealed the law of contributory negligence that still prevails in many jurisdictions, and that they have gone a long way toward repealing the other rules of negligence in favor of a system modeled upon the workmen's compensation statutes. The law of torts stated in law books bears little resemblance to the law of torts administered by juries. According to "the law" in many states—meaning the statements found in the opinions of appellate court judges—a plaintiff cannot recover at all if his own negligence contributed in any degree to his injuries. Juries, however, in case after case allow recoveries where plaintiffs are partially at fault.[90] Again according to "the law," it is irrelevant and immaterial that the defendant may carry liability insurance. But not to juries. Many of them simply do not think it just—at least in a close case— to make an individual bear a loss which can be spread out among many policy holders in an insurance company.

These observations cannot be supported by definite proof, but neither are they susceptible of disproof. And few experienced trial judges, trial lawyers, insurance adjusters, ex-plaintiffs, or ex-jurors will deny their validity. The only thing which can prevent a jury from "taking the law in its own hands" is the judicial control already discussed.

It must not be supposed from what has been said that there is a perpetual tug-of-war between judge and jury over the law to be applied. Most rules of law are sufficiently in accord with common conceptions of fairness that a jury is perfectly willing to apply them. Some are so far out of line that even the judges wink when they are circumvented by juries.

Presumably the jury deliberates by going through some such mental processes as have just been described. But we cannot be too sure. Perhaps the result is reached by flipping a coin. If so, nothing can be done about it in many states. This is because of a rule that jurors cannot "impeach" their own verdicts.[91] A juror's account of how a verdict was reached is not to be used for the purpose of invalidating it. The reason for the rule is to prevent litigants from pestering the jurors after they have finished their jobs and to give finality to their verdicts.

When the jury has arrived at its decision, it comes back into the courtroom and the foreman announces the verdict. Then the jury may be "polled"—that is, each juror may be asked whether he individually agrees in the result announced.[92] The purpose is to make sure that the questions submitted to the jury have been decided by the required number of jurors. In civil cases, many jurisdictions allow a verdict to be reached by a majority of a five sixths or some similar fraction of the jurors. If the required degree of unanimity is not present, the judge will send the jury back for further deliberation or will order a new trial. If it is present, the verdict stands. However, no probing is allowed into the mental operations by which the verdict was reached.

After rendition of the verdict, the losing party may ask the judge to set it aside. Two motions are available for this purpose.

## The Motion for Judgment Notwithstanding the Verdict

The more dramatic is the "motion for judgment notwithstanding the verdict," or, as it is sometimes more properly described, the motion to change the answers of the jury on a special verdict or to set aside a general verdict and enter judgment in accordance with the evidence.[93] It presents to the judge the same problem that was presented by the motion for a directed verdict. He decides it according to the same criterion—what a reasonable jury would do if confronted with the same evidence. In other words, the question is whether reasonable persons could have reached the verdict that this jury has, in fact, reached. It may seem strange that a judge should be allowed to decide that a "reasonable" jury could not have reached the conclusion that this particular jury reached, but the power being exercised is fundamentally the same as that involved in deciding the motion for a directed verdict. The only substantial difference between the two motions is that one is made before the case is submitted to the jury, whereas the other is made after it has been decided by the jury. The effect of granting either motion is the same: a final judgment, without any retrial by the jury which heard the case or any other, unless the appellate court should reverse the trial judge's determination.

Why should such a motion be allowed? Ought not the judge to direct a verdict if the evidence is so clear that reasonable persons could reach only one conclusion? Theoretically, yes; but there are two practical reasons for preferring the motion for judgment notwithstanding the verdict. One is that the judge has more time to consider the evidence on such a motion than when deciding, under the excitement and pressure of trial, whether to direct a verdict. At the trial, the lawyers are ready to make their final arguments and the jurors are waiting to receive instructions. An adjournment to give the judge time to think over the problem presented to him would not be feasible. After the verdict has been rendered, however, he is no longer rushed.

The other reason for preferring a judgment notwithstanding the verdict over a directed verdict is that it may save the time and expense of a retrial. If the trial judge directs a verdict, and then is reversed by the appellate court because it believes that reasonable people could differ on the evidence, a new trial must be had so that a jury may decide. If, instead, he submits the case to the jury and then enters judgment notwithstanding the verdict, the result of an appellate reversal is entirely different. All that needs to be done is to reinstate the original verdict and enter judgment accordingly. No new trial is necessary.

### The Motion for a New Trial

The other motion after verdict, though not so spectacular in operation, is of more frequent use. It is the motion for a new trial.[94] There are several grounds upon which a trial judge may grant a new trial—because the verdict is "against the evidence," or because the damages are excessive or inadequate, or because of errors committed during the trial, or because of newly discovered evidence, or merely "in the interests of justice." The granting of such a motion is not a final determination disposing of the case, as is the granting of a motion for judgment notwithstanding the verdict. Its effect, rather, is to set aside the verdict and require another trial by another jury. The trial judge has very broad power in this area, and an appellate court will rarely interfere with his discretion.

The test, at least in some jurisdictions, of the trial judge's power to grant a new trial on the ground that the verdict is "against the evidence" is whether reasonable persons could disagree as to the issues which were before the jury.[95] If the evidence is such that they could disagree, and the trial judge feels that the jury has reached a wrong result, he may set the verdict aside and grant a new trial. It will be recalled that the test on the motion for a directed verdict was phrased in the same terms—whether reasonable persons could disagree. If so, the case was submitted to the jury. Thus the judge is given virtually one hundred percent control. Whenever the case is one upon which reasonable persons could disagree—in other words, whenever the case is for the jury— the judge has the power to grant a new trial. Whether many judges exercise such power is another question, to be discussed in a moment.

The power to grant a new trial on the ground of excessive or inadequate damages is scarcely less broad than the power to grant a new trial on the ground that the verdict is "against the evidence." In some cases it is perfectly clear that such power ought to be vested in the judge. If, for example, the plaintiff is suing on a promissory note for $1,000 and the jury brings back a verdict for $500, no one would doubt that the judge ought to set it aside. It would be evident that the jury had not properly decided the question of liability, but had returned a compromise verdict. However, most cases in which the power is exercised are not of this type. They are cases where the damages are not susceptible of accurate measurement—tort cases involving pain and suffering or other situations in which the damages are equally a matter of judgment or guesswork.[96]

In granting a new trial the judge is not deciding the case finally, for the assumption is that the case will be retried before another jury. But at least he is preventing the jury that heard it from deciding. And since there is a practical limit to the number of new trials that a litigant can suffer without going broke, but no legal limit (in most jurisdictions) to the number of new trials that a judge may grant, the net

CIVIL LITIGATION

result in any given case may very well be that the judge is deciding it on the motion for a new trial.

Hence, even if the power of a judge to finally decide a case directly, by motion for a directed verdict or for judgment notwithstanding the verdict, is limited, his power to grant a new trial gives him so much control over the results reached by juries that it ought to satisfy even the most vigorous opponents of trial by jury.

## A General View of the Relationship of Judge and Jury

Now, having completed our examination of the devices by which cases or particular issues in them may be taken away from the jury, we can see that we have departed very far from the oft heard maxim that questions of fact are for the jury and questions of law for the court. Perhaps the maxim should be modified to read "questions of fact are for the jury unless the judge decides them, and questions of law are for the judge." Even that would probably have to be qualified by adding "unless the judge wants the jury to decide some issues of law."[97]

There is a tremendous variation between judges as to their willingness to exercise the powers that they possess. Some are naturally positive men who tend to see all things in black or white with no intermediate grays. When they hear a case they are sure of what its result should be. Furthermore, they are sure that anyone who disagrees with them is being unreasonable. These judges will often and vigorously exercise their powers. On the other hand, there are some judges of a very different temperament, who are never sure, and who always see two sides to any question even though practically everyone else can see only one side. These judges will seldom exercise their powers.

In the final analysis, a proper relationship between judge and jury is maintained only by self-restraint on the part of the judges themselves, reinforced by the pressure of public opinion. Trial judges are usually hesitant about using their powers, and to their hesitation is added the control exercised by the judges sitting in appellate courts.

100

## Issues of Fact Determined by Judge Alone

In this and the preceding chapter, we have been assuming a case in which all issues of fact are potentially for the jury to decide—that is, a common law action where trial by jury has been duly demanded, and where there are no equitable issues. Sometimes, however, a case involves equitable as well as legal issues, for a complaint may contain several causes of action, some legal and some equitable; and an answer may set forth any defense or counterclaim which the defendant has, whether formerly equitable or legal. If there are mixed issues, the judge submits only the legal issues of fact to the jury, and decides the equitable issues of fact for himself. It is only with respect to the former that questions arise as to the roles of judge and jury—for example, whether a nonsuit should be given, and what questions should be submitted for a verdict. As to equitable issues, the judge proceeds like a jury to reach his findings of fact.

Some trials are conducted by a judge alone, without any jury at all sitting. That happens if the case involves only equitable issues or if the parties waive their right to trial by jury. Such trials are in fact more common than trials conducted with a jury, but we do not discuss them in detail because they are less complicated and less difficult than jury trials. One who understands the nature of a jury trial will have no difficulty in understanding a trial by the court alone.

The essential differences are these: First, the admission of improper evidence is not likely to be as important in a trial by the judge alone as in a trial before a jury.[98] The theory is that the judge is competent to disregard improper evidence after hearing it, but that a jury may be unduly influenced by evidence which ought to have been excluded ("you can't unring a bell"). Second, there are no problems as to the relationship of judge and jury. With the judge deciding issues of fact as well as issues of law, difficult decisions as to the scope of his authority are eliminated. Third, there is no verdict. Its place is taken by a document called "findings of fact and conclusions of law," in which the judge states his determinations as to the factual and legal issues of the case.[99]

It is not unlike a special verdict, and the mental process by which the judge makes his findings is very similar to that of the jury in reaching a verdict. The judge may also submit, along with his findings of fact and conclusions of law, a reasoned opinion similar to that rendered by an appellate court, but this is not necessary, and indeed, not even customary.[100]

## Chapter 6

## JUDGMENT AND EXECUTION

In the absence of a successful motion to set aside the verdict, a judgment follows it both in time and substance. Unlike the verdict, representing conclusions reached by the jury, a judgment represents the determination of the judge.

If a special verdict (one which, it will be recalled, does not state which party has won) has been rendered, the judge reaches his judgment by applying substantive law to the facts found by the jury. This is a logical process, as a few examples will demonstrate. The substantive law of torts in states which follow the traditional doctrine of contributory negligence is that one whose negligence is the sole cause of another's injury is liable for the damages suffered by that person, but that if the injured person was partly to blame, however slight his fault, he recovers nothing. The jury renders a special verdict that the defendant was negligent, that the plaintiff was not, that the defendant's negligence was the proximate cause of the plaintiff's injuries and that the damages suffered by the plaintiff amounted to $5,000. From this, the conclusion logically follows in the form of a judgment that the plaintiff recover $5,000 from the defendant. If on the other hand, the special verdict differed from the one just given by stating that the plaintiff was slightly (10 percent) at fault in causing the injury, the judgment would be in favor of the defendant, leaving the plaintiff without a remedy. Had the case been tried in a state which had abolished the doctrine of contributory negligence in favor of the doctrine of comparative negligence, the special verdict just considered would result in a judgment for the plaintiff for $4,500 ($5,000 minus $500).[1]

If the jury renders a general instead of a special verdict, the judge's job is even simpler. That is because the jury, presumably acting in accordance with the judge's instructions, already has applied the law to the facts to reach its decision.

Unless the judge grants one of the motions discussed in the preceding chapter, his clerk has no choice but to enter a judgment which will carry out the verdict.[2]

If a general verdict with interrogatories has been used and if the answers to the interrogatories are consistent with each other and with the general verdict, the judgment follows these combined jury findings in the absence of a successful motion to set aside the verdict. If the answers to the interrogatories are consistent with each other but inconsistent with the general verdict—if, for example, in a contributory negligence state the jury should render a verdict for the plaintiff but at the same time find that he was partly to blame for his injuries—the judge may (1) enter judgment based on the answers to the interrogatories on the assumption that specific findings ought to control over a general conclusion; or (2) return the case to the jury for further consideration; or (3) order a new trial. If the answers to the interrogatories are inconsistent with each other—if, for example, the jury should find that the defendant was not negligent but that his negligence caused the plaintiff's injuries—the judge is not in a position to render judgment; he must either return the case to the jury for further consideration or order a new trial.[3]

If the case was tried without a jury, judgment is entered upon the basis of the judge's own findings.[4] If the jury has resolved some issues and the judge others (as in a case involving both legal and equitable issues of fact) judgment is based upon the composite result of the jury's verdict and the judge's findings.

### Granting or Denying a Remedy

The judgment is a formal document, sometimes prepared by the winning lawyer but always signed by the judge or his clerk. It embodies the net result of the case. No reasons are given. If in favor of the defendant in an ordinary lawsuit, it merely says in substance that the plaintiff's complaint is dismissed—for example, "that the plaintiff take nothing, that the action be dismissed on the merits, and that the defendant recover of the plaintiff his costs of action."[5] If in favor of the plaintiff, it states that a certain remedy is granted—for example, "that the plaintiff recover of the defendant the sum of $10,000 with interest thereon at the rate of 6 percent as provided by law, and his costs of action."[6]

What remedy is granted in a particular case is not wholly or even ordinarily subject to the discretion of the judge, but rather a matter of substantive law. As remarked before, every rule of substantive law can be regarded as a statement of the factual conditions for granting a particular remedy, whether money damages, the return of personal property, the recovery of possession of real estate, an injunction, or a decree for the specific performance or rescission or reformation of a contract.

A court is not limited to granting or denying the precise remedy asked by the plaintiff in his complaint unless judgment is entered by default.[7] If there has been a trial, the judge grants whatever relief the plaintiff is entitled to on the basis of the evidence and the law, regardless of what he asked in the complaint.[8] Thus, if the plaintiff sought specific performance of a contract to buy a carload of wheat, he would not be entitled to that remedy (because wheat is not unique), but the court would award him damages measured by the difference between the contract price and the market price of the wheat at the time and place specified in the contract for delivery.

### Costs

Besides granting or denying a remedy, the judgment normally awards "costs" to the winning party, payable by the losing party. The purpose is to reimburse the winner, at least in part, for the expenses he incurred in the litigation—expenses which would have been saved if the loser had done in the beginning what the final judgment declares he should have done.

Costs, however, are ordinarily limited to relatively minor expenses incurred for court filing fees, travel reimbursements to witnesses, etc. They do not cover the major expense of attorney's fees paid by the prevailing party. The reason for so limiting costs is the belief that the threat of heavier costs might deter people from asserting claims or defenses that they believe to be well-founded. The facts are not always so easy to ascertain or the law so easy to find that a litigant should be severely penalized for making an honest mistake; the courthouse doors must be kept open to persons of modest means as well as to those who can afford substantial monetary risks in conducting litigation that turns out in the end to be unsuccessful. So run the arguments for limited, modest awards of costs.

What these arguments overlook is that modest costs may encourage frivolous claims and defenses while discouraging some legitimate claims and defenses. If one has a doubtful claim or defense, what is there to lose by asserting it? If it is rejected, all the litigant has gambled is his own out-of-pocket expenses, not those incurred by the other side. If one has a valid claim in a case involving a small amount of money or property, why sue when the expenses of litigation will equal or exceed the amount at stake and not be recoverable from the other side? That would be throwing good money after bad. Why assert a meritorious defense if defending will cost as much as yielding to the other side's demand?

The general American rule on costs (which is contrary to that followed in England) is subject to a number of exceptions, some judge-made and some created by statute.[9] In specified situations where it is thought to be in the public interest to actively encourage litigation—as in cases involving complaints by consumers or persons who have been deprived of their civil rights or victims of anti-trust violations—the exceptions allow the prevailing party to recover his attorney's fees as well as his miscellaneous disbursements.

Once the amount of costs has been determined by the clerk of the court (on application of the winning party, of course), it becomes part of the judgment, to be enforced like any other judgment for money.

## Execution

The judgment in itself does not necessarily accomplish anything. It merely grants or denies a remedy, usually in rather abstract language. It does not carry the remedy into effect, as by putting the money "granted" to the plaintiff in his pocket. Something more is needed if the defendant does not voluntarily pay up.

That something is execution. Here we must distinguish between legal remedies and equitable remedies.[10] Legal remedies are those granted in actions which formerly would have been tried in courts of common law, whereas equitable remedies are those granted in actions which formerly would have been tried in courts of equity.

Legal remedies are executed by the sheriff.[11] If the judgment is for the recovery of money, and the defendant does not pay, the plaintiff applies to the clerk of court for a "writ of execution." This paper directs the sheriff to seize property of the defendant, sell it at public auction, retain enough for his own fees, and, with the proceeds, pay the plaintiff the amount of his judgment. The balance is turned over to the defendant. In this manner, or by voluntary payment, the judgment is "satisfied," that is, paid.

This forcible method of proceeding to collect a money judgment is supplemented by the effect given the judgment as a "lien." When the judgment is rendered, or in some states when it is "docketed" (recorded) in the office of the county clerk, it becomes a charge ("lien") on any real estate owned by the defendant in the county. Even if the real estate is not sold to satisfy the judgment, the defendant is hampered in disposing of it. The amount of the judgment is a claim enforceable by sale of the property, no matter who owns it. A purchaser from the defendant must take the property subject to this lien.

If the judgment is for the recovery of specific property, the sheriff forcibly, if necessary, takes it from the defendant and hands it over to the plaintiff unless this has already been done at the commencement of an action of replevin.

If the judgment is for the recovery of possession of real estate (ejectment), the sheriff, if necessary, will forcibly remove the defendant, his family and his goods from the property.

Equitable remedies are enforced in a different fashion.[12] Historically, the equity court did not use the services of sheriffs. Its determinations (called "decrees" instead of judgments) were designed to operate "in personam," meaning directly upon the defendant. This is clear when we consider the most common and dramatic remedy of equity—the injunction. In substance the injunction orders the defendant to act or refrain from acting in a certain manner—for example to stop throwing refuse on the plaintiff's property. It is served upon the defendant. If he disobeys it, that fact will be determined at a judicial hearing, called a "contempt proceeding," and if he still stubbornly resists, the judge will commit him to jail or subject him to a continuing and accumulating fine until he is willing to comply.

It is evident that the equity method of enforcing its remedies is highly effective in most situations. There are some situations, however, where it is ineffective, as, for example, where the defendant is an exceptionally stubborn person or where he leaves the jurisdiction. Consequently, supplemental devices have been developed enlisting the aid of sheriffs, as in the case of common law judgments, to help in the enforcement of equity decrees. One such device is a "writ of assistance" to recover possession of real property awarded in an equity action. It operates like common law ejectment.[13] Moreover, in the last century and a half statutes have been passed giving the same effect to some types of equity decrees as if the defendant had complied with them. For example, a decree for specific performance of a contract to convey real estate formerly would have required the defendant to make out a deed. Under more modern practice, the decree itself operates as a deed, or at least authorizes the sheriff to convey the property in accordance with the court's directions.[14] Modern execution, though based upon common law and equity methods, does not preserve unchanged the ancient distinctions between them. It is largely statutory today.

Sometimes no enforcement of a judgment is needed. This may be because the defendant voluntarily complies with it, or because the judgment itself is sufficient, as in an action for a declaratory judgment. All that is sought in such an action is a declaration of rights. The same is true in an action for divorce alone where neither alimony nor the custody of children is sought or in a proceeding to change a person's name.

When enforcement is needed, actually securing satisfaction presents more serious difficulties than are suggested by the preceding discussion. If, for example, the plaintiff does not know what property the defendant owns or if the defendant is concealing his property or if he has placed it in the name of another, the plaintiff may encounter substantial trouble. He cannot rely upon the initiative or diligence of the sheriff to find property belonging to the defendant. Indeed, the sheriff before taking any action will ordinarily demand a bond to indemnify himself against liability for seizing the wrong property or too much or too little of it. As always in a lawsuit, responsibility rests upon counsel to take the initiative.[15] To aid him, "supplementary proceedings" have been devised. In such proceedings the "judgment creditor" (formerly the plaintiff) is allowed to examine the "judgment debtor" (formerly defendant) under oath for the purpose of discovering what assets he has which can be reached by execution. It is also possible in such proceedings to secure an order that the defendant turn over whatever property is discovered.[16] When such an order is granted, the legal remedy becomes very much like the equitable remedy, for the defendant is subject to punishment for contempt in the event of disobedience. Statutes on supplementary proceedings also often authorize injunctions to prevent the disposition of property or receivers to keep it intact or even the sale of property to satisfy judgments.[17]

In addition to supplementary proceedings, other procedural devices exist to aid the judgment creditor in securing what has been granted to him by a judgment. By the procedure known as "garnishment," a debtor of the judgment debtor (his bank or his employer, for example) can be forced to pay what is owed to the judgment creditor instead of the judgment debtor. Also, the judgment creditor may be helped by "attachment." Earlier in the proceedings when he was only the plaintiff and before judgment had been entered, he may have caused the sheriff to "attach" (seize, either physically or symbolically) property belonging to the defendant. This would have created a "lien" on the property, giving the plaintiff priority over certain other creditors if the defendant's property turned out to be insufficient to satisfy all his debts. Attachment is considered a "provisional," as distinguished from final remedy, being designed only to protect the plaintiff's interests while his action is pending. Garnishment can also be used as a provisional remedy—in other words, before as well as after judgment. In that case, the employer or other person owing money or property to the defendant would have been warned that he was required, at his peril, to hold the money or property pending the outcome of the action and to deliver all or some of it to the plaintiff if he should prevail. These and other devices available in aid of execution, including actions to set aside fraudulent conveyances, are the subject of an advanced law school course on debtor-creditor relationships. That course, in addition to providing a more detailed consideration of execution than is possible here and revealing the complexities of sorting out the conflicting claims of diverse creditors, will drive home the moral that it is not always wise to press execution too hard. The judgment debtor, if insolvent either because of the rendition of the judgment against him or otherwise, may be forced or may voluntarily go into bankruptcy and so be relieved of liability.

Not all property is subject to execution. In every jurisdiction there are statutes, sometimes extremely complicated, exempting specified property. For example, it is commonly provided that a judgment-debtor's homestead cannot be taken, nor the clothing off his back, nor the family Bible, nor the tools of his trade, etc.[18]

## Interstate Enforcement of Judgments

If no property subject to execution can be found within the state, the plaintiff may be able to go after property in another state belonging to the defendant. The traditional way of doing so would be to start a new lawsuit, since an execution has no force outside of the state where the judgment was rendered. In the second lawsuit, the plaintiff would merely allege the first judgment and the fact that it remained unsatisfied. No retrial on the merits would be required or allowed because the United States Constitution compels every state to accord "full faith and credit" to the judgment of a court of a sister state. The only ground upon which the defendant might be able to resist the second suit would be lack of jurisdiction in the first court to render the original judgment. If the first court did have jurisdiction, the second court would render its own judgment accordingly, upon which execution could be issued to reach property in the second state.[19] In recent years, a simpler procedure has been devised. Instead of bringing a new action in a sister state on the original judgment, the plaintiff needs only register the judgment by filing a certified copy in the second state. When so registered, it has the same effect as if it had been rendered in the second state.[20]

## Res Judicata

In addition to granting a remedy and providing the basis for its execution, a judgment has another important effect. That is to finally and conclusively terminate the controversy between the parties. After a party has had his full day in court, he should not be permitted to retry his case. There is no assurance that a second trial would be any better than the first. Litigation must end somewhere.[21]

A judgment can be set aside only by an appeal[22] or by an application addressed to the court which rendered the judgment to vacate it,[23] or by an independent action to enjoin its enforcement on the ground that it was procured fraudulently.[24] Any other method of attacking it will be ineffective.

This effect of a judgment is commonly described as "res judicata," although other more precise terms are being used increasingly, particularly "claim preclusion" and "issue preclusion" or, as the latter is sometimes called, direct or collateral "estoppel."

## Claim Preclusion

Claim preclusion means that once a valid and final judgment on the merits has been entered, neither party is allowed to relitigate the same claim. They are precluded not only as to the issues actually litigated in the first action, but also as to those that might have been litigated then. If the plaintiff loses the first action, his original claim ceases to exist, being barred by the judgment. He cannot successfully sue again on the original claim even though he goes to a different court, offers better evidence, hires a more skillful lawyer or relies on a different legal theory for recovery. If the plaintiff wins the first action, again his original claim ceases to exist, being merged in the judgment, and a new claim arises in his favor on the judgment. Since he is precluded from litigating again not only the issues that were tried on the first action but also those which might have been tried, the consequences of his having "split" his "cause of action" in his first effort are serious. If he suffered personal injuries and property damage but sued only for the property damage, recovering judgment, he would be barred from seeking recovery for his personal injuries in a later action.[25] If, as a landlord, he successfully sued his tenant for one month's rent when three month's rent were due, he would be barred from recovering rent for the other two months.[26] If, as a merchant, he successfully sued a charge-account customer for one of several unpaid items on the bill, he would be barred from seeking recovery for the other unpaid items.[27] Over the course of many years, courts have defined and redefined in specific situations the dimensions of a single cause of action (or claim) which cannot be split for purposes of res judicata.[28]

Just as the plaintiff is precluded from litigating the same claim more than once, so is the defendant. When the plaintiff's original claim ceases to exist by being merged in the judgment, the defendant's defenses, whether they were asserted or not, also cease to exist. A judgment by default is just as conclusive as one entered after a contest.[29] If proceedings are instituted to execute a judgment against the defendant for $1,000, he cannot effectively argue with the sheriff that he owes nothing or less than the amount of the judgment. If the plaintiff, attempting to collect his judgment, follows the defendant to another state where the defendant owns property and there sues him again, relying on the original judgment, the defendant cannot relitigate the case on the merits. The first judgment is binding and will be enforced by the second court because of the "full faith and credit" clause of the United States Constitution.[30]

By a valid judgment is meant one rendered by a court having jurisdiction. If the question of jurisdiction was not litigated in the first action, it can be litigated in the second, but that is the only question open. If the second court decides that the first court had jurisdiction, it has no choice but to respect and enforce the judgment, no matter how erroneous on the merits it may appear. If it decides that the first court lacked jurisdiction, the judgment is void. However, if the question of jurisdiction was litigated in the first action, the adjudication binds the second court. It has no power to reconsider even that issue afresh.[31]

A judgment is binding not only on parties to the action in which it is rendered, but also on those in "privity" with them. These are persons (sometimes called "privies") who have such a close relationship to the parties that they too, in the interests of fairness and judicial economy, ought to be foreclosed from relitigating the matters decided.[32] Thus an insurance company, having the power to control the defense of a tort action against the owner of an automobile insured by it would be as much bound by the judgment in that action as the owner himself.[33] Similarly, a person who inherited or purchased land from another and thus became a successor in title would be bound by a judgment against the former owner fixing the boundaries of the land.[34]

113

*Issue Preclusion*

Beyond precluding the parties and those in privity with them from relitigating the same claim, the judgment precludes them from relitigating the same issues that they have already litigated even if those issues arise in connection with a different claim. This is called "issue preclusion." Suppose that two motorists, A and B, are involved in a collision and both are injured. A sues B, alleging that B's negligence caused the collision. B denies that he was negligent and asserts that A's negligence caused the collision. A trial is held and A wins, recovering damages for his injuries. Now B sues for the injuries he suffered in the same accident, claiming that he was free of negligence and that the cause of the collision was A's negligence. Although B's claim is obviously not the same as A's, the first judgment is conclusive as to the issues actually litigated, namely whether A, B, or both were at fault. The result in the second case is a foregone conclusion under principles of res judicata—judgment for A (who was the winning plaintiff in the first action and the defendant in the second).[35] Issue preclusion, unlike claim preclusion, is concerned only with issues that were actually litigated, not with those that might have been but were not litigated.

Since issue preclusion comes into play when a different claim is asserted than the one originally litigated, an important and interesting question arises as to the consequences of the judgment, if any, for persons who were neither parties to the first action nor in privity with those parties. Suppose, for example, that two people are injured when the taxi in which they are riding crashes into a telephone pole. One passenger sues for his injuries, alleging negligence on the part of the taxi driver. The case is tried and results in a judgment for the plaintiff against the taxi driver. Now the other passenger sues for his injuries. He was not a party to the first action, nor in privity with the first passenger. His claim is different from and independent of the other claim, but it raises an identical issue—whether the taxi driver was negligent. Can the second passenger take advantage of the first passenger's judgment? Is the taxi driver precluded from relitigating his alleged negligence? The traditional answer to both these questions is "no." It is based on the rationale that unless both parties to the second action are bound by the prior judgment, neither is; there must be "mutuality of estoppel."[36] In the situation supposed, had the judgment gone the other way—in favor of the taxi driver,—the second passenger would not have been bound by it. The court had not acquired jurisdiction over him and he had never had his day in court. To give the judgment binding effect as to him would be to deprive him of his constitutional right to notice and the opportunity to be heard.[37] From this it follows by traditional reasoning that the taxi driver is not bound either.

The traditional rule makes little sense and does nothing to alleviate needless burdens on the judicial system. As remarked in a leading case: "No satisfactory rationalization has been advanced for the requirement of mutuality. Just why a party who was not bound by a previous action should be precluded from asserting it as res judicata against a party who was bound by it is difficult to comprehend."[38] If the person *against* whom the plea of res judicata is asserted was a party or in privity with a party to the earlier litigation, that is enough to satisfy the requirements of due process. That person had a full opportunity to litigate and did litigate the identical issue presented in the second action. He should be bound by the result and not allowed to relitigate that issue.

Such is the approach that today has been adopted by many courts. Under it, our hypothetical case would result in the taxicab driver being bound by the first judgment as to his liability. He would not, of course, be bound as to the amount of damage suffered by the second passenger because that issue was not litigated. While the newer approach generally yields a sensible result, it creates difficulties in some situations. A disaster involving a train or an airplane, for example, may result in injury to hundreds of people. If one of them sues and loses, the other passengers are not bound by the result; if another passenger also sues and loses, they are still not bound; but if one passenger finally succeeds, the railroad or airline may thereafter be foreclosed from relitigating the central question of liability.[39] This seems unfair and may explain why some courts are unwilling to abandon the requirement of mutuality—or at least to abandon it completely.

The doctrine of res judicata, it must be emphasized, is concerned only with the binding effect of judgments on parties and those in privity with them. Unlike the doctrine of stare decisis or precedent, dealing with the effect of general legal principles enunciated in earlier cases, to be considered in the next chapter, it does not affect all persons similarly situated.

# Chapter 7

## APPEAL

Just as relatively few cases that are filed reach trial, so also relatively few cases that are tried—only about 10 percent—are appealed.[1] Review is not automatic. Most litigants, having had their day in court, are not disposed to go further. They may be unhappy with the judgment, but realize that it would be futile to spend time and money on what probably would be an unsuccessful effort to secure its reversal or modification. Since most appeals result in affirmance,[2] there is no point in taking an appeal unless there is a reasonable likelihood that the reviewing court can be persuaded that the trial court committed serious error or otherwise reached an unjust result.

Any party aggrieved by the judgment may appeal. Normally this means the party who "lost." But sometimes the "winner"—for example, a plaintiff who has been awarded damages which he considers inadequate—is aggrieved too.

### The Purpose and Nature of Appellate Review

The purpose of taking an appeal is to have another court look at the case in the hope that it will reverse or modify the adverse decision. Why should any litigant be allowed this second chance? Why indulge the natural desire of a loser to have another tribunal substituted for the one that ruled against him?

One reason we allow appeals is because we believe that greater knowledge, skill and objectivity can be brought to bear upon a case by an appellate court than by a trial court. The appellate court consists not of one judge, but of several senior judges—at least three, sometimes five, seven or nine —who are paid higher salaries and whose jobs carry more prestige. They act as a collegial body, trading viewpoints back and forth and applying their combined intelligence, experience and wisdom in reviewing the proceedings below.[3]

117

Another reason lies in our desire to achieve uniformity in the law. Even if all judges in a state were equally competent, appeals still would be needed to iron out differences that inevitably would arise between them.[4]

From these two reasons for allowing appeals arise two partially conflicting notions as to the function of an appellate court. The first is that it exists in order to make sure that cases are decided correctly. The second is that it exists in order to clarify and expound the law, filling in gaps in the existing rules and sometimes modifying them when they appear obsolete or otherwise unjust.

If the first idea were carried to its logical extreme, we would allow a completely new trial in the appellate court, with witnesses, a jury and all the other incidents of an original trial. Such appeals are allowed in some states from judgments of justices of the peace and similar tribunals (frequently presided over by laymen rather than legally trained judges).[5] But these "trials de novo," as they are called, do not represent the usual pattern.

If the second idea were carried to its logical extreme, the appellate court would be converted into a sort of second legislature. Not many cases could be appealed to it, only those involving undecided or otherwise difficult questions of law. Some schemes of appellate review, though again not representing the usual pattern, approach fairly close to this idea. The United States Supreme Court, for example, has discretionary power over a very large part of its jurisdiction. Few appeals can be taken to it as of right. Most cases reach the Court by way of a "petition for certiorari," asking review because of the importance and uncertainty of the questions of law involved. This explanation was given by a former Chief Justice of the Court:

> The Supreme Court is not, and never has been, primarily concerned with the correction of errors in lower court decisions. The debates in the Constitutional Convention make clear that the purpose of the establishment of one supreme national tribunal was, in the words of John Rutledge of South Carolina, "to secure the national rights and uniformity of judg-

ments." The function of the Supreme Court is, therefore, to resolve conflicts of opinion on federal questions that have arisen among lower courts, to pass upon questions of wide import under the Constitution, laws, and treaties of the United States, and to exercise supervisory power over lower federal courts. If we took every case in which an interesting legal question is raised, or our *prima facie* impression is that the decision below is erroneous, we could not fulfill the Constitutional and statutory responsibilities placed upon the Court. To remain effective, the Supreme Court must continue to decide only those cases which present questions whose resolution will have immediate importance far beyond the particular facts and parties involved. Those of you whose petitions for certiorari are granted by the Supreme Court will know, therefore, that you are, in a sense, prosecuting or defending class actions; that you represent not only your clients, but tremendously important principles, upon which are based the plans, hopes, and aspirations of a great many people throughout the country. Lawyers might be well-advised, in preparing petitions for certiorari, to spend a little less time discussing the merits of their cases and a little more time demonstrating why it is important that the Court should hear them. What the Court is interested in is the actual, practical effect of the disputed decision—its consequences for other litigants and in other situations. A petition for certiorari should explain why it is vital that the question involved be decided finally by the Supreme Court. If it only succeeds in demonstrating that the decision below may be erroneous, it has not fulfilled its purpose.[6]

A much more common type of appeal, which prevails in most states, represents a compromise between the two ideas. It does not involve any new trial or the direct taking of evidence in the appellate court. Instead the appellate court reviews, on a paper record of what transpired below, errors claimed to have caused the trial court to reach an improper decision. It ordinarily lies as of right by statute (though in most states it is not constitutionally guaranteed) from all final judgments and from some intermediate orders.[7]

## The Scope of Review

Upon appeal from a judgment, the appellate court can review not only errors alleged to have taken place in the entering of judgment, but also any alleged errors committed in earlier stages of the case which may have affected the final result.[8] Thus, even though in some states an order denying a motion to dismiss the complaint is appealable as soon as it is entered, the defendant may wait until the case has been tried and then if he loses, raise the question upon appeal from final judgment. If the appellate court concludes that the motion should have been granted, i.e., that the complaint did not state a valid claim (and that no subsequent proceedings have cured its defects) it will reverse the judgment.

Not all types of errors are subject to appellate review, however. A lawyer cannot argue a case before an appellate court as though it were a jury. He must be complaining about mistakes made by the trial judge. Errors of the jury are constitutionally insulated against review unless they were caused, permitted or confirmed by the judge. Thus, if a party complains of a judgment against him on the ground that the evidence does not warrant it, he must phrase his objection in terms of the trial judge's improper refusal to grant his motion for a directed verdict or for judgment notwithstanding the verdict or for a new trial. It is useless to argue merely that the jury reached an unwarranted decision.[9]

Furthermore, an appeal does not reach even all errors of the judge. The party complaining must have been hurt by the error—i.e., it must be "prejudicial" to his rights. If "harmless" it is overlooked. If, for example, the trial judge improperly excluded certain evidence but later admitted it, or if he granted a continuance that was not justified—nobody would have been hurt enough to justify reversal.[10] In addition, certain rulings are considered as being within the trial court's discretion and therefore ordinarily not subject to appellate scrutiny. For example, the trial judge is usually sustained in his decision whether to use a special or a general verdict[11] and in his ruling on a motion for a new trial, whether he grants or denies it.[12]

120

Equally important, the party complaining of an error must have tried to protect his rights below, as by making a motion that was denied, or resisting one that was granted, or urging an objection that was overruled, or otherwise taking appropriate steps to make clear his position and give the judge an opportunity to rule correctly.[13] There are two exceptions to this rule: one clear exception deals with the court's lack of jurisdiction[14] and another rather hazy exception allows the appellate court to notice "plain" error.[15] But generally speaking, unless a lawyer is alert in the trial court, his client's rights are lost before the case goes up on appeal. It is the same story that we have encountered before: a judge is not expected to be infallible, to do justice by himself, or even to rule correctly without the assistance of counsel; he is subject to reversal only for errors which he had a proper chance to avoid.[16]

Finally, the party complaining of a trial court error must persist in his position at the appellate court level. If he is urging reversal only because of the amount of damages awarded, the appellate court will not consider errors that may have occurred in determining the question of liability; if he is questioning liability only, the court will not consider the amount of damages awarded.[17]

Because of the limited scope of appellate review, the questions argued on appeal are almost inevitably less diffuse than those which were litigated at trial. When the stage of appeal is reached, the focus is sharp and narrow on the controlling issues of the case.

The limitations as well as the strengths of the type of appellate review described in dealing with questions of fact are evident. The upper court is confined to a written record of what went on in the court below. It does not see or hear the witnesses. The subtleties of the trial atmosphere, the tone of voice of the judge, the facial expressions of the parties, the gestures of counsel are gone. Hence most appellate courts disclaim any attempt to pass on the weight or credibility of the evidence on the theory that such matters can best be determined by the jury and the trial judge.[18] Happy to confine themselves as much as possible to questions of law, some appellate courts when reviewing rulings on questions of fact, as in connection with the motions discussed in Chapter 5, narrowly restrict their inquiries and refuse to upset jury verdicts if supported by any evidence.[19] Others require that verdicts be supported by "substantial" evidence.[20] Still others, while paying lip service to the roles of the jury and the trial judge, determine for themselves what inferences can be drawn from the evidence.[21] The difference between the various approaches is hard to define concretely. It is difficult even to state with precision the rules which apply in any single jurisdiction. The main limitations on the scope of appellate review are self-imposed, and even they are not always followed.

## Mechanics

So much for the function and scope of an appeal. What about the mechanics?

The party seeking review serves a "notice of appeal." Here is what such a document looks like:[22]

...... Court

| | |
|---|---|
| A.B., Plaintiff : | File No. ........ |
| v. : | Notice of Appeal |
| C.D., Defendant : | |

Notice is hereby given that C.D., defendant above named, hereby appeals to the ........ Court from the final judgment entered in this action on the ...... day of ......... .

(S) ...................

................................

(Address)

.........19........

Though it gives little information beyond the bare fact that an appeal is being taken, this document is vitally important. It must be served on the opposing party and filed in the trial court within a limited period (usually 30 days) after rendition of the judgment or order challenged. If not served and filed in time, the aggrieved party's right to appellate review disappears. Other steps in the appellate process may be delayed beyond the time limits fixed for them, but not this first step.[23] After the notice of appeal is filed, the party taking the appeal becomes known as the "appellant" and the other party as the "appellee" or "respondent." Appellate courts tend to use these terms in referring to the parties—a practice that is confusing to readers of appellate opinions, however understandable it may be from the viewpoint of the appellate judges themselves and the litigants directly involved.

Simultaneously with the filing of the notice of appeal, the appellant must furnish an "undertaking on appeal." This is a document, ordinarily executed by a surety company, guaranteeing the payment of costs which may be awarded on the appeal.[24] It does not guarantee payment of the judgment itself, nor does it prevent the winning party from issuing execution on property during the pendency of the appeal. Execution of a money judgment can be stayed only if the appellant furnishes in addition a "supersedeas bond."[25] Such a bond, also normally executed by a surety company, guarantees payment of the judgment itself in the event of affirmance, or so much of the judgment as may be affirmed. In the meantime it suspends execution.

When these preliminaries have been completed, a record is prepared so that the appellate court may see the errors complained of. It consists of the formal papers in the case (pleadings, verdict, judgment, etc.) and, as far as relevant to the questions to be raised on appeal, a transcript of the court stenographer's shorthand notes taken at the trial.[26] It is the responsibility of the appellant's lawyer to order and pay for this transcript.[27] Unless an appeal is taken, the court reporter's notes are ordinarily not transcribed. A transcript is expensive, sometimes running $3 or $4 a page. The court reporter, although paid an official salary for his work in court, is entitled to be paid for his labor outside of court in making the transcript.[28] The transcript may be supplemented or corrected by stipulation of the parties or order of the trial court as may be necessary to make it reflect accurately what occurred in the court below.[29] This batch of papers, called collectively the "record on appeal," and constituting the central foundation for appellate review, is assembled by the clerk of the trial court and transmitted to the appellate court.[30] This is supposed to be done with a fixed time—say 40 days—after filing of the notice of appeal, but in fact is often long delayed because of the time needed to get the court reporter's transcript.

Some jurisdictions require that the record be printed or otherwise duplicated, so that copies will be available for the convenience of all members of the court.[31] Others require only an abridgment to be printed, usually as an appendix to the appellant's brief.[32] In such jurisdictions, only those portions of the record which need to be considered in determining the questions raised on appeal are reproduced.

Sometimes the abridgment contains only a small part of the record, as where the sole question on appeal is the admissibility of a particular piece of evidence. Sometimes it contains a large part, as where a ruling on a motion for a directed verdict is involved, calling for the appellate court's consideration of all the evidence. The job of preparing the abridgment of the record falls on the lawyer for the party taking the appeal, but if his version is not accurate or complete enough, the opposing lawyer can insist upon the inclusion of such omitted portions of the record as he thinks necessary.[33]

Each side then prepares a brief. That of the appellant points out the errors complained of and attempts to show why the appellate court should reverse or modify the judgment. That of the appellee is defensive, attempting to show either that the trial judge ruled correctly or that his errors were not sufficiently prejudicial to warrant reversal or modification of the judgment. Despite their name, briefs tend to be lengthy documents, often running 25, 50 or more pages. After summarizing the facts of the case and the issues on appeal, they cite and discuss at length statutes, cases and other authorities deemed by the lawyers to be relevant.[34]

Briefs are exchanged between the opposing parties and enough copies are filed with the court to provide one for each judge and an additional number for miscellaneous law

APPEAL

libraries.[35] These documents provide the main working basis for the court's determination, although the full record on appeal is available for study whenever the briefs and appendices prove inadequate.

The appellant's brief is due within a fixed time (say 40 days) after the record on appeal is filed; the appellee's within a fixed number of days thereafter (say 30); and then the appellant may submit still another document called a "reply brief" within a certain number of days (say 15) after that. These times, fixed by statute or court rule, are subject to extension by court order or stipulation of the parties.[36] Even if all stated time limits are strictly observed, several months are likely to elapse between the entry of judgment in the trial court and the completion of the appellate paperwork required of the parties. With the generous extensions of time that are often allowed, many more months may go by before the case is ready to be considered on appeal. Still to come are oral arguments, which may not be reached for several weeks or months more.

Oral arguments necessarily duplicate to some extent the written briefs already filed, and might therefore be eliminated. They are dispensed with in many nations of continental Europe.[37] In England, on the other hand, it is the written briefs that are dispensed with. There, sole reliance is placed upon lengthy oral arguments of counsel, in which they quote extensively from the record on appeal and the legal authorities on which they rely.[38] The American pattern is a hybrid of these two, permitting and sometimes requiring both oral and written arguments, with increasing emphasis on the latter. Oral arguments are strictly limited in duration—15 minutes, a half hour or an hour to each side[39]—and counsel are discouraged from quoting any material that the judges can read for themselves in the papers on file. The lawyer for the appellant speaks first, then the lawyer for the other side, followed by rebuttal from the first speaker, much as in a formal debate.[40] However, if the judges have read the briefs in advance (a practice that is increasing), much of the time allowed counsel may be consumed in answering questions put to them by the judges.

Cases are not heard and decided one at a time, with the judges announcing their decision from the bench immediately after the close of oral arguments, as in England. Instead, an American appellate court typically hears oral arguments in five or six cases a day for several days running and then adjourns for several weeks while the judges write their opinions. After preliminary conferences between the judges in which they tentatively agree on the results to be reached, the cases they have heard are divided among them for the writing of opinions, either on the basis of assignment by the presiding judge or a numerical rotation system. The judge to whom a particular case has been assigned reads the briefs of counsel (perhaps he has done this once before in preparing for oral argument), consults the record on appeal so far as he considers that necessary, studies the statutes, cases and rules that have been cited, conducts independent research into the law if he is not satisfied that counsel have covered the ground adequately, and prepares a reasoned opinion disposing of the case. In these tasks, he is assisted by his "law clerk," typically a recent law school graduate. The draft opinion is circulated among other members of the court for their comments and suggestions and in the hope that they will agree with the conclusion set forth and the reasons given in support of it. A single opinion for the entire court is the ideal, but if unanimous agreement cannot be reached, an opinion representing the views of the majority will suffice. Any judge in the minority is entitled to write a dissenting opinion espousing a contrary result or a concurring opinion agreeing with the result but for different reasons than are expounded in the majority opinion. All this takes time, and it may be weeks or months after oral argument before the appellate court's decision is made public.[41]

One reason for devoting so much time and effort to the preparation of written opinions is to improve the decisional process. When judges are forced into the discipline of explaining the reasons for the results they reach, they cannot easily indulge in snap judgments. Another reason is to satisfy disappointed litigants that their contentions have received careful attention. The most important reason, however, is to assure so far as possible that the legal principles and rules that result as a by-product of the decision of specific cases are developed thoughtfully and without undue haste.[42] Each decision becomes a precedent, governing like cases that may arise in the future.

The court's decision will be to affirm the judgment below, reverse it, modify it or order a new trial. Then the record will be sent back to the trial court for such action there as the appellate court has indicated. The directions to the lower court will be contained in a formal document known as a "remittitur" or "mandate."[43]

As in the trial court, there are costs to be paid by the losing party, but again the costs fall short of actual expenses because they do not include attorney's fees for the winning party.[44] Appeals are expensive, which is one of the reasons why relatively few cases of all that are tried in courts of original jurisdiction are reviewed on appeal.

The role of lawyers in the appellate process should not be underestimated. Their briefs and arguments are of crucial importance. Appellate courts, no less than trial courts, are dependent upon lawyers. Not only do the courts have no facilities for conducting independent investigations into the facts; their facilities are inadequate for conducting independent investigations as into the law. Most appellate courts are burdened by heavy caseloads. If the lawyers who argue cases before them do not perform their jobs properly, the judges may not be able to do their jobs properly either. When that happens, the blame is not attributable to the courts alone. Private lawyers must be held accountable in large measure not only for bad decisions, but also for bad rules of law, because, as we shall see in a moment, decisions are law.

### The Doctrine of Precedent

Appellate opinions are published, widely disseminated and permanently preserved in official and unofficial reports.[45] They do more than dispose of the particular cases in which they are rendered. They enunciate principles and rules to govern lower courts in all similar cases. They create rights and duties for individuals. They become law as surely as statutes passed by the legislature. They constitute the basic raw material for casebooks which law teachers assemble and law students study.

We are dealing here with the doctrine of "precedent," or, as it is sometimes called, "stare decisis." In essence, it can be expressed thus: a decision in one case obliges the court which rendered it and all inferior courts to decide like cases in the same way. Courts in other jurisdictions are not so bound, although, in the absence of precedents of their own, they will at least consider the decision as "persuasive."[46] In this doctrine, we see the realization of one of the functions of an appeal discussed at the beginning of this chapter—that of laying down uniform rules of general application.

Juries and trial judges do not make law in the same sense that appellate courts do. Verdicts are not published for future guidance in other cases. They determine only the legal consequences of specific cases. Ultimately patterns of decision may grow up in particular areas—for example, in auto accident litigation—which will enable skilled lawyers to predict with fair accuracy the outcome of future cases, but their predictions must be based upon trial court observation, not library study. The law made by juries is truly "unwritten" and evanescent. It cannot be cited in future cases. What has been said about jury determinations applies also, generally speaking, to the determinations of trial judges. Although some decisions by trial judges (particularly in the federal courts) are published, most are not. If not published, they are not available to the bench and bar generally and so cannot be cited as precedents for future cases.

We are now in a position to further differentiate the doctrine of precedent from the doctrine of res judicata, discussed in the last chapter. That doctrine deals with the effect of a judgment in determining the facts of a particular case or the application of law to those facts. It is conclusive only on the parties to the lawsuit in which it is rendered and a few other persons standing in a close relationship to them. Under the doctrine of precedent, on the other hand, all persons who in

APPEAL

the future become involved in fact situations like the one where the decision was rendered are bound by the legal principles enunciated therein.

The law embodied in judicial decisions differs markedly in form from statutory law. Indeed, many opinions do not seem to be laying down rules for the future at all. The reader must extract the precedent from the discussion. He cannot safely pick a particular passage and say, "This is it," but must frame the rule himself on the basis of the facts discussed by the court and the actual decision made. It is not unusual that other readers will disagree with him. Unlike statutory rules, judicial rules have no fixed and indisputable textual form. Nevertheless, once the rule is ascertained by the court which is to apply it, it is just as binding as if it were spelled out in a statute.

It is useful at this point to distinguish between "holdings" and "dicta." A "holding" is what we have been discussing— a rule necessary to the court's decision on the facts before it. It may be expressly stated, or, as we have seen, implied. A "dictum," on the other hand, is a statement in the court's opinion which is not necessary to the decision—for example, a remark about a hypothetical case not before the court. Such a statement, though not to be treated lightly, does not have the same force as a holding.[47] It may be followed in later cases if the court still considers it sound, but the court will feel free to re-examine the question. Nonetheless some leading cases are remembered more for their dicta than their holdings.[48]

We have talked about the "binding" force of precedent. Perhaps that is misleading, because courts can and occasionally do overrule their own previous decisions. Most appellate judges, however, believe that certainty and stability in the law are so important that they do not feel free to reconsider every problem anew. Hence, though they may entertain grave doubts about the wisdom or fairness of an earlier decision, they do not necessarily undertake to correct it. That, they usually say, is a job for the legislature. But not always. If the legislature has long been derelict in its duty to correct

129

a notoriously unjust rule of law, a court may step in and do the job itself.[49] If a constitutional interpretation has proved unwise, the court which rendered it may feel obliged to alter its previous ruling because the legislature is incapable of doing so and because of the slow and cumbersome process of securing a constitutional amendment.[50]

Without the doctrine of precedent, the character of American law would be drastically changed. Law schools would not operate as they do today. They would require students to devote most of their attention to statutes instead of spending so much time studying the opinions of appellate courts. The fact is, however, that statutes cover only a fraction of the total law in force today in the United States. The bulk of our law of contracts, torts, property, etc. is found in judicial decisions.

Laymen often criticize lawyers and judges for their devotion to precedent. To an extent, the criticism is justified, for undoubtedly a tendency exists on the part of some members of the profession to apply old rules to new situations mechanically, even blindly. To be balanced against such abuses, however, is the consideration that if the doctrine of precedent were abolished, judges would be free to operate according to their individual, private notions of right and wrong throughout the entire area of human relations not covered by statute. Perhaps laymen would be even more alarmed at that prospect.

It is questionable, however, that the judges would in fact act much differently than they do today. Though each judge might be free to make law as he wished, he could not help knowing something about how problems similar to the one before him had been handled in the past by other judges. His inclination, therefore, would be to avoid the labor of working out a solution for himself by adopting one already formulated. Also, he would probably take the view that one person ought to be treated as another person is treated in similar circumstances, and so would conclude that it is not only convenient but also right to do what has been done before if the ideal of equal justice under law is to be achieved. Appellate decision making is never, and never can be, a matter purely of ethics, morality and justice. Those considerations are always present, but so is history in the form of existing decisions as well as statutes.

## Levels of Review

The foregoing discussion deals with a single level of review, which is all that is provided in about half the states. In the remaining states, the volume of cases to be reviewed is so large that intermediate appellate courts have been established between the trial courts and the highest state court (usually, but not invariably called its "Supreme" court). In these states, two stages of review for a single case are possible and indeed necessary in some situations to resolve differences of opinion that develop between intermediate courts. A case can be appealed from a trial court to the intermediate court for that part of the state in which the trial court is located as a matter of right. Thereafter, further review is ordinarily allowed only in the discretion of the highest court, which chooses the cases it will hear on the basis of their general importance and the need for establishing uniform rules of law throughout the state.[51] At this level, the lawmaking function of appellate review tends to assume greater importance than the function of correcting errors in particular cases. The procedure followed at both the intermediate and the highest level is basically the same.

Not all cases stop at the highest court of the state. Further review is possible in the Supreme Court of the United States, but only if a case involves a federal question of controlling importance.[52] State courts are required to follow federal law, whenever it is applicable. Most of their cases, however, are not affected by it. They typically involve torts, contracts, property and other areas of law where there is no federal legislation and where no federal constitutional questions are raised. On matters of purely state law, the highest state court has the final word, and the Supreme Court of the United States is powerless to interfere. Thus if a state court should abolish its common law doctrine of contributory negligence, its decision would not be subject to further review.[53]

In the few cases where federal questions are raised in a state court, they may or may not be controlling. If a state court should invalidate a local statute on the ground that it violated both the state and the federal constitution, the state ground of decision—the court's interpretation of its own constitution, on which it has the final say—would be controlling and render academic the question of whether the statute also violated the federal constitution.[54] If, on the other hand, the state court should hold the statute invalid solely because it violated the federal constitution, the federal question would be controlling. Similarly, if a state court based its decision solely upon its interpretation of a federal statute, the federal question would be controlling.

In such cases, further review in the Supreme Court of the United States would be possible. But it would not be accorded as a matter of right. As indicated earlier, that Court exercises a very large degree of control over its own docket by means of granting or denying petitions for writs of certiorari. It can in its discretion deny review even of a case where a controlling federal question is involved. The only situations where it must grant review of a state court decision as a matter of right are (1) where the state court has held a federal statute or treaty invalid; or (2) where it has upheld a state statute against the contention that it is repugnant to the Constitution, treaties or laws of the United States.[55] Such conflicts of sovereignty are rare.

Including both cases that can be appealed as a matter of right and those that can reach the Court only by its permission, only about 60 cases a year coming from all of the 50 states combined are reviewed on the merits by the Supreme Court of the United States.[56] The limited capacity of the total American judicial system to provide ultimate, authoritative answers to the many questions of federal law that are not presently settled on a nationwide basis will be explored further in the next chapter.

# Part II

# MORE COMPLEX LITIGATION

**Introductory Note**

Part I of this book was devoted to the basic or most common type of lawsuit, where one local person was suing another in a local court on a claim arising locally and governed by local law. Now we shift our attention to more complex litigation, first considering cases where there are nonlocal elements: (1) where the claim arises elsewhere or is governed by the substantive law of another jurisdiction, and (2) where the opposing parties are residents of different states. After dealing with such cases, we shall go on to cases where there are multiple claims or multiple parties or both.

# Chapter 8

## THE DUAL SYSTEM OF STATE AND FEDERAL COURTS

In Chapter 1, the court system of a single state was outlined. In the entire United States, however, 51 court systems are in operation, one for each of the states and another for the federal government. Each state, moreover, has its own distinctive body of law, substantive and procedural; and the federal government provides still another set of laws, superimposed upon those of the several states.

The United States does not have a unitary government like that which prevails in England and many other nations. Instead, legislative, executive and judicial powers are divided between the federal government and the states. The United States Constitution establishes a federal government of limited powers. It is given control over external affairs—national defense, foreign relations and the like—and over some domestic affairs, such as currency, the postal service and interstate commerce, but not over all domestic concerns. The states are generally free to regulate activities within their own borders subject only to restrictions imposed by the Constitution as interpreted by the Supreme Court of the United States. They cannot raise their own armies, establish tariff barriers or otherwise interfere with the operation of the central government; and they cannot deprive any person of due process of law or the equal protection of the laws. Otherwise, however, they are free to establish and amend their own constitutions and under them to exercise legislative, executive and judicial powers as they see fit, but only within their own borders.

The result is that the laws and legal institutions of the several states differ one from another, sometimes radically. There is no national law of torts, contracts, property or matrimonial affairs. If one should ask what the American grounds for divorce are, or what the American formalities for execut-

135

ing a valid will are, he could get no quick and simple answer that was accurate, but only a lengthy exposition of the law of each of the 50 states. Both statutory law and judge-made law vary from state to state. The legislature of Tennessee is under no obligation to conform to what the legislature of Connecticut or any other state does; and the courts of Texas are not bound by decisions of the courts of Illinois or any other state. There is no such thing as general national common law, not even in the Federal Courts.

In a nation where people travel freely and transact business across state lines, operating sometimes under one set of state rules and sometimes under another, and where they are also subject to federal laws, lawyers must ascertain what courts are competent to handle controversies that arise and which laws will be followed by those courts. We shall first consider cases handled by state courts, and then turn our attention to those handled by federal courts.

### State Courts and Cases from Sister States

A state court is not limited to dealing with claims that arise locally and are governed by local law. It is equally competent to deal with claims arising elsewhere and governed by the laws of sister states. Most actions are "transitory," meaning that they can be brought wherever the defendant can be served with process. The justification is clear: otherwise a person who committed a wrong in one state could go elsewhere and escape liability for his conduct, leaving the injured person without redress.

But what law governs in deciding a claim arising outside of the "forum" (the place where the action is brought)— local law or that of the state where the claim arose or that of some other state? The traditional answer is as follows: the substantive law of the state where the events giving rise to the lawsuit took place governs, but is applied in accordance with the procedural rules of the forum.[1] Several considerations justify the substantive law choice. One is the idea that each state has power to regulate persons, things and activities within its own borders, and a corresponding duty to refrain from interfering with matters outside those borders. Another is the belief that people ought to behave in accordance with the law of the state where they are at the time they act. Finally it is thought that their rights and duties ought to be fixed at or before the time they act and not vary depending upon where a lawsuit arising out of their conduct later happens to be brought. These considerations are reinforced by Article IV section 7 of the United States Constitution, reading as follows: "Full Faith and Credit shall be given in each State to the public Acts, Records and judicial Proceedings of every other State." Nevertheless, many courts in recent years have departed from the traditional view. They say that the governing substantive law ought to be that of the state having the greatest interest in the outcome of the litigation, that the "center of gravity" of litigation ought to determine which substantive law governs. The problem of choice of law is too complicated to explore further here. It is considered in depth in advanced law school courses in "Conflict of Laws."

Once a decision has been made to apply the substantive law of another state, it is not unduly difficult for a court in the forum to discover and understand that law. The necessary books are available in any respectable law library; the language in which they are written and the underlying conceptions on which they are based are the same as those that prevail locally. Differences exist, to be sure, from state to state, but there is sufficient homogeneity in American law considered as a whole to enable judges and lawyers to cope with the laws of sister states. If they can carry on research into questions of local substantive law, as they frequently must do even in purely local cases, they should be equally capable of studying and understanding the substantive law of a sister state.

As for procedural law, different considerations are relevant. In accordance with the principle that each state can control activities within its borders, the state of the forum alone has the right to determine how its litigation shall be conducted. Moreover, procedure is not intended to define the rights and duties of the parties and thus determine the outcome of litigation. It is concerned with the mechanics of litigation—how and where an action is brought, how the parties plead, what evidence is admissible and so forth. Ordinarily, therefore, it would be foolishly doctrinaire to make reference to the law of a sister state all inclusive. Finally, to apply the procedure as well as the substantive law of the sister state would be extraordinarily cumbersome and difficult. Judges and lawyers have a hard enough time mastering the multifarious details of procedure of their own state without being burdened with trying to learn on a case-to-case basis the procedure of every state. Especially is this so in view of the fact that a great many procedural rulings, such as those on the admissibility of evidence, may have to be made in the course of a single case and often on the spur of the moment, without extended research.

Although most civil actions are transitory, a few, notably those involving real property, are considered "local," meaning that they must be brought in the state where the events giving rise to them took place.[2] This is understandable where judgment is sought directly affecting the property, as in an action of ejectment. If such an action is successful, the sheriff removes the defendant from the property, by force if necessary, and restores possession to the plaintiff. It would be presumptuous for a court of one state to send its officers into another state (where in any event they would have no authority to act). On the other hand, where the judgment sought does not directly affect the property, there is little justification for treating an action as local. Where a plaintiff sues for trespass to real estate, he seeks a money judgment for damages, the same kind of judgment given in most ordinary tort and contract actions. Nevertheless, the courts of most states, following ancient precedent, treat trespass to real property as local.[3] A few states have broken away from the old rule either by statute or judicial decision.[4] When an action is treated as local, whether justifiably or not, the state of the forum is necessarily also the state where the claim arose; and the governing law, substantive as well as procedural, is local.

THE DUAL SYSTEM OF STATE AND FEDERAL COURTS

## Cases in State Courts Arising Under Federal Law

State courts are empowered to handle not only claims arising under local laws and the laws of sister states, but also those arising under federal law. This follows from Article VI of the United States Constitution, reading as follows:

> This Constitution, and the Laws of the United States which shall be made in Pursuance thereof; and all Treaties made, or which shall be made, under the Authority of the United States, shall be the supreme Law of the Land; and the Judges in every State shall be bound thereby, any thing in the Constitution or Law of any State to the Contrary notwithstanding.

When Congress passes a statute giving rise to civil liability, unless it restricts enforcement to the federal courts (which it rarely does),[5] enforcement can be sought in a state court even against that court's desire. A state court cannot escape its responsibility by claiming that it is too busy or by asserting that the federal law is contrary to local public policy.[6]

When the plaintiff brings a claim arising under federal law in a state court, it often happens that the court must interpret the meaning of the federal law, whether it be in the form of a constitutional provision, a statute or a treaty. It may also be called upon to determine the constitutional validity of a federal statute—whether it is within the limited powers conferred on Congress or whether it conflicts with some provision of the United States Constitution. Finally it may have to strike down a provision in the state constitution or a state statute if it conflicts with a valid federal rule. It must decide the case to the best of its ability (although realizing of course that ultimate review may be possible in the Supreme Court of the United States).

The jurisdiction of state courts over claims based on federal law is for the most part concurrent with that of federal courts, the choice between tribunals being made in the first instance by the plaintiff, subject to possible removal of case to federal court.[7] Regardless of which tribunal hears the case, the governing substantive law to be applied—federal—is the same. As to procedure, however, the same principle encountered before in dealing with claims arising under the laws of sister states applies: the law of the forum governs. In short, federal substantive law is applied according to local state procedure.

## Federal Court Structure

The United States Constitution defines and limits the judicial power of the federal government. The jurisdiction so defined is not plenary, authorizing federal courts to handle every kind of case that arises in the nation, but is restricted to particular kinds of cases, the most common and important being those between citizens of different states and those arising under the Constitution, laws and treaties of the federal government.[8] The Constitution also establishes the Supreme Court and defines its limited and little used original jurisdiction but leaves to Congress the delineation of its more important appellate jurisdiction.[9] Equally subject to Congressional control is the composition of the Court. We have long been accustomed to having nine judges, but that number could be increased or decreased by Congress.[10]

As extensive as is Congress' control over the Supreme Court, even more extensive is its power over the lower federal courts. These are not established by the Constitution itself; their very creation and continued existence is left to Congress, as is their jurisdiction and organization. Congress has power to abolish them, and to create new courts supplementing or supplanting those now in existence.[11]

At the present time, there are three levels of regular federal courts.[12] At the trial level are District Courts; above them, Courts of Appeal; and at the apex of the federal judicial structure, the Supreme Court of the United States.

## United States District Courts

At the trial level, the nation is divided into about 90 districts, each of which has a United States District Court. In heavily populated areas, a single state may contain as many as four districts, each manned by several judges; in less densely populated areas, the boundaries of a federal district may be coterminous with those of the state, and a single judge may serve the entire area. Every state has at least one federal district, and no federal district extends into more than a single state.[13]

The federal district courts are courts of original jurisdiction, trying cases in the first instance. They are on the same level as state trial courts, neither above nor below them. A state case cannot be appealed to a federal district court. It must proceed up through the state system to the highest state court which is empowered to deal with it. If it is ever to enter the federal system, it can do so only through the Supreme Court of the United States.

Unlike state trial courts of general jurisdiction, federal trial courts exercise strictly limited jurisdiction. They are limited by the Constitution and Congressional enactments to two main types of cases: those arising under federal law and those involving adverse litigants of different states.

*Cases Arising Under Federal Law*

Cases based in federal law ("federal question cases") are not very numerous in relation to the total litigation of the nation because of the limited legislative power of the federal government, already discussed. Most cases arise under state rather than federal law. Furthermore, not all federal question cases can be brought in federal court. In some, but not all, of them, the amount in controversy must involve $10,000 or more. If less than $10,000 is involved in such a case, it must go to a state court. If more than $10,000 is involved, it can go initially into either a state or federal court, depending upon the desires of the plaintiff; but then the defendant has a right at the outset of proceedings if he so desires, to remove it to a federal court, where it will proceed as if it had originally been brought there.[14]

In dealing with a federal question case, a federal court, like a state court, has no choice but to apply federal substantive law. Unlike a state court, however, which follows its own state procedure, it operates according to federal procedure.

## Diversity of Citizenship Cases

Cases between citizens of different states, usually called "diversity of citizenship cases" comprise the second main category of federal jurisdiction. Congress has restricted the jurisdiction of federal district courts over such cases to those involving "complete" diversity of citizenship[15] and $10,000 or more in controversy. The fact that a $10,000 lawsuit between residents of different states may be brought in a federal district court, does not mean that it must be brought there. It can equally well be brought in a state court; and once brought there it can be removed by the defense to a federal district court only if none of the defendants is a resident of the state in which the action is brought.[16] Congress is now seriously considering abolishing diversity jurisdiction completely, thus restricting the federal courts to cases arising under federal law.

There are a few kinds of litigation over which Congress has vested exclusive jurisdiction in the federal courts, notably those involving bankruptcy, patents, copyrights, and admiralty, but these are specialities which account for relatively little judicial business.

### The Law Followed in Diversity Cases

When a federal court is handling a diversity of citizenship case, it follows the Federal Rules of Civil Procedure but is obliged to follow state substantive law. Until 1938 the reverse was generally true. Federal courts, except in equity cases, were governed procedurally by the Conformity Act which commanded them to conform "as nearly as may be" to the procedure of the states in which they were sitting.[17] Substantively, they were free to apply their own conception of "the common law" in any case not governed by statute.[18] In both respects, results were unsatisfactory. Procedural rules, ranging from bad to mediocre, varied needlessly from one federal court to another. Substantive precedents created by federal courts diverged from those created by state courts, so that the outcome of a given case often depended upon whether it was tried in a state or federal court.

In 1938, the Supreme Court of the United States, pursuant to authority granted by Congress,[19] promulgated the Federal

Rules of Civil Procedure to apply uniformly to all civil cases in all federal district courts. In the same year, it rendered the landmark decision of *Erie Railroad v. Tompkins*,[20] which declared that henceforth in diversity cases federal courts were bound to follow state law, judge-made as well as statutory. The substantive change came about partly because of a slowly dawning realization that there was no transcendental body of common law existing apart from the authority of a particular government, and partly because of a hearkening back to fundamental constitutional principles governing the relationship between the states and the federal government. The common law of New York was a reality, consisting of the decisions of its courts and backed by their authority, as was the common law of every other state; but there was no "brooding omnipresence in the sky," to use Justice Holmes' phrase,[21] from which judges could, through their own mental operations, pluck rules of decision for every case that came before them. The federal government, being one of limited powers, was not authorized to make law generally, but only to enact statutes within the scope of its enumerated powers; and there was nothing in the Constitution which empowered federal judges to make laws that Congress was prohibited from enacting. The federal courts, therefore, had been following an unconstitutional course of conduct for over a century. There was and could be no such thing as a federal general common law.

When a choice has to be made between conflicting state rules in a transitory action brought in a federal court by reason of diversity of citizenship, the federal court must refer to the conflict of law rules of the state in which it is sitting and abide by them.[22] If these rules indicate that local state law governs, the federal court follows that law; if they indicate that the law of another state governs, the federal court follows that law. This formula is designed to assure that a federal court handling a diversity of citizenship case reaches the same result that would be reached if the case were pending in a court of the state where the federal court is sitting. It curtails but does not eliminate "forum shopping."[23]

When, as often happens, the governing state law for a diversity case is not clear, a federal court is confronted with a difficult problem. It may itself attempt to resolve the uncertainty, reasoning from analogy and principle, just as it would do if it were a state court confronted by the same problem, meanwhile realizing that its decision may have little value as precedent and that authoritative resolution of the problem will have to await a decision of the highest court of the state. Or it may abstain from deciding until the parties, in another proceeding brought in a state court, have secured an authoritative resolution of the problem. Or it may, if fortunate, be able to certify the question to the Supreme Court of the state whose law controls for a definitive answer.[24] The difficulties that federal courts encounter in ascertaining state law are neither unique nor insuperable. They are fundamentally the same as those encountered by state courts in ascertaining federal law or the law of sister states. All courts are occasionally forced to decide cases when they are unsure of the correct answers.

### Choosing Between State and Federal Trial Courts

From the foregoing description of federal question cases and diversity cases, it is apparent that federal courts, except for the few cases entrusted exclusively to them, duplicate the work of state courts. State courts can handle practically all civil cases that federal courts can handle and a great many more besides—those that involve no federal question, those where the parties are not of diverse citizenship, those which involve a smaller amount in controversy than is required in federal courts.

How then do litigants choose between state and federal courts when there is a choice?[25] They cannot do it on the basis of substantive law because, as we have seen, the same substantive law is applied to the same type of case in either a federal or a state court. The choice must be based on other factors. One such factor is procedure. While many states follow the federal pattern of procedure, others do not. A lawyer may believe that one set of procedural rules is more favorable to his client than the other; and he, himself, may

144

feel more comfortable with the rules most familiar to him. Another factor is personnel. The judges and jurors in an available state court may strike a lawyer as more likely to be favorable to his contentions than the judges and jurors in an available federal court, having been chosen in a different way and operating in a different psychological atmosphere; or vice versa. Still another factor is calendar condition. An available federal court may be either more or less current in its work than an available state court, and hence likely to reach the case at hand for trial sooner or later than the state court.

## United States Courts of Appeals

Above the District Courts are eleven United States Courts of Appeals, one for the District of Columbia, but each of the others covering three or more states. They hear appeals from the federal district courts within their respective geographical areas. They have no power to hear appeals from state courts.

## The Supreme Court of the United States

At the top of the federal judicial hierarchy is the Supreme Court of the United States. It is a unique tribunal because it is empowered to hear appeals not only from the lower federal courts, but also from state courts. Nevertheless, it exercises a limited jurisdiction. It is not authorized to review all types of cases coming from the state courts, but only those which present federal questions of controlling importance. If the supreme court of a state were to drastically change its common law as by abolishing the doctrine of comparative negligence in tort cases or the requirement of consideration in contract cases, or if it were to invalidate a state statute on the ground that it violated the state constitution, there would be nothing for the Supreme Court of the United States to review. On questions of purely state law, the supreme court of the state has the last word, not the Supreme Court of the United States. If on the other hand, the basis of a state supreme court decision were the interpretation or validity of a federal statute, there would be a federal question appropriate for resolution by the Supreme Court of the United States. Not even all federal questions of controlling importance, however, are subject to mandatory review in the Supreme Court. The volume of litigation is too great to allow the Court to handle all cases that parties would like to bring to it or even that the members of the Court itself would like to consider. Cases appropriate for review can come not only from the eleven United States Courts of Appeals and the 50 state supreme courts, but also, in exceptional circumstances, from lower courts, state[26] as well as federal.[27] For this reason, Congress has given the Supreme Court control over most of its own docket. The only cases that can be "appealed" as of right are those which involve what might loosely be called a conflict of sovereignty—when a federal court of appeals holds a state statute invalid as violating the United States Constitution or when a state court invalidates a federal statute or upholds its own state statute against the claim that it violates the United States Constitution.[28] Other kinds of cases can reach the Supreme Court only by its permission. The party seeking review submits a "petition for certiorari."[29] All nine Justices study the petition and the response to it from the other side. If four of the nine Justices agree that the case involves not only a controlling federal question, but also that it is of such national importance that it merits consideration by the highest tribunal in the land, the court grants a "writ of certiorari," bringing the papers up for hearing and decision on the merits.[30] Although the Court receives upwards of 4,000 petitions for certiorari each year, it grants very few of them. It decides on the merits only about 125 cases a year, including those appealed to it as of right. The consequence is that many federal questions, on which there ought to be definitive rulings binding throughout the nation, remain unresolved for long periods of time. The decision of a question of federal law by a state supreme court is binding only within that state and only in the lower courts of that state. The decision of such a question by a United States Court of Appeals is binding only within its circuit on the lower federal courts located there. Thus, if a new federal statute of ambiguous import were enacted, a decision on its meaning by the United States Court of Appeals for the Second Circuit would not be binding on any federal court outside of that circuit and not even in any state court within the circuit. A decision as to its meaning by the Supreme Court of California would not be binding on the courts of any other state or even on the federal courts in California. There is, in consequence, a serious paucity of authoritative national law. Only the Supreme Court of the United States can make decisions that are binding throughout the nation, and it does not have enough time, energy or resources to make enough of them to satisfy the national need. Thus, in addition to the diversity of state law, already discussed, there is a very considerable diversity of federal law, theoretically national in scope, but in fact uncertain in meaning until declared by the Supreme Court of the United States.[31]

## Chapter 9

## NONRESIDENTS AND FOREIGN CORPORATIONS

Just as a court can handle transitory actions wherever they arise, including those governed by the laws of other jurisdictions, so also it can handle cases in which some or all of the parties are nonresidents or foreign corporations. It is not restricted to cases involving only local people.

In order to render a valid judgment, a court must possess not only jurisdiction over the subject matter—the competence to handle the general type of case presented, as discussed in Chapters 1 and 8 but also jurisdiction over the parties. This means power to handle the specific case presented, binding the particular parties involved in the litigation. If a court lacks either type of jurisdiction, any judgment rendered by it is void, subject not only to direct attack on appeal, but also to collateral attack whenever an attempt is made to enforce the judgment either in the place of its rendition or elsewhere.

There is no difficulty in acquiring jurisdiction over the plaintiff, whether he is a local resident or not. By bringing the action, he acknowledges the court's power and submits himself to it. This is true not only with respect to his own claim but also with respect to any claim that the law of the forum allows the defendant to assert against him.[1]

Nor is much difficulty encountered in acquiring jurisdiction over the defendant in the type of case discussed in Chapter 1—where he is a resident of the state in which the action is brought and served with process in that state. Problems arise mainly where an attempt is made to serve a nonresident individual or a foreign corporation.

### Pennoyer v. Neff

Current rules on jurisdiction can best be understood in the perspective of history, beginning with the leading American case on the subject, *Pennoyer v. Neff,* decided by the Supreme

Court of the United States in 1878.[2] The facts of the case were as follows: Mitchell, a lawyer, sued his client Neff in a state court of Oregon to collect legal fees. Neff was outside the state and was not personally served with process in the state. Instead, Mitchell had the summons published in an Oregon newspaper in accordance with a local statute. Neff did not appear, and judgment by default was entered against him. Thereafter Mitchell had execution levied on Neff's Oregon real estate, and the land was sold by the sheriff at public auction to Pennoyer. Subsequently, Neff returned to Oregon and brought an action of ejectment against Pennoyer in a federal court in Oregon, seeking to eject him and recover the property. Neff claimed that the original judgment against him was invalid for lack of jurisdiction and consequently that the sheriff's sale of the property to Pennoyer was without lawful authority. Pennoyer disagreed, and their dispute eventually reached the Supreme Court.

Starting with the proposition that each state had power over persons and things within its own borders, the Court posited two types of jurisdiction: over the person of the defendant (jurisdiction in personam) based on his physical presence; and over things in which he claimed an interest (jurisdiction in rem) based on the location of those things within the state. By exercising jurisdiction over the defendant personally, the court could do indirectly what it could not do directly: affect things outside its borders, as when it ordered the defendant to convey land located elsewhere. By exercising jurisdiction over local things, the court also could do indirectly what it could not do directly: affect persons outside the state by cutting off or limiting their rights to things under the control of the court, as where it foreclosed a mortgage on local property belonging to a nonresident. A judgment in rem was effective only with respect to the property involved in the action. It imposed no personal obligation or liability on the defendant. A judgment in personam, on the other hand, imposed personal liability on the defendant. If it were a money judgment, it could be collected out of any property the defendant owned, wherever located, and whether acquired before or after the lawsuit. If no property within the state could be found, proceedings could be instituted in another state where the defendant owned property, and the courts of that state were required to give full faith and credit to the judgment of the original court.[3] The case could not be retried on its merits in the second state. The only question open was whether the first court had jurisdiction. If it did, the judgment was good and as binding in the second state as it was in the first.

## Jurisdiction in Personam

The primary way of acquiring jurisdiction over any defendant, resident or nonresident, said the Court in *Pennoyer v. Neff*, was by delivering a summons to him personally while he was within the borders of the state where the action was brought. This not only gave him notice of the suit and the opportunity to defend, but also satisfied the historic notion that jurisdiction was based on physical power—the idea that the only judgments permissible were those which the court, through its officers, was capable of enforcing. At one time in the history of English law, the defendant was taken into custody, just as in a criminal case, to await the judgment of the court. We had long since dispensed with the need for acquiring or maintaining physical custody of the defendant in a civil case, but the idea persisted that it was necessary, at least symbolically, to assert the state's power over the defendant while he was within its borders. Such symbolic assertion of power was accomplished by handing a summons to him. It made no difference how long he had been in the state or how long he intended to stay. He might just be passing through momentarily, but still he would have to defend the case on the merits, however inconvenient that might be for him, or suffer judgment to be entered by default, carrying the same consequences as if it had been entered after a contest.[4]

Personal service of a summons within the state, however, was not the sole basis for jurisdiction in personam recognized in *Pennoyer v. Neff*. Jurisdiction, said the Court, could also be conferred by the defendant's consent, either given in advance, as by the appointment of an agent within the state to receive service of process,[5] or given after commencement of the action by the defendant's "appearance" in court to contest the merits without challenging the court's power.[6] In such situations, the defendant was not subject to the physical power of the state at the time the action was commenced, but he was treated as if he were.

Thus, even at the time of *Pennoyer v. Neff*, the court recognized bases of jurisdiction in personam other than physical power over the defendant. Later cases, as we shall see, have enormously expanded such bases, and at the same time have separated the idea that there must be some relationship between the defendant and the state where he is being sued from the idea that he is entitled to fair notice and an opportunity to defend. As long as personal service within the state was the primary, almost the exclusive, method of acquiring jurisdiction, both requirements were satisfied, and there was little or no need to clearly differentiate between them.

## Jurisdiction in Rem

Returning now to jurisdiction in rem, the Court in *Pennoyer v. Neff* distinguished two types of such jurisdiction. One was where the claim in litigation was specifically related to a thing within the state—for example, an ejectment action in which the plaintiff sought to acquire possession of property from the defendant, or an action to partition property, dividing it between the plaintiff and the defendant, or an action of eminent domain to condemn the defendant's property and appropriate it for a public use.

This type of in rem jurisdiction covered not only physical things like real property and chattels, but also intangible things like the status of a person (whether married or unmarried, for example). The Court was willing to stretch the concept this far in an attempt to explain and justify the jurisdiction that courts were exercising over divorce cases when one of the parties, being a nonresident, was not subject to the personal jurisdiction of the court.[7]

The second type of in rem jurisdiction recognized in *Pennoyer v. Neff*, even harder to explain, was where the plaintiff's claim was personal, unrelated to specific property, but where the defendant owned property within the state which could be applied to satisfy any judgment that might be rendered in favor of the plaintiff. But, said the Court, ownership by the defendant of property within the state at the time of execution of the judgment was not enough. Jurisdiction should not depend upon facts to be ascertained after judgment was rendered because a defendant owning property at the commencement of the action could dispose of it before judgment, or one not owning property originally could acquire it after judgment. Jurisdiction should depend upon bringing specific property of the defendant under the court's control before judgment. This could be accomplished by "attachment"—seizing the property physically or symbolically as security for the judgment ultimately to be rendered. This concept in effect allowed the plaintiff, as if by magic, to convert an in personam claim into an in rem claim.[8]

Dominated by the idea of physical power over things and persons within the state and by the idea that a state could act only within its own borders, the Court paid little attention to the importance of giving fair notice to the defendant. It held that publication of the summons in a newspaper within the state was sufficient notice to justify in rem jurisdiction (on the dubious theory that the owner of property would always know what was happening to it). At the same time, the Court held that personal service outside of the state was totally ineffective either in an in rem or an in personam proceeding (presumably on the even more dubious theory that a summons would become invisible if it crossed a state boundary).

### Recent Developments

Since *Pennoyer v. Neff* was decided, a century has elapsed and many later cases dealing with jurisdiction over litigants have come before the Supreme Court. The old landmark still stands, but it has been severely buffeted by time. It is still true that there must be some connection between the defendant and the state before its courts can exercise jurisdiction over him or his property; and most of the bases of jurisdiction recognized in the old case still stand as firm as ever. Nevertheless, current rules bear only a family resemblance to those set forth in *Pennoyer v. Neff*. The major developments can be briefly summarized as follows:

1.  It is now recognized that the requirement of fair notice is quite distinct from the requirement that there be some connection between the defendant and the state where he is being sued. Both elements are necessary and constitutionally mandated, so that neither standing alone will support jurisdiction. But there are now many different bases of jurisdiction and many different types of permissible notice. All that is necessary to satisfy due process is that any proper basis of jurisdiction be combined with any type of permissible notice.

2.  Notice is viewed more realistically than at the time of *Pennoyer v. Neff*. A summons reaching the defendant outside the state is recognized to be just as legible as one served within its borders. Publication of a summons within the state is recognized for what it is—a very questionable method of letting the defendant know that he is being sued. Furthermore, fair notice is just as essential in an in rem proceeding as in an in personam proceeding. Both affect the rights of people, not just things. What is required in either type of proceeding is notice realistically and reasonably calculated in the circumstances to inform the defendant that he is being sued and give him an opportunity to defend.[9] Such notice includes personal delivery of the summons outside of the state,[10] delivery of it to a person of suitable age and discretion at the defendant's home or place of business,[11] and delivery of it through the mail.[12] Publication is permissible only as a last resort, when the defendant's identity or whereabouts are unknown or he is intentionally avoiding a better means of service.[13]

3.  The defendant's presence within the state at the commencement of the action, his appearance or his consent in advance are no longer the sole bases for in personam jurisdiction. No longer controlling are ideas of territorial sovereignty and physical power. Now it is enough if the defendant has such "minimum contacts" with the state that maintenance of

the suit does not offend "traditional notions of fair play and substantial justice."[14] Such minimum contacts can be found if the defendant is domiciled in the state[15] or does business there[16] or does an isolated act there which gives rise to a claim against him,[17] even if he does an act outside of the state knowing or having reason to know that it might cause injury within the state.[18] The same activities that justify jurisdiction over nonresident individuals also justify jurisdiction over foreign corporations.[19]

4. The distinction between jurisdiction in personam and jurisdiction in rem seems to be disappearing. In a recent case, the Supreme Court of the United States held that a defendant could no longer be subjected to jurisdiction in rem solely on the basis of attaching property owned by him within the state where suit was brought. Other "minimum contacts" between him and the state, of the type required for in personam jurisdiction, were needed. The Court intimated that only a single type of jurisdiction, judged by the single standard of "minimum contacts," would henceforth be recognized.[20]

Thus far we have been discussing the constitutional bases of jurisdiction and the constitutional requirements as to notice —in other words, what the Supreme Court will permit a state to do under the due process clause of the Fourteenth Amendment. A state, however, is not compelled to exercise its constitutional power to the fullest extent permitted.[21] Unless it takes advantage of Supreme Court decisions by the enactment of legislation, its courts are not likely to do so by striking out on their own, and prospective plaintiffs are not helped. In short, two problems are present in each case: (1) is service of process in compliance with state law? and (2) is such service in the circumstances within the limits of the state's constitutional power? If the answer to the first question is negative, the second question becomes theoretical.

As might be expected, most states are not reluctant to take advantage of their full constitutional power to subject nonresidents and foreign corporations to the jurisdiction of their courts through the passage of various forms of "long arm statutes."[22] By doing so, they provide a convenient forum for local citizens having claims that otherwise might

have to be asserted in the courts of distant states. In opening the doors of their courts for resident plaintiffs, they
also open them for plaintiffs from other states, who under
the United States Constitution are entitled to all "privileges
and immunities" enjoyed by local citizens.[23]

The net result of expanding the bases of jurisdiction and
easing the requirements of notice is that in many situations
plaintiffs today have a wide choice of courts. Assume that
a person domiciled in New York, while driving his auto in
California, is involved in an accident which injures a California
resident; and assume further that the New Yorker has a
department store in Pennsylvania, has appointed an agent
for the service of process in New Jersey, and spends January,
February and March of each year vacationing in Florida.
The Californian could bring an action in Florida based on the
defendant's presence at the time of service of process, or in
New York based on domicile, or in Pennsylvania based on the
defendant's doing business there, or in New Jersey based on
consent given in advance, or in California based on the tort
committed there. Similar examples could be multiplied. Particularly vulnerable to suit in many alternative forums are
large corporate defendants that have places of business all
over the nation.

In some situations, a defendant may be able to invoke the
doctrine of "forum non conveniens" and persuade a court
that has jurisdiction over him or his property to dismiss the
action nevertheless. The basis would be that the forum
chosen by the plaintiff was highly inconvenient for the parties
or witnesses or that the psychological atmosphere surrounding the forum was so fraught with prejudice as to make a
fair trial impossible. If the court agreed, it would dismiss
the action, remitting the plaintiff to suit in a more appropriate
forum. If, however, the court found reasonable justification
for the plaintiff's initial choice of forum, the action would be
allowed to proceed.[24]

The choice of one forum over another would rarely control
the outcome of litigation if all courts followed a uniform set
of choice of laws rules. Whatever court was chosen would

apply the same substantive law, while following local law only in matters of procedure. Procedure, in theory at least, would not determine which side would prevail. Unfortunately, however, choice of laws rules are not uniform throughout the nation. They vary widely from state to state. The consequence is that a plaintiff, carefully comparing the choice of laws rules that would be applied in the various courts that are open to him, may be able to do some "forum shopping." In other words, he may be able to choose a court that will apply the substantive law favoring his contentions and disfavoring those of his opponent. As noted earlier, forum shopping as between a state court and a federal court in the same state has been substantially eliminated by *Erie R.R. v. Tompkins*.[25] But it still persists as between courts of different states. Furthermore, since each federal court is required to follow the choice of laws rules of the state in which it is sitting,[26] forum shopping as between a federal court in one state and a federal court in another state also persists.

### Federal Courts

Our discussion of jurisdiction over litigants has concentrated thus far on state courts. Still to be considered are the federal courts. The rules governing them are not greatly different. They too must possess both jurisdiction over the subject matter (discussed in the preceding chapter) and jurisdiction over the parties. Again the plaintiff, by bringing suit, subjects himself to jurisdiction, so that the only difficulty is in securing jurisdiction over the defendant.

Contrary to what might be expected, federal process ordinarily does not run nationwide. Instead, the normal territorial limits are the borders of the state in which the federal district court sits.[27] Within those borders, the Federal Rules specifically authorize (1) personal service on an individual or on an officer, managing agent or general agent of a corporation; (2) substituted service (leaving a copy of the summons and complaint at the defendant's "dwelling house or usual place of abode with some person of suitable age and discretion then residing therein") ; and (3) service upon any

157

agent "authorized by appointment or by law to receive service of process."

In addition to these provisions, the Federal Rules sanction state methods of serving process and, more important, incorporate by reference valid state laws governing jurisdiction over nonresidents and foreign corporations.[28] Because of these provisions, state "long arm" statutes become operative in federal courts, and the constitutional doctrines enunciated in *Pennoyer v. Neff* and related cases growing out of it become as relevant in defining the jurisdiction of federal courts as in defining the jurisdiction of state courts. So far as jurisdiction over litigants is concerned (not jurisdiction over subject matter) a federal court can act whenever a state court located in the same place can act. All of the constitutional bases of jurisdiction recognized in the state court—presence, consent, appearance, doing business, whatever—are also available in the federal court.

## Venue

Qualifying the broad jurisdiction over litigants that federal courts can exercise are rules on venue.[29] A federal question case ordinarily must be brought only where all defendants reside or where the claim arose.[30] A diversity of citizenship case ordinarily must be brought where either of those requirements is met or where all plaintiffs reside.[31] If the defendant is a corporation, it can be sued wherever it is incorporated, licensed to do business or is doing business.[32] The federal rules on venue are more restrictive than state venue rules in the sense that they sometimes deny a plaintiff access to a federal court that possesses both jurisdiction over the subject matter and jurisdiction over the defendant. They are less restrictive than state rules because of a provision allowing the transfer of cases from district to district nationwide.[33] State venue rules ordinarily allow the transfer of cases from county to county within the state court system, but it may well be that no county in the state is an appropriate forum because of local prejudice or inconvenience to parties and witnesses.

The operation of federal venue rules can be illustrated hypothetically. Assume that the plaintiff is a resident of California and the defendant a resident of New York and that the claim arose in Illinois; and assume that the defendant is physically present in Texas. Personal service of a federal summons in Texas would give the federal district court there jurisdiction over the defendant, but the venue would be improper. If the defendant did not object, the case would proceed, because improper venue (like jurisdiction over the defendant, but unlike jurisdiction over the subject matter) can be waived; but if the defendant did object, the court would be obliged to dismiss the case or "if it were in the interest of justice" transfer it to a district in which it could have been brought—i.e., in California, New York or Illinois. Even where venue is proper, the court has power to transfer a case to another district where it could have been brought "for the convenience of parties and witnesses, in the interest of justice."[34]

# Chapter 10

## MULTIPLE CLAIMS AND MULTIPLE PARTIES

While most lawsuits involve a single claim between a single plaintiff and a single defendant, others are more complex. These are the main subject of this chapter. In addition to considering rules designed to prevent litigation from being too spacious and unwieldy, we shall also examine rules designed to prevent it from being unduly narrow and restricted. Our aim is to discover the permissible limits, maximum and minimum, on the scope of a lawsuit.

### Joinder of Claims

Sometimes a plaintiff has several claims against the same defendant. If so, he need bring only one lawsuit, regardless of the nature of his claims, even if they are totally unrelated to each other. Thus he could join a claim for damages for personal injuries sustained in an auto accident with a claim for specific performance of a contract to sell a piece of real estate. The claims would have to be separately stated and numbered in the complaint, but otherwise the federal pattern of procedure imposes no restriction on the "permissive" joinder of claims.[1] When several unrelated claims are asserted in a single action, confusion may result at trial. However, there is a safety valve in the trial judge's discretion to order separate claims tried separately if he anticipates such difficulty.[2]

One qualification needs to be added as to federal courts because of their limited jurisdiction over subject matter. Every claim asserted must normally satisfy federal jurisdictional requirements—that is, involve diversity of citizenship or a federal question. However, if a claim not within federal jurisdiction arises out of a "common nucleus of operative facts" with another claim over which the federal court has jurisdiction, the two may be joined.[3] The court is then said to have "pendant" or "ancillary" jurisdiction over the former.

161

## Splitting a Cause of Action

A plaintiff who fails to join closely related claims, pursuing only one, may later find that he has lost any chance of redress for the others. This is because of the rule against "splitting a cause of action," a branch of the law of res judicata. It is rooted in the idea of using the judicial system economically and preventing harassment of the other side. A litigant is not allowed unreasonably to subdivide what ought to be a single claim into several and bring successive lawsuits when one would do. Thus it would be unreasonable for a person who had suffered personal injuries and property damage in an auto accident to sue first for one type of injury and later for the other;[4] and it would be equally unreasonable for one to whom several installment payments on a contract were due to sue first for one installment, then for another, then for still another and so forth.[5] If separate torts or separate contracts were involved, the plaintiff would be allowed to sue for one and postpone action on the other because each would be considered as giving rise to a separate cause of action. However, as already indicated, separate actions would not be necessary in view of the liberal rules governing permissive joinder of claims.

## Counterclaims

The fact that a person is sued as defendant does not mean that he has no claim against the plaintiff. He may have a claim arising out of the same transaction or event as the plaintiff's claim (as where both parties to an auto accident are injured, each blaming the other) or one that is wholly independent and unrelated. It may be greater in amount than the plaintiff's claim or less; and it may require the same type of remedy—for example, damages—or a different type—for example, an injunction.

Just as the rules permit the plaintiff to assert as many claims as he has and require him to assert some, so also they permit the defendant to assert as many counterclaims as he has and require him to assert some. If a counterclaim arises out of the same event or transaction as the plaintiff's claim, it is "compulsory" under the Federal Rules and in

162

states that follow the federal pattern.[6] Unless asserted, it is lost and cannot be made the basis of a later lawsuit. In other states, there is said to be no such thing as a compulsory counterclaim. Nevertheless, much the same result is reached under the principles of res judicata (more specifically "collateral estoppel"). If A sues B for damages arising out of an auto accident, and B, defending on the ground of contributory negligence but not asserting a claim for his own damages, loses, he will not be allowed to relitigate the question of fault in a subsequent lawsuit.[7] It follows that B's claim will be lost as a result of the first lawsuit regardless of the fact that he was not required to assert it as a counterclaim. Only if he had defaulted would the claim remain alive, because then it would not have been litigated. As this example shows, the same facts that give rise to an affirmative defense often also support a counterclaim, the difference being that the former is aimed only at defeating the plaintiff's claim whereas the latter seeks a remedy in favor of the defendant against the plaintiff. Whenever the defendant is seeking affirmative relief in his favor, the appropriate vehicle is a counterclaim.

Different considerations apply to a counterclaim that does not arise out of the same transaction or event as the plaintiff's claim. There is no compelling urgency that it be dealt with in the same lawsuit. The evidence relevant to one claim will neither support nor defeat the other; and there is some possibility that confusion will result if the two are combined in a single lawsuit. Nevertheless, the rules give the defendant the option of asserting a "permissive" counterclaim or bringing his own action. Why offer him the first option? One reason is that unfairness might result if separate lawsuits were required when both parties had valid claims. They might race to judgment on their separate claims, and the one who recovered judgment first might collect on it and squander the money, making himself "judgment proof" before the other could bring his claim to judgment. Another reason is to save time and money for both parties and the public by making a single lawsuit do the work of two or more.[8]

In the federal courts, the defendant must satisfy federal jurisdiction requirements independent of those established by the plaintiff if he wishes to assert a permissive counterclaim. Since it arises out of a different transaction than the plaintiff's claim, it cannot be considered ancillary to the main action.[9] If he asserts a compulsory counterclaim, on the other hand, no independent grounds of jurisdiction are needed.[10]

## Joinder of Parties

Thus far we have been considering cases that are still relatively uncomplicated—where, although several claims may be involved, there is only one plaintiff and one defendant. Now we turn our attention to cases where additional parties, plaintiff or defendant or both, may be involved.

At common law, the rules governing multiple parties were rigidly bound up with the forms of action and took little account of the practicalities of litigation. No distinction was made between those who had to be joined as plaintiffs or defendants and those who might optionally be made litigants. If persons had joint rights or obligations, they had to be joined as litigants. If their rights or obligations were separate, they could not be joined.

The Federal Rules of Civil Procedure relating to the joinder of parties are derived historically from equity rather than common law precedents. Their keynote is flexibility; and a pragmatic view is taken of the desirability of avoiding an unnecessary multiplicity of lawsuits.

### Permissive Joinder

If several persons have individual claims arising out of the same transaction or event and if there are questions of law or fact common to their claims, they may join as plaintiffs in a single lawsuit.[11] Thus if a dozen strangers were riding in a bus when it collided with a truck, each would not be required to sue the truck driver separately, as at common law. All of their claims arise out of the same event—the collision—and they all involve the same question of fact as to how the accident happened and the same question of law as to the duty owed them by the truck driver. Therefore they could all join as plaintiffs in a single action. Some aspects of their claims would be individual—the amount of damage suffered by each—but the court could deal with these issues after resolving the basic question of liability; and the entire controversy could be determined in a single action.

Much the same rule applies to defendants: if the claims against several defendants involve common questions of fact or law and if they arise out of the same transaction or event, the several defendants can be joined in a single lawsuit. Thus in the hypothetical accident supposed, the passengers might wish to sue not only the truck driver, but also three others: the owner of the truck, the bus driver, and the owner of the bus. They would be permitted to assert in one action their 12 individual claims against the four separate defendants. Individual questions would arise not only as between plaintiffs, but also as between defendants, covering the extent of liability of each. But again, the court could deal with these issues after determining the common issues about how the accident occurred. Thus a single lawsuit could do what previously might have required many.

*Required Joinder*

Consistent with and complementary to the idea that persons having substantially similar interests may be joined as plaintiffs or defendants is the idea that some persons are "necessary," even "indispensable" as parties. These terms, seemingly synonymous, have been judicially distinguished nevertheless. A "necessary" party is one who should be joined if jurisdiction can be obtained over him; an "indispensable" party is one who must be joined if the lawsuit is to proceed. Thus in an action by a landlord against a sublessee to forfeit a lease because of acts of the sublessee, the original tenant is held to be an indispensable party since a decree of forfeiture would deprive him of his lease.[12] But in an action by a state against lessees operating oil wells to prevent waste of natural gas, the lessors are held to be only necessary parties who should be brought in if jurisdiction can be obtained over them; if not the action can proceed

CIVIL LITIGATION

without them.[13] Despite decisions like those just mentioned, confusion between "necessary" and "indispensable" parties persists. The latest and probably most successful attempt to clarify the distinction is contained in the 1966 amendments to the Federal Rules, where pragmatic and realistic standards are laid down, requiring the court to thoughtfully consider the extent of prejudice that would be suffered by existing parties and absent persons if those absent persons are not joined in the action.[14]

## Real Party in Interest

Closely related to the concept of necessary and indispensable parties is the concept that every action must be brought in the name of "the real party in interest."[15] This means a good deal less than it seems to say. It boils down simply to the proposition that an action must be brought by one who has the right under substantive law to the remedy sought. Thus a trustee, being legal owner of the trust assets, may sue to collect money owing to the trust from a third person without joining the beneficiaries. The beneficiaries may not sue in such a situation. If, however, the trustee is mismanaging the assets for his own selfish purposes, the beneficiaries can sue him, their right having been given legal recognition in the Court of Chancery.[16] In short, the real party in interest rule could be repealed without noticeable effect. It came into existence and still persists only because of an anachronistic common law rule, now long abolished, that the assignee of a "chose in action" (claim) could not sue in his own name, but only in the name of his assignor.[17] Modern real party in interest rules merely clarify and give specific illustrations of how the substantive law works in a few recurring situations.

## Impleader and Cross Claims

It sometimes happens that a person who might have been made party to a lawsuit is not originally joined. If so, one of the existing parties may insist on bringing that person in.[18] One reason would be to pass on to him part or all of the liability being asserted against the existing party. Thus an employer, sued on the theory of respondeat superior for a tort committed by his employee, could implead the employee and assert a claim against him for reimbursement. The original plaintiff, ordinarily having the right to choose his own adversary or adversaries, could, but would not be required to, assert his own separate claim against the employee. Another reason for impleading a third person would be for an existing party to assert his own independent claim against that person. This claim, however, must arise out of the same transaction or event as the original claim and involve common questions of law or fact.[19]

If there are multiple parties on either side, any one of them may assert a "cross claim" against a co-party.[20] Thus if a passenger in a taxi, injured when it collided with a private automobile, sued both the taxi driver and the driver of the other car, either defendant could assert a cross claim for his own injuries suffered in the accident against the other defendant.

## Intervention

Intervention, the reverse of impleader, describes the procedure whereby a third person, not originally made party to a lawsuit, is allowed to come in to assert a claim or defense of his own. If that claim or defense presents merely a question of law or fact common to the main action, as where a third person injured in the same accident as the plaintiff in an existing lawsuit wishes to come in and assert his own claim against the defendant, intervention is in the discretion of the court. It can refuse permission if the intervention would prejudice or delay a determination of the rights of the original parties.[21] If, on the other hand, the interest of the third person in the property or transaction involved in the suit is such that he could not as a practical matter adequately protect it without being made a party, intervention is not discretionary, but a matter of right.[22] An example would be where A sued B, claiming the right to certain perishable property, and C, not a party, also claimed the right to the same property. A judgment between A and B would not be res judicata so far as C was concerned; but as a practical matter the judgment might well render academic whatever rights C had in the property.[23] Since his rights are not adequately represented by either existing party, he should be allowed to intervene not only in fairness to him, but also in the interest of avoiding a multiplicity of lawsuits— one of the objectives of modern rules governing the joinder of claims and parties.

## Class Actions

Sometimes all the persons who ought to be parties to a given controversy are so numerous that it would be impossible to accommodate all of them and their lawyers in a single courtroom. For this situation equity invented the class action. It allows one person or a small group of persons to sue on behalf of themselves and all others similarly situated. It also allows one person or small group of persons to be sued as representatives of others similarly situated. The judgment sought is one that will bind not only the parties directly involved in the litigation, but also all members of the group on whose behalf or against whom the suit is brought.[24]

The class action represents a radical and potentially dangerous departure from traditional ideas of jurisdiction and res judicata, for its object is to affect the interests of persons who may never have had an opportunity to participate in the litigation—who may indeed never have heard of its existence. Against its potential danger must be balanced its potential value in affording efficient redress to large numbers of persons who have suffered legal injuries but whose individual stakes are too small to warrant incurring the cost and trouble of individual suits—for example, stockholders of a corporation being looted by its officers, consumers who have been overcharged by a utility company, or environmentalists suffering from polluted air or water. As a practical matter, such persons are likely to secure no redress at all unless it is available in the form of some group remedy. The great advantage of the class action over organizing all members of the class and getting them to join as plaintiffs is that one person or a few can volunteer to act on behalf of the entire group. Their motive for so volunteering may be altruistic;

168

but in some cases, where the recovery of a large sum of money is sought in behalf of a large group, their motive may really be the motive of the lawyer who represents them. If the suit is successful, he is compensated not on the basis of what he has accomplished for his immediate clients; his fee is fixed by the court on the basis of the benefit conferred on all members of the group.[25]

A familiar form of class action is the derivative shareholders suit.[26] Assume that the directors and officers of a corporation have been mismanaging its affairs and enriching themselves at the corporation's expense. The corporation has suffered directly and its stockholders have suffered indirectly in the sense that their shares are worth less than they would be if the corporation had been properly managed. In this situation, the corporation should sue its directors and officers; but since the malefactors control the corporation, no action is taken. Minority stockholders may demand that appropriate action be taken, but if their demands go unheeded (or if it is clear that any demand would be futile) they must seek redress on their own. The vehicle for seeking redress is the derivative stockholders action. A few of the minority stockholders retain a lawyer (or perhaps the lawyer, winking at ethical restraints, finds the clients), and suit is brought on behalf of these few and "all others similarly situated," meaning all the remaining stockholders, who may number in the thousands or even hundreds of thousands. The directors and officers are named and served as defendants, and so is the corporation itself for two reasons: (1) by failing to bring action itself, it has placed itself in a position antagonistic to the plaintiffs; and (2) it must be a party to the action so that if there is any recovery of damages from the directors, it can be paid into the corporate treasury. If the court finds that wrongdoing occurred as alleged, it enters judgment against the individual defendants in favor of the corporation. The court also fixes the legal fees to be paid to the plaintiff's lawyer out of the sums recovered, taking into account the benefits conferred on the entire class. The case cannot be settled or dismissed without the approval of the court after such notice as it directs to stockholders not directly represented in the litigation.[27]

Not all class actions are derivative, nor do all of them seek large monetary recoveries with correspondingly large legal fees. For example, a class action might be brought on behalf of owners of land (whether their ownership was joint or several) near a proposed hydroelectric dam to enjoin its construction, or on behalf of persons claiming to be deprived of their civil rights to enjoin public officials from discriminating against them.

In order to qualify as a class action that will result in judgment having res judicata effect—finally determining issues of fact as well as issues of law—on persons not actually made parties, two main prerequisites are necessary. First, the numbers of the class to be affected must be so numerous that actual joinder of them in the litigation is not practicable. Second, those who act as representatives of the class must fairly represent its interests. Implicit in the second prerequisite are two more requirements spelled out in Federal Rule 23: (1) that there be questions of law or fact common to all members of the class and (2) that the claims or defenses of the representative parties be typical of the claims or defenses of the class.[28]

Under the current federal rule, further restrictions of a complicated nature are imposed, presumably because of the fear of departing too widely from traditional notions of jurisdiction and res judicata. These restrictions have mainly to do with giving appropriate notice to members of the class to be affected, and having a judicial determination that the class action is "manageable" as well as "superior to other available methods for the fair and efficient adjudication of the controversy." They have been troublesome where the only basis for bringing a class action is the existence of questions of law or fact common to all members of the class. As a result, the courts thus far have frustrated many consumer class actions because notice, the cost of which must be borne by named plaintiffs, is too expensive.[29] They have also disallowed class actions brought on behalf of the victims of common disasters like train wrecks, midair collisions between jumbo jets, or ship sinkings because they are considered too unmanageable, particularly in view of the fact that individual questions as to damages may be thought to predominate over common questions relating to liability.

Whether the rules can or will be revised to make them less cumbersome so that class actions can justly and safely be extended to areas where they are not yet permitted remains to be seen. The question is highly controversial, for many people passionately in favor of class actions are confronted by others who are passionately opposed to them.

It should be noted that some lawsuits which are not formally class actions, but ones brought only on behalf of or against named parties, have much the same effect as class actions because of the combined effect of the doctrines of stare decisis and res judicata.[30] In a multi-district case involving a mass disaster caused by an airline crash, the 5th United States Circuit Court of Appeals recently said:

> Appellants approach the case as though it were purely a private contest . . . This approach is a nostalgic luxury no longer available in the hard-pressed federal courts. It overlooks the much larger interests which arise in litigation such as this. Each case in the consolidated case was private in its inception. But the number and cumulative size of the massed cases created a penumbra of class-type interest on the part of all the litigants and of public interest on the part of the court and the world at large. The power of the court must be assayed in this semi-public context.[31]

### Interpleader

Interpleader (to be distinguished from "impleader," discussed earlier) deals with the situation where one person holds money or property that is subject to conflicting claims by rival claimants.[32] The stakeholder is indifferent as to which claimant prevails; his concern is to avoid double liability and double litigation. A judgment in favor of one of the claimants would not be res judicata as to the other, because in general only parties to a judgment are bound by it.[33] Suppose that an insurance company, having written

171

a life policy on Mr. X payable to his wife as beneficiary, is confronted after his death with claims from two different women, each claiming to be the widow of X and therefore entitled to the proceeds of the policy. The real dispute is between the women; the insurance company, caught in the middle, wants to pay the money it owes and get out of their cross fire. In these circumstances, the company is allowed to bring an action of interpleader, naming the two women as defendants, paying the insurance money into court to await its judgment (or posting a bond to the same effect) and thereupon be released from further liability.

Interpleader can also be used defensively. If the stakeholder, before bringing his own action, is sued by one of the claimants, he can cause the other claimant to be made a party to the litigation and enjoin independent litigation by both claimants.

At one time, the stakeholder had to have no adverse interest against any claimant if he wished to take advantage of the remedy of interpleader. Such is no longer the rule; the stakeholder's interest as well as those of the claimants can be resolved in a single litigation.[34] Thus, in the hypothetical insurance case just discussed, if the insurance company denied liability—perhaps on the ground that the insured had committed suicide—the question of whether it was liable at all could be resolved along with the question of which claimant, if any, was entitled to the proceeds.

When the rival claimants are residents of different states, interpleader ordinarily cannot be brought in a state court because the court cannot obtain personal jurisdiction over them by service of process within the borders of the state.[35] The same difficulty would prevent resort to a federal court were it not for a special interpleader statute passed by Congress greatly relaxing the ordinary jurisdictional and venue requirements for federal courts.[36] Under this statute, (1) diversity of citizenship is required only as between rival claimants, not as between plaintiff and defendants; (2) process runs nationwide, not merely within the borders of the state where the federal court is sitting; (3) the amount in controversy needed is only $500, not $10,000; and (4) venue is proper in any federal district where one or more of the claimants resides. Where normal federal jurisdictional and venue requirements can be met, federal interpleader is available under Rule 22 of the Federal Rules of Civil Procedure.

## Consolidation and Severance

Through the procedural devices described in this chapter, litigants and their lawyers are allowed great flexibility in molding a lawsuit to fit their controversy, whatever its shape may be. The responsibility is primarily theirs, as in deciding what claims or parties to join and whether to assert a permissive counterclaim. In some situations, however, judicial approval or consent is necessary—for example, as to whether permissive intervention will be allowed or whether a class action may be maintained.

In spite of these devices, further flexibility needs to be given judges to enable them to make sure that lawsuits as framed by the parties are neither too broad nor too narrow. Accordingly they are vested with wide discretionary power to consolidate or sever actions for purposes of trial, so that the public interest will be served by using the judicial system wisely and economically.[37] Thus, where many persons injured in a common disaster sue separately, a common trial on the question of liability may be ordered. Or where a plaintiff has joined totally unrelated claims or a defendant has interposed a counterclaim having nothing to do with the plaintiff's claim, the court may order separate trials of the issues, especially if there appears to be a danger of confusing the jury by treating the issues together. Even in a simple lawsuit, with one plaintiff asserting a single claim against one defendant, the court can order separate trials of particular issues. This is sometimes done in personal injury actions: a separate trial is ordered on the issue of liability alone, to be followed if necessary by another trial on the issue of damages. If liability is resolved against the plaintiff, the second trial becomes unnecessary; and if resolved in his favor, the case may be settled, thus again saving the time and expense of determining damages.

# Part III

# LAW, EQUITY AND THEIR MERGER

### Introductory Note

Our analysis of a modern lawsuit reveals at least two vital problems which cannot be understood without reference to history. They are:

1. The mode of trial—whether with or without a jury; and
2. The availability of one type of remedy as against another.

The two problems are intimately related, for the mode of trial generally depends upon the remedy sought. The key to their solution lies in the separate development of "law" and "equity" in England. Certain remedies were available only in the Court of Chancery, or "equity" as it was commonly called. In that court juries were not used. Other remedies were available only in the courts of common law, where juries were used.

When law and equity were merged beginning about a century ago, two sets of rules had developed in the separate courts to determine when particular remedies would be granted. These were rules of substantive law, and were not changed by the merger. Furthermore, the right to trial by jury was preserved only where it previously had been enjoyed—that is, in cases which prior to the merger would have been tried in the common law courts.

In tracing the development of law and equity and their merger, our interest will be concentrated on such parts of the story as are still important to an understanding of modern American procedure. That means that many details and many collateral developments will be omitted, and that our attention will shift from England to America at the time when English law was imported into this country. No specific date can be assigned, but 1776, the date of the American Declaration of Independence, will do as a focal point. The objective will be to get a picture of English civil justice at that time—in particular, what area was covered by common law and what by equity—as a background for the developments in America.

Before beginning, it is necessary to guard against an ambiguity in the term "common law." In one sense (among many) it is used to describe judge-made law as distinguished from statutory law; in another, to describe that body of law which was developed in the common law courts as distinguished from that developed in Chancery. Both meanings are common, but the second is intended whenever the term is used in this Part.

## Chapter 11

## THE COMMON LAW

The history of English law is the story of expanding royal power in deciding disputes. In 1066 when William the Conqueror landed in England, the king was supposed to deal only with disputes involving his own tenants-in-chief—persons who held land directly from him. By 1776 his courts were open to all subjects as a matter of course.

### The Writ System

The early setting of royal justice was feudalism—a form of social organization based upon military prowess.[1] The most powerful man was "king." When he conquered a territory he owned it, and because he owned it, he governed it. Governmental power was not thought of as something distinct from land holding, but as an incident of it; and land holding was an incident of military conquest. When the king granted a portion of his land to one of his supporters, who thus became a "tenant-in-chief," the power of governing went along with it.[2] And when the king's tenant-in-chief (now a "lord") in turn subdivided the land among his tenants, or "vassals," again the power of government went with the land, until a person was reached who had no vassals under him. He was called a "serf."

One of the jobs of government was deciding disputes. The feudal idea was that each lord maintained his own court and had jurisdiction over his own tenants.[3] In feudal theory, therefore, the king was justified only in handling disputes which involved his own direct tenants,[4] or which were otherwise beyond the power of the other courts—as, for example, where a dispute arose between tenants of two different lords or where one of the parties was so powerful that he would not submit to the court of any lord below the king. Any attempt to extend jurisdiction beyond this area was likely to be resented as usurpation.[5]

177

The English kings following William had no intention of restricting themselves to their proper jurisdiction in the narrow feudal sense. On the other hand, they dared not suddenly proclaim that they would do justice in all cases for all subjects throughout the realm. Any such dramatic assertion of power would have been resisted, probably by force. What they did, therefore, was to proceed cautiously, almost stealthily, attempting to justify each forward step. The English system was not created in a single stroke as a rational, coherent scheme of substantive law, procedure and legal administration. It was the product of slow evolution.[6]

The development took place chiefly through a system of "writs." Originally these were written commands given by the king or in his name. When two men became embroiled in a controversy, one of them would seek the king's aid in the form of such a writ. The other man was given an opportunity to show why he should not be compelled to do as ordered, and if he availed himself of it, a decision became necessary. The job of deciding such disputes was delegated by the king to advisers. Later forms of writs (see the writ of trespass, *infra*) merely commanded the defendant to appear in court to answer the demand of the plaintiff.[7]

Gradually patterns of delegation grew up, whereby certain types of cases came to be handled as a matter of course by certain groups of advisers.[8] Ultimately three distinct courts emerged—the Court of King's Bench, the Court of Common Pleas and the Court of Exchequer.[9] Their individual histories do not concern us, for when they were fully mature, all handled the same types of cases in substantially the same manner.[10] The law developed and applied by them is now known to us as the common law.

Writs were issued by the Chancellor, an important royal official and the king's right-hand man. By the year 1200 a number of different writs, each covering a different type of factual situation, were in existence, and being granted as a matter of course upon payment of fees.[11] No action could be started in a royal court without such a writ, for it alone conferred jurisdiction on the court to handle the case. At the same time, it limited that jurisdiction: only the precise claim specified in the writ could be heard—no other.[12]

The scope of the early writs was limited. Most of them concerned land litigation,[13] a subject of overwhelming importance in feudal times,[14] and one, therefore, in which the king was vitally concerned. In general, they could be used only to recover the possession of "freehold" land,[15] meaning land held at a rather high level in the feudal hierarchy. The names of such writs are no longer important, for they were all replaced by the writ of ejectment which we shall consider later.

Writs which did not deal with land were few and narrowly circumscribed. "Covenant" could be used to recover for breaches of sealed contracts;[16] "debt" to recover liquidated sums of money owing;[17] "detinue" to recover from a bailee a chattel wrongfully detained or its value, at the option of the bailee;[18] and "replevin" to recover a chattel unlawfully "distrained."[19] All except replevin were in practice largely superseded by the writ of trespass and its offshoots, which we shall consider in more detail.

Replevin is a special case. It lay relatively quiescent until a century or two ago, when it blossomed into vigor. In the early period, it was used to recover possession of a chattel unlawfully distrained.[20] Distress was a form of self-help permitted in the middle ages, whereby a person could seize the goods of another and hold them for some obligation owing from their owner.[21] For example, if A discovered B's cattle doing damage on his land, he could hold them until the owner made amends. Similarly, a feudal lord could seize goods owned by his tenants who had failed to make payments or render services owing.[22] Within the narrow scope indicated, the action provided a highly effective remedy. At the commencement of the action, upon the plaintiff's posting a bond, the goods in question were recaptured by the sheriff and turned over to the plaintiff. Then a trial would be held to determine who had the right to possession. If the plaintiff won, he kept the goods and in addition recovered damages for their detention. If he lost, they were returned to the

179

defendant. However, the action did not cover wrongful taking generally, as by theft, nor wrongful detention at all, as by a bailee who refused to return goods.

The narrow scope of the action continued until at least Blackstone's time. Writing shortly before the American Revolution, he referred to it as being limited to cases of wrongful distraint. At a later date, the action was extended and improved. Provision was made for the defendant to post a "redelivery bond" and so retain possession of the goods pending the outcome of the action; and the remedy was extended to all cases of wrongful taking and all cases of wrongful detention of chattels.[23]

The action is of great present day importance, particularly in connection with conditional sales contracts. Under such a contract, the seller retains title until final payment. If the buyer defaults in paying installments, the seller can recover the goods by means of this action. The remedy is available whenever the right to possession of a chattel is in issue. The term replevin is still in common use to describe an action for the recovery of specific property, and is heard frequently in connection with the law of personal property and sales.[24]

As for the other ancient writs, it is enough for our purpose to realize how narrow they were in scope. They did not cover ordinary wrongs done to ordinary people. The man in the street (or in feudal terms, "the man in the field") was not likely to be vitally interested in remedies for the recovery of freehold land, or in writs dealing with such formalized transactions as bailments, sealed contracts, and contracts for liquidated sums of money. Humble men were much more in need of remedies for torts and breaches of simple contracts. The writs which we have discussed would not help a man if he were physically beaten up by another, or if someone wrecked his house, or refused to pay him for work done on an informal understanding that he would receive reasonable pay. For wrongs such as these, no remedy existed in the king's courts in the year 1200.[25]

The creation of new royal writs was not an easy matter. Each one represented an extension of the king's power at the expense of the great feudal lords. At stake was not only what we today would call judicial power but also legislative power, for it was beginning to be realized that the issuance of new writs amounted to the creation of new substantive law, and hence, new rights and duties.[26] If the king deliberately short-circuited the feudal courts, as he sometimes did, grumblings were heard. There is a provision in Magna Charta (1215) prohibiting the use of certain royal land writs in cases of disputes between vassals of a lord when those men owed allegiance primarily to the lord rather than the king.[27] In 1258, a general prohibition against the creation of new writs by the Chancellor was enacted.[28] Twenty-seven years later, an enactment now known as the Statute of Westminster II conceded a limited authority to the Chancellor to create new writs, but only for situations similar to those already covered by existing writs.[29] No general authority was granted for the indiscriminate creation of new writs. Nevertheless, as we shall see, the authority was sufficient to allow the Chancellor to introduce many variations on existing writs and thus pave the way for the ultimate broad scope of the common law.[30]

The result of the writ system was that law developed in a number of separate compartments. Each writ had its own precedents, procedural and substantive.[31] There was the law of trespass, the law of covenant, the law of debt, etc.,[32] but no conception of procedural or substantive law in general, no conscious effort to define wrongs and provide remedies for them. If there was no writ to fit the plaintiff's case, he had no right which could be vindicated in the common law courts.

Furthermore, as we shall see, the divisions created by the writ system were arbitrary, and from the modern point of view, quite unnecessary, if not meaningless. Vastly different wrongs were sometimes comprehended within a single writ, whereas closely related wrongs often fell under different headings. So long as the writ system remained in force, substantive law was "secreted in the interstices of proce-

181

dure."[33] Also there was great difficulty in attempting to fit new fact situations under the old writs. A wrong choice, if not fatal, was at least enough to throw the plaintiff out of court and force him to start again through another door.[34]

If the writ system was as unsatisfactory as indicated, why did people seek royal justice? Why was the king's justice preferred over that dispensed in the feudal courts? The reason must have been that the feudal courts were even less satisfactory.

The king's courts provided these advantages:

(1) Trial by jury could be had in the action of trespass and in all actions which developed out of it.[35] This was a much better method of determining facts than the older methods in vogue in the local courts—chiefly trial by battle and trial by compurgation.[36] Trial by battle decided issues by strength (either personal to the litigant or purchased by him). The man who prevailed in the fight prevailed at law.[37] Trial by compurgation was not much of an improvement. A number of persons would swear in a set, ritualistic form of words that a litigant had told the truth. Any slip in repeating the formula destroyed the value of the oath, whereas a letter perfect recitation (though founded on nothing but perjury) established the case.[38] Both of these ancient modes of trial were based upon a superstitious search for divine guidance in the determination of disputes.[39] For a time, they were used in the royal courts in connection with the early forms of action discussed in this section, but once trespass and its offspring gained ascendancy, the older forms of action were all but obliterated, and with them the ancient modes of trial.[40]

The new method of trial was by jury. The germ of the institution was imported with the Norman kings, and with the development of the action of trespass it grew into the normal method for deciding disputed issues of fact. It was a monopoly of the royal courts. It was a more rational, less supernatural approach even in its rudimentary beginnings than the older methods of trial. The jurors were "neighbor-witnesses," relying upon their own knowledge in deciding cases.[41] Today, as a result of gradual changes over the centuries, they are usually neither witnesses nor neighbors, but persons who acquire their knowledge in the courtroom and decide solely upon the evidence.[42]

(2) Royal justice was convenient. Itinerant justices, the predecessors of our modern travelling judges, went from community to community to preside at trials.[43] The formal papers were sent to the full courts sitting in Westminster for the determination of difficult questions of law and for entry of judgment, but trials were local.

(3) A legal profession developed in and around the king's courts.[44] Judges, being specialists, became skilled at litigation, and so did the lawyers who practiced before them. As experts, presumably they were able to dispense more satisfactory justice than laymen.

## The Forms of Action

The common law did not exist apart from the writs.[45] Its scope was the sum of the scope of the individual forms of action, each limited and controlled by a particular writ.[46] Furthermore, equity, as we shall see, acted only where the common law courts did not. Hence, its scope also depended upon the scope of the forms of action. The forms of action are no longer important as such in procedural law in most jurisdictions (at least they are not supposed to be), but they must be reckoned with in delineating the respective areas formerly occupied by common law and equity in order to understand modern remedies and modes of trial. The forms of action also have a continuing significance in substantive law, for out of them has developed much of the basic law in effect today. For example, the law of torts is based largely on trespass, case and trover, and the law of contracts largely on assumpsit, debt and covenant.[47] It is by examining these ancient forms of action that we learn why the most common remedy given today is a judgment for money damages, the situations where that remedy is available, and the fact that trial by jury can be had where it is sought. It is from them also that we discover what other situations warrant trial by jury and what other remedies can be given after such a trial.

As we noted in discussing the early writs, the most elementary wrongs were not covered in the king's courts at an early date.[48] It was only with the development of the action of trespass in about 1250 that royal justice broke out of the feudal barriers which had confined it.[49] Until then, it was sporadic, tentative and cautious.

A writ of trespass took the following form:

> The King to the Sheriff greeting. If A shall make you secure for the prosecution of his claim, then put X through gages and safe pledges that he be before our justices, etc., on such day to show wherefore by force and arms he made assault on said A at Trumpington and beat and wounded and maltreated him so that his life was despaired of . . . and other enormous things did, to the great damage of him the said A and against our peace: and have there the names of the pledges and this writ.[50]

It will be observed that the new writ was based upon the idea of "the king's peace"—a favorite justification in medieval eyes for the expansion of royal justice. The early conception was that certain roads, certain fortifications, certain persons, and certain days were entitled to the king's peace, and that violence which breached it was an offense not only against the person injured but also against the king. Hence the king had an interest in punishing such violence in his courts. Before long, the concept was extended to cover all persons in all places at all times.[51] In this way all serious crime came under the jurisdiction of the king's courts. More important from our point of view, the writ of trespass developed to give private redress to the person injured. Redress took the form of a judgment for damages, enforced, if necessary by the sheriff seizing and selling enough of the defendant's property to raise the money. (See Chapter 6).

Important in itself for extending royal justice into the area of common wrongs, the new writ was also important for its collateral influence. Out of it grew a number of other writs destined to swallow up the earlier writs and to formulate most of the common law.[52] In it, the institution of trial by jury matured.

The development of the common law out of the action of trespass resembles the growth of a tree.[53] The trunk is trespass, which starts growing in the year 1250. Branching off from it about 1400 is a main limb called "case." Case, in turn, throws out 2 branches: one called "assumpsit," developing about 1500; and the other "trover," developing half a century later. Meanwhile, another big limb grows out from the trunk itself about 1500. It is called "ejectment."

## Trespass

Originally trespass covered only obvious wrongs against persons and property. There were three forms of the action, all half criminal in nature, and all resulting in money damages.[54] One covered assault and battery; another (called "trespass de bonis asportatis") the taking of chattels; and the third (called "trespass quare clausum fregit") injuries to land.[55] Common to all three was the idea of violence—a breach of the king's peace.[56] The injury had to be "direct."[57]

The distinction between direct and indirect injuries, however, was not easy to draw. This is illustrated by the famous "Squib Case."[58] There the defendant threw a firecracker into a crowded market place. It landed on the stall of A, a merchant. He picked it up and threw it so that it landed on the stall of B, another merchant. B, reacting in a similar fashion, threw it away from his stall. It exploded in the plaintiff's face, as a result of which he lost an eye. He sued in trespass. There was no doubt among the judges as to the defendant's liability. The only question was whether trespass would lie—in other words, whether the injury was direct. If so, trespass was proper; if not, an action on the case, which we shall consider in a moment, was necessary. A majority of the court decided that trespass was a proper remedy.

It is interesting to look at the plaintiff's declaration in the famous case. It reads as follows:

> This is an action of trespass and assault wherein the plaintiff declares, that the defendant on the 28th day of October 1770, with force and arms, (to wit) with sticks, staves, clubs and fists, made an assault

185

upon the plaintiff at Taunton in the county of Somer-
set, and greatly bruised, wounded, and ill treated him,
so that his life was greatly despaired of, and then
and there, threw, cast and tossed a lighted squib,
consisting of gunpowder and other combustible materials, at and against the said plaintiff, and struck
the said plaintiff on the face therewith, and so
greatly burnt one of the eyes of the said plaintiff,
that the plaintiff underwent and suffered great and
excruciating pain and torment for a long time, (to
wit) for the space of six months then next following,
and afterwards wholly lost his said eye and the sight
thereof. . . .

That the defendant afterwards, (to wit) on the
same day and year aforesaid, with force and arms
(to wit) with sticks, staves, clubs and fists at Taunton aforesaid, made another assault upon the plaintiff, and there again beat, bruised, wounded and ill
treated him so that his life was greatly despaired
of, and the other wrongs, etc., to the great damage,
etc., and against the peace, etc., to the plaintiff his
damage of 500£ and therefore he brings suit, etc.[59]

The emphasis, it will be noted, is upon violence, a breach
of the king's peace, direct injury. There is no plain and concise statement of the facts, but on the contrary, much talk
about "beatings," "woundings," and similar outrages which
never happened in an attempt to bring the case within the
writ. The plaintiff, having chosen trespass, had to tailor his
allegations of fact to fit it.

The term "trespass" is still used, but usually with a much
more narrow meaning than at common law. Today it normally signifies only a wrongful invasion of some one else's
land—what formerly would have been called more precisely
trespass quare clausum fregit. The other types of trespass
at common law, insofar as they were not swallowed up by
some of the later forms of action which we are about to consider, are called today "assault," "battery" and "false imprisonment" and are sometimes lumped together under the
broad heading of "intentional torts."[60] Trial by jury can still
be had in any action based upon such a wrong and a judgment
for money damages is still the remedy.[61]

## Case

The other writ which the plaintiff might have used in the Squib Case was "trespass on the case," or more simply, case. Writs by that name began to have a recognizable form in about the year 1400.[62] The same theory which justified the chancellor in issuing the writ of trespass also justified his issuance of its offspring, case—the king's peace was threatened by indirect as well as by direct injuries. The same remedy was given: money damages.

Case lay for indirect injuries. If the defendant cut a rope by which the plaintiff's boat was moored so that the boat was lost or wrecked, trespass would lie for the cutting of the rope,[63] but an action on the case was the proper remedy to recover for injuries to the boat itself. If the defendant stole timber from property owned by the plaintiff but leased to another, the proper action would be case.[64] Trespass, limited to direct injuries, protected only possession. If the defendant shot at the plaintiff, trespass was proper, but if he shot at a customer of the plaintiff so that the plaintiff lost business, there would be no violence or direct injury to the plaintiff's body or goods or land, and so only case would lie. If the defendant slapped the plaintiff, trespass would lie; but if he called him a bad name, case was the proper remedy. If the defendant stole property from plaintiff, trespass would lie; but if he tricked him into handing it over, case was the proper remedy. If the defendant threw a log at the plaintiff, trespass would lie; but if he negligently cut down a log and left it lying in the road so that the plaintiff tripped and fell, case was the proper remedy.[65]

Out of the action of case developed most of the law of negligence, the law of defamation and the law of deceit.[66]

Hard as it was to define the distinction between trespass and case, courts normally required the plaintiff to choose either one writ or the other. If he proved a right to recover in trespass, having commenced an action on the case, his labor was in vain.[67] The courts were not authorized to try any kind of action, but only the kind specified in the writ. In some situations, the two remedies were concurrent, and the plaintiff could use either one;[68] but usually a choice was necessary.

It was natural that the courts should stretch the writs somewhat out of shape in attempting to do justice in individual cases.[69] Particularly so in view of the fact that the cases were originally tried by itinerant justices, with questions of law postponed until they could be decided by the full courts sitting in Westminster.[70] Thus it would often happen, as in the Squib Case, that by the time the court came to consider whether the plaintiff had chosen the correct writ, the action already had been tried. Despite the theory that a writ limited jurisdiction, it made little sense to turn the plaintiff out without a remedy after he had proved facts which would entitle him to some remedy under another writ. Hence we find strange decisions defining trespass, and in the process thoroughly confounding direct and indirect injuries. For example, a court held that a man whose daughter had been seduced could bring trespass against her seducer on the theory that the woman was a chattel which had been directly injured.[71] The doctrine of "trespass ab initio" represented similar reasoning. One who under authority of law had come into the possession of another's goods but subsequently misused them could be held liable in the owner's action of trespass. The theory was that the defendant's misuse of the goods related back to the time when he originally obtained possession, thus making him a trespasser ab initio.[72] This was fiction, but it saved cases. All sorts of such hairline distinctions were drawn between trespass and case. They were necessary until the abolition of the forms of action, but interest in them today is mainly antiquarian.

The term case is no longer in common use. Injuries formerly redressed in that form of action are called today simply "torts."[73] The mode of trial is by jury and the remedy a judgment for money damages.

### Trover

Out of the action on the case developed trover[74] in about 1550. Originally it was merely one of many species of actions on the case. When a pattern was established that case would lie whenever the plaintiff had lost goods and the defendant had found and refused to give them back, trover as a distinct form of action was born. A new writ evolved to cover that type of situation specifically. Before long, courts extended trover to cover situations where the plaintiff had not lost the goods, but had bailed them to a person who refused to return them. The loss and finding became fictitious. Later courts extended trover to cover the wrongful taking of goods. Here trespass could be "waived." Finally the action came to be used in any case of "conversion," meaning any unauthorized exercise of dominion over property owned by another. Conversion might take the form of taking, detaining, destroying or misusing any chattel. Thus the action preempted the entire field of the misuse of chattels. The remedy given was always money damages.

Trover is interesting not alone because of its practical importance, but also because its history is instructive in the development of the entire system of royal justice. It shows how courts used fictions to develop the law—how a particular writ could be expanded through interpretation. It shows how trespass and its offspring invaded the area once covered by the ancient writs—in this instance, detinue and replevin.[75] Finally, it shows what a variety of wrongs could be comprehended within a single writ—wrongs unrelated except for the rather fortuitous fact that all of them could be redressed in the same form of action.

The term trover is no longer in common use, but the concept of conversion developed in this form of action, is a very familiar one in the law of personal property and torts.[76] Modern actions for conversion call for trial by jury and money damages.[77]

### Assumpsit

Another form of action which developed out of case was assumpsit, appearing around 1500.[78] The name has fallen into disuse today, but not the law developed in this form of action. Assumpsit underlies most of our modern law of contracts, and much of that branch of law known variously as "quasi-contracts" or "restitution" or "unjust enrichment."

Many of the indirect injuries covered by case arose where the defendant, having promised to do something for the plaintiff, had done it badly. For example, he had cut the plaintiff while shaving him, or lamed the plaintiff's horse while shoeing it. Essential to recovery in such cases was the fact that the defendant had undertaken (assumpsit) to perform his job properly.[79] If he had not so undertaken, it was difficult for the medieval mind to understand why the plaintiff had any just complaint. The ordinary medieval conception of a wrong was one committed by a stranger, as in a trespass. If, however, the defendant had not only embarked on a job for the plaintiff, but also had undertaken to do it properly, it seemed proper to hold him responsible. An action on the case would lie in such a situation.[80]

Suppose, however, that the defendant did not commit any affirmative wrong, but merely failed to do what he had undertaken. Did that entitle the plaintiff to a remedy? This was a hard step to take, for it amounted to making "mere" agreements enforceable. Only a few special types of contracts had been enforced previously in the king's courts. Covenant lay for breaches of sealed contracts;[81] debt for the recovery of liquidated sums of money;[82] detinue for the wrongful detention of a chattel by a bailee.[83] There was no action which covered breach of contract generally. The question, was, therefore, whether courts should use the action of case to enforce promises other than those covered by the older writs. After some hesitation, the answer was yes.[84]

"Nonfeasance" (the failure to do something) was now no less a wrong than "misfeasance" (doing something wrong). If A delivered a horse to B to be transported across a river by boat, and B pushed it in the river, trespass would lie. If B lost the horse through negligence, having undertaken to transport it safely, case would lie. If B did no harm to the animal, either intentionally or negligently, directly or indirectly, but merely failed to perform his agreement, a special type of case, which became known as assumpsit, would lie.[85]

The importance of this development can hardly be overestimated. It meant that courts would enforce express contracts generally, subject only to the requirement (developed chiefly in this form of action) that they were supported by consideration.[86] Plaintiffs thenceforth would receive compensation for the losses they suffered from breaches of their contracts, including their expectancy of gain if the contracts had been performed.

Assumpsit was later extended to cover implied contracts. The first step in this direction was taking over the field formerly occupied by the action of debt.[87] In order to understand this development, it is necessary to say a few words about that action. It was triable in one of the king's courts, but by an ancient and unsatisfactory procedure. Instead of trial by jury, compurgation could be used at the option of the defendant.[88] Furthermore, the action was based upon a presupposition which is hard for us to understand today. A debt was thought to be very much like a chattel[89]—something that the defendant had granted or conveyed to his creditor. The grant was considered exhausted when the debt was created. No continuing promise was conceived.

Of course, if the debtor made a later express promise to pay the debt, the new action of assumpsit, with its simpler and more rational procedure, would lie.[90] But what if there were no such new express promise? About 1600 the courts held that assumpsit covered this situation on the rationale that the defendant, being indebted, had impliedly promised to pay.[91]

This, too, was an important step, for no longer was there any necessity for an express promise. It was enough if the circumstances surrounding plaintiff and defendant in their dealings with each other were such that a promise could be implied in fact. Thus if A worked for B without any specific agreement as to how much he was to be paid, the courts implied from B that he would pay the reasonable value of the services ("quantum meruit"). Or if A furnished goods or materials to B without any express agreement as to payment, the courts implied a promise that B would pay their reasonable value ("quantum valebat"). This new type of assumpsit, covering implied promises, was called "indebitatus" or "general" assumpsit to distinguish it from "special" assumpsit, which covered express contracts.[92]

Having taken the step of implying promises in fact and enforcing them, the courts took one step further. They also implied promises "in law."[93] Such promises were pure fiction.[94] The courts were really fabricating a remedy against a defendant who ought to pay something even though he never had any intention of doing so.[95] Since in such a situation he should have made a promise, he was treated as though he had. If by mistake he received a payment intended for the plaintiff, he was held liable. If he wrongfully acquired money or property of the plaintiff or in any other way became unjustly enriched at the expense of the plaintiff, he was held liable. This is the beginning of the law of quasi-contract,[96] a most confusing description except in the light of the history we have just traced.

With this final development, assumpsit encompassed a wide variety of wrongs, unrelated except as they might be put within the rubric of a single form of action. The entry of the common law courts, through the avenue of quasi-contract, into the area of "equity and good conscience" was both explained and limited by the growing jurisdiction of the Court of Chancery. The story of Chancery, which was at this time busily engaged in taking care of frauds and mistakes and thus indirectly influencing the development of the common law, is reserved for the next chapter.

For all forms of assumpsit, the standard remedy was and still is available: money damages.[97] The mode of trial was and still is by jury.

Besides developing much of the substantive law that prevails today, the action of assumpsit also had a permanent influence on pleading. The "common counts" were allegations used in declarations in assumpsit. They covered many situations in remarkably terse language. Still considered proper pleading in most jurisdictions (surprisingly), they are the inspiration for several of the model complaints set forth in the Federal Rules of Civil Procedure.[98]

## Ejectment

Ejectment developed directly out of trespass.[99]

The form of trespass applicable to land cases was quare clausum fregit, initiating an inquiry into why the defendant broke the "close" (enclosure) of the plaintiff.[100] Related as it was to conceptions of violence and a breach of the king's peace, trespass protected all persons who claimed a right to immediate possession of land.[101] It made no difference whether the person molested was a man of high or low estate, for a serf might be expected to fight for his farm as violently as a lord for his castle. Hence, the writ protected not only freeholders claiming land by feudal tenures, but also lessees claiming land by contract, and even serfs who were mere tenants at will. Furthermore they were protected even against the lords and owners themselves.[102]

The only difficulty with the action was that it could be used only to recover a money judgment. The land itself could not be recovered.[103] In that respect the remedy was less effective than that given by the ancient land writs protecting freeholders.

In about 1500, the common law judges began to award possession of the land itself as a remedy in place of damages.[104] This was the beginning of the action of ejectment.[105]

The action was an important one because it dealt with land, the most important form of wealth at the time.[106] It was an interesting one because it was the first action of continuing importance at common law in which some remedy other than money damages was given. All of the others resulted in money judgments, except replevin and detinue. In replevin, it was possible to recover a specific chattel, but the scope of the action was so limited that the remedy was not very important until recent times. In detinue a chattel could be recovered also, but only if the defendant was willing to surrender it. He had the option of paying its value.[107] In ejectment, the successful plaintiff recovered possession of the land itself, and the defendant had no option. As was true of all other common law remedies, the sheriff executed the judgment. Just as in the case of a judgment for money damages the sheriff would seize and sell the defendant's property, so in carrying out a judgment of ejectment, he would forcibly remove the defendant from the property in question.[108]

In addition to giving an especially desirable remedy, the action of ejectment had all the other advantages of trespass and its other offspring, namely, trial by jury, and a relatively simple and speedy procedure.[109] It was natural, therefore, that all persons desiring to obtain possession of land would wish to use the new remedy.[110] The difficulty was that freeholders already had other remedies, theoretically adequate. Since the ancient land writs were available to freeholders, they were not entitled directly to use the action of ejectment.[111]

However, the remedy was so desirable that medieval lawyers found a way to overcome the difficulty.[112] The first method was by having a freeholder who claimed possession of land adversely held by the defendant make a lease of the land to some friend. The lease was designed only to give the freehold owner the benefit of the new action. The owner's friend would hang around the premises until the defendant threw him off. Then an action of ejectment would arise in favor of the friend, although the owner would really prosecute it.

This procedure was somewhat dangerous to the friend. So the claimant introduced another actor into the farce—a second friend. Now the claimant would make a lease of the land to the first friend, and the second friend would gently kick the first friend off of the land. Then an action of ejectment would arise by the first friend against the second friend, and the second friend, claiming no interest in the land, would advise the true defendant to defend the action.

The procedure was still cumbersome, however. It involved two men going through a pantomime, the execution of a lease, and other unnecessary and foolish hocus pocus. The final step was to merely pretend that a lease had been entered into and the lessee had been evicted. Now the plaintiff sent notice to the defendant to come in and defend, signing it "your loving friend" over a fictitious name. The defendant was allowed to defend the action only on condition that he did not dispute the making of the lease or the ejectment. Thus, the fictitious action of ejectment came to be the normal method of recovering possession of land and trying title to it.[113] It soon supplanted the ancient land actions. The term ejectment is still used to describe an action by which possession of land can be recovered. Trial by jury is available.

The action of trespass of real estate continued, however. It was used in all cases except where the plaintiff was deprived of possession—in other words, in all cases of injury to the land or things growing on it or attached to it. By the time of the development of the action of ejectment, the concept of direct injuries to land had become very much attenuated. Merely stepping on a neighbor's lot without his permission was a trespass. The step was the only violence involved, and the only injury was crushing the blades of grass under foot. The idea of the king's peace, in this as in the other forms of action, had been left far behind, if not forgotten.

## Extraordinary Remedies

In addition to deciding private disputes, the common law courts played an important part in controlling official action. They did so by means of "prerogative writs," granting what have come to be known as "extraordinary remedies." In dealing with these remedies, the common law courts, contrary to their usual practice, did not use juries.[114] Still very much alive in the field of public law, these remedies are useful in private litigation as well, particularly that involving corporations. We shall do nothing more than attempt to indicate what they are.

*Mandamus* is used to compel an officer—public or corporate —to perform some duty. The duty must be clear and not of such a nature that the official is vested with discretion to decide whether to act or not. Thus, mandamus could be used to compel a motor vehicle bureau to register an automobile; or to force a corporate officer to permit a proper inspection of the company's books; or to require a lower court to exercise jurisdiction in a given case. The first step in the proceeding might be the issuance of what is called an "alternative writ," commanding that the defendant do the thing asked, or else show cause why not. If he failed either to perform or to justify his refusal, a "peremptory writ" would issue, unequivocally commanding him to perform.

*Quo Warranto* is used to inquire into the authority by which an individual or corporation presumes to exercise some office, privilege or franchise granted by the government. If proper authority cannot be produced, the unauthorized activities must cease. Thus, quo warranto would be the proper remedy if a police chief were illegally appointed or elected; or if a corporation were acting beyond its rightful powers; or if the deposed treasurer of a corporation refused to surrender his office.

*Habeas Corpus* is a celebrated remedy because of its historic and continuing importance as a safeguard of personal liberty. It is used to inquire into the cause of the detention of any person under restraint and to release him if the restraint is illegal. It would be the proper remedy if a man were under arrest and held by the police without charges being preferred against him; or if he were in prison for a crime after being convicted by a court without jurisdiction; or if a child whose custody had been awarded in divorce proceedings to his mother were kidnapped by his father.

*Prohibition* is used to restrain an inferior court or administrative body from acting in excess of its jurisdiction. Thus, it could be used to prevent a justice of the peace from deciding a case involving $1,000,000; or to stop a state conservation commission from dealing with a labor dispute. It could not, however, be used to delay a trial to correct an erroneous ruling by the judge on such a matter as the admissibility of evidence. An appeal is considered adequate for that purpose. Indeed, the adequacy of other procedures, like appeal, is an important limitation on the use of all the extraordinary remedies. As in the case of mandamus, procedure in prohibition in some jurisdictions contemplates the issuance of both an alternative and a peremptory writ.

*Certiorari* is used to compel an inferior court or an administrative body to certify and transmit a record of its proceedings in a particular matter to a superior court for the review of claimed jurisdictional errors. Thus, it could be used if a lower court, authorized only to give money judgments, granted an injunction; or if a board of bar examiners undertook to revoke a physician's license to practice medicine. The United States Supreme Court, as we saw in Chapter 12, uses "certiorari" as a means of bringing up records from lower courts for appellate review. This differs from the common law practice in that review is not limited to jurisdictional questions.

Mandamus, quo warranto and habeas corpus, can be used against public officials generally and against private individuals or corporations. Prohibition and certiorari, on the other hand, can be used only against courts and administrative bodies exercising judicial or "quasi-judicial" functions. Nevertheless, their utility in private litigation is evident, for they control those agencies in their dealings with private cases.

The various extraordinary remedies overlap one another to such an extent that it is often difficult to know which should be used in a particular situation. Also, despite a maxim that they are not to be used to perform the functions of an appeal, there is an overlap there too. For example, very close questions are raised when a convicted defendant in a criminal case brings habeas corpus or certiorari; or if a party to a civil action suffering an adverse ruling on a jurisdictional issue brings prohibition or mandamus. Because of such uncertainty and confusion, and also because of wide variations from one jurisdiction to another as to the use made of the various extraordinary remedies, the modern trend is to try to define by statute the scope of each or to combine them into a unified statutory proceeding. This development follows the pattern of an earlier reform (to be discussed in

Chapter 13), whereby the ordinary forms of action were abolished in favor of a single form of civil action.

## Common Law Procedure

Despite the proliferation of writs and vast expansion of the jurisdiction of the royal courts to cover most ordinary disputes between subject and subject, the common law remained compartmentalized in the forms of action. It lacked any generalized concept of a civil action with procedure of general application. Only actions of trespass, assumpsit, trover, ejectment and the like existed. Each form of action had its own substantive content and its own specialized rules of procedure.[115] These procedural rules became rigid and stereotyped even as the substantive content of the various forms of action expanded to cover a vast number of situations never originally envisaged.[116]

Mention has already been made of how trover, originally designed to cover a situation where the plaintiff had lost some article and the defendant had found it and refused to give it back, expanded to cover any unauthorized exercise of dominion over property owned by another. Despite the remarkable expansion of substantive common law so accomplished, the language of the writ and that of the "declaration" —the common law name for what we now call a complaint— remained the same.[117] Thus one who was suing to recover the value of a carload of wheat or the contents of a warehouse or a stable of race horses was still required solemnly to allege that the property in question was "casually lost" by the plaintiff and "found" by the defendant.[118] What really had happened between the parties did not appear in the pleadings; it would be disclosed only when the case came to trial. Thus the main purposes of pleading—to disclose to each party the contentions of the other, to eliminate surprise, to avoid unnecessary expense in preparation for trial and unnecessary adjournments, and to enable courts to dispose of some cases on issues of law without a trial on the facts—were frustrated.

Mention also has been made of the action of ejectment, originally designed to enable tenants to recover possession of the land of which they had been unlawfully deprived, but expanded over the course of centuries to allow owners of land the same remedy.[119] The fictions by which this expansion was accomplished, even more elaborate than those used in the action of trover, have already been described. They were embalmed in stereotyped language in writs and declarations about two non-existent persons ("John Doe," the alleged lessee, and "Richard Roe," the alleged ejector), a lease that was never made, and an incident (the ejectment) that never took place. Even the identity of the parties was not disclosed. The real plaintiff was identified only as the lessor of the fictitious John Doe. The real defendant was not named in the main body of the document but only as the recipient of an appended letter from fictitious Richard Roe, reading substantially as follows:

> I am informed that you are in possession of, or claim title to, the premises in this declaration of ejectment mentioned, or some part thereof, and I being sued in this action as a casual ejector only, and having no claim or title to the same, do advise you to appear on the first day of the next term in his Majesty's court, and then and there, by rule of the same court, to cause yourself to be made defendant in my stead, otherwise I shall suffer judgment therein to be entered against me by default, and you will be turned out of possession.[120]

The common law propensity to twist facts to fit them into formally unchanged rules of law did not yield a result materially different from that produced by our modern propensity to remold old rules to fit new situations by overruling or distinguishing precedents. The goal was the same then as now: to adapt law to changing conditions. As people continue to develop, altering their life styles, their ideas and their ideals, and as new inventions and discoveries accelerate the process, the task of adapting law to a changing society remains inexorable. Much of the job of adaptation has to be done by lawyers and judges in the process of adjudication, for legislation is not and never has been equal to the task of keeping pace with the rate of social change.

The rigid, fictional and stereotyped pleadings for plaintiffs at common law were matched by equally unsatisfactory pleadings for defendants. What we call the answer today was then called a "plea." Its most common form was the plea of "general issue," which varied in meaning from one form of action to another.[121] For example in both trespass and case (closely related tort actions) the plea of general issue was "not guilty." In the former, the defendant was not allowed to prove that he was justified in his conduct, whereas in the latter he was allowed to offer such proof.[122] The meaning of the plea therefore depended not on the language used, but on precedent. In the action of debt, the plea of general issue was "nil debet," which could be roughly translated as "I do not owe." It permitted proof of any fact that would defeat the plaintiff's claim—not only that no debt had ever been contracted, but also that the claim was barred by res judicata, the statute of frauds or the statute of limitations, or that payment had been made or a settlement agreed upon.[123] Receiving such a plea, the plaintiff would not have a clue as to what the defendant was going to litigate at trial.[124] In another closely related contract action, assumpsit, the plea of general issue was non assumpsit, which could be roughly translated "I did not promise." At one time in English history, this plea was substantially as broad as the plea of nil debet, but at another time so narrow that it restricted the defendant to proving only that he had not made the promise alleged. The defendant was not allowed to prove that the claim was barred by res judicata, the statute of limitations or the statute of frauds, or that payment had been made or a settlement agreed upon.[125] Again the meaning of the plea of general issue depended almost entirely upon precedent. Language and logic were not sufficient to allow one reading the declaration and the plea to understand what was at issue between the parties.

In those forms of action where the plea of general issue was narrow in scope, the defendant might have to enter a "Plea in confession and avoidance" in order to prove facts exonerating him from liability[126]—in assumpsit, for example, that the plaintiff's claim was barred by res judicata or a previous settlement between the parties. The defendant was required to plead the facts on which he relied "specially" as opposed to the plea of general issue. Here technicalities multiplied because common law judges were enamoured of the idea that every lawsuit could be reduced to and disposed of upon the basis of a single issue, either of law or fact.[127] The defendant was not allowed to deny the plaintiff's allegations and at the same time to plead new matter in avoidance of those allegations. Nor was he allowed to deny the allegations while simultaneously challenging their legal sufficiency by demurrer.[128] In short, the defendant had to choose a single line of defense at his peril. If he failed in his chosen course of action, the case was decided against him finally. He did not enjoy the freedom that the present day defendant enjoys of asserting more than one type of defense to the plaintiff's claim.

In pursuance of the common law insistence upon reducing every lawsuit to a single issue, further pleadings were required if the defendant entered a plea in confession and avoidance. To the new matter asserted by the defendant, the plaintiff would have to either demur or deny or file a "replication," containing more new facts in avoidance of the defendant's new facts. Then could follow a "rejoinder" by the defendant, a "surrebutter" by the plaintiff and so on until special names for these pleadings were exhausted.[129] All this in the name of reducing the lawsuit to a single issue, upon which it could be decided! As noted in our analysis of a modern lawsuit, pleadings today seldom go beyond the complaint and the answer.

In addition to the procedural difficulties already described, the common law lacked any machinery for discovering facts in advance of trial or for disposing of cases without trial where there was no genuine issue of material fact. It was also woefully inadequate in dealing with complex controversies involving multiple claims or multiple parties. Every lawsuit had to fit into one of the forms of action. Such procedural devices as interpleader, class actions and joinder of diverse claims could not be found in the common law courts. They were developed only in equity.

In summary, common law procedure, as distinguished from substantive common law, was a horror in the 18th century—rigid, hypertechnical and cumbersome. Reform was badly needed. As we shall see, it got under way in the middle of the 19th century.

# Chapter 12

## EQUITY

Despite the broad development of the forms of action discussed in the last chapter, royal justice was never completely confined to the common law courts. The king's subjects frequently petitioned him to dispense justice in situations where the common law courts were unwilling or unable to act.[1]

Common law inadequacies could be summarized under the following headings:

1. REMEDIES. Substantially all the forms of action yielded only money judgments.[2] The only important exception was the action of ejectment which could be used to recover the possession of real property.[3] There was no practicable remedy for recovery of possession of a chattel, because replevin, as we have noted, was limited to cases of unlawful distress, and detinue allowed the defendant the option of returning the chattel or paying its value.

The greatest deficiency in common law remedies was the lack of any machinery to prevent future wrongs, or to force a defendant to perform a contract or other obligation.

2. HARSH RULES. Some of the rules the common law courts administered were harsh and contrary to common notions of fairness. They emphasized formalism and ritual, particularly in contract and property law. The tendency was to insist upon a literal interpretation of anything in writing.

3. JURY TRIALS. While trial by jury was a vastly better method of determining facts than the methods which it supplanted, it had disadvantages: juries were sometimes incapable of understanding complicated transactions; and they were sometimes subject to corruption or intimidation by powerful men.[4] Thus, the character of prospective liti-

gants sometimes determined the feasibility of resort to the common law courts.

4. BLIND SPOTS. Some institutions and areas of conduct were not covered by the common law at all. Conspicuous were trusts and the administration of estates of persons who had died.⁵

Because of such inadequacies, the king received many petitions for his personal justice. The number was so great that he delegated the handling of them to his Chancellor. The Chancellor already had important duties in the administration of royal justice, for it was he who supervised the issuance of the writs needed to start the common law actions. His function in that area was more administrative than judicial. When he undertook the additional job of deciding the special petitions presented to the king, his judicial function came to predominate.⁶

At first there were no limitations upon the Chancellor's jurisdiction.⁷ He operated in the same areas as the common law courts and gave the same remedies. Such duplication of effort could not long be tolerated. During the fourteenth century, the principle was established that the Chancellor would not act where there was an "adequate" remedy at common law either by way of an ordinary form of action or an extraordinary remedy.⁸ This vague test left the Chancellor a large area of discretion, but it became sharper as precedents were established, defining where Chancery would act and where it would leave the common law courts to act.

Furthermore, equitable remedies came to be differentiated from legal remedies. The maxim was that equity acted "in personam," meaning against the person.⁹ The judgment, or "decree" as it was called, took the form of a command to the defendant to do or refrain from doing a certain act. If he disobeyed, he was in contempt of court and subject to imprisonment until he was willing to comply. There was normally no reliance, as in the common law system, upon the help of sheriffs. Beginning in the seventeenth century, some departure was made from this norm (see Chapter 6), but basically the method of equity enforcement was as stated.[10]

At first the Chancellor decided cases without reference to any fixed rules of substantive law or procedure. His standard was "equity and good conscience"—a fact which gave rise to a famous quip that the only measure in Chancery was "the Chancellor's foot."[11] The Chancellors neither systematically preserved their decisions, nor consciously adhered to precedent. During the seventeenth century, however, it became customary to appoint lawyers rather than ecclesiastics to the post of Chancellor. Gradually the doctrine of precedent developed, and came to operate in Chancery much the same as it operated in the common law courts.[12]

From the very beginning, no jury was used in equity. Perhaps this was because of the fact, already mentioned, that equity jurisdiction was sometimes predicated upon the claim that juries were subject to intimidation and corruption;[13] perhaps because Chancery's procedure was modelled upon the procedure of the ecclesiastical courts,[14] where juries were unknown.[15] Whatever the reason, it is clear that the judge determined all issues of fact as well as of law.[16]

Furthermore, from the beginning there was no system of writs in equity such as prevailed at common law. The procedure of Chancery in the initial stages of suit was flexible.[17] This is probably the reason why modern procedure in this area is modeled more closely on equity practice than on common law practice.

### Relation of Law and Equity

Equity was never a complete body of law. It consisted of a collection of miscellaneous rules, because Chancery acted only in situations where the common law courts did not provide an adequate remedy. The point is made by Maitland in his classic "Lectures on Equity" as follows:[18]

> We ought not to think of common law and equity as of two rival systems. Equity was not a self-sufficient system, at every point it presupposed the existence of common law. Common law was a self-sufficient

system. I mean this: that if the legislature had passed a short act saying "Equity is hereby abolished" we might still have got on fairly well; in some respects our law would have been barbarous, unjust, absurd, but still the great elementary rights, the right to immunity from violence, the right to one's good name, the right to ownership and possession would have been decently protected and contract would have been enforced. On the other hand had the legislature said, "Common Law is hereby abolished," this decree if obeyed would have meant anarchy. At every point equity presupposed the existence of common law. Take the case of the trust. It's of no use for Equity to say that A is a trustee of Blackacre for B unless there be some court that can say that A is the owner of Blackacre. Equity without common law would have been a castle in the air, an impossibility.

For this reason I do not think that any one has expounded or ever will expound equity as a single, consistent system, an articulate body of law. It is a collection of appendixes between which there is no very close connexion. If we suppose all our law put into systematic order, we shall find that some chapters of it have been copiously glossed by equity, while others are quite free from equitable glosses. Since the destruction of the Star Chamber we have had no criminal equity. The Court of Chancery kept very clear of the province of crime, and since the province of crime and the province of tort overlap, it kept very clear of large portions of the province of tort. For example, before 1875 it would grant no injunction to restrain the publication of a libel, for normally the libel which is a tort is also a crime and it was thought, and rightly thought, that such a matter should not be brought before a court where a judge without any jury tried both fact and law. Indeed if you will look at your books on tort you will find that on the whole—if we except the province of fraud—equity has had little to do with tort, though it has granted injunctions to restrain the commission of nuisances and the like. The law of contract has been more richly provided with equitable appendixes. The power of the Chancery to compel specific performance, and its power to decree the cancellation or rectification of agreements brought numerous cases of contract before it, and then it had special doctrines about mortgages, and penalties, and stipulations concerning time. Property law was yet more richly glossed. One vast appendix was added to it under the title of trusts. The bond which kept these various appendixes together under the head of Equity was the jurisdictional and procedural bond. All these matters were within the cognizance of courts of equity, and they were not within cognizance of the courts of common law. That bond is now broken by the Judicature Acts. Instead of it we find but a mere historical bond—"these rules used to be dealt with by the Court of Chancery"—and the strength of that bond is being diminished year by year.

Perhaps Maitland overstated his case. In the heterogeneous collection of rules called equity there was a common starting point—the principle that "equity and good conscience" were controlling.[19] This principle was translated into various maxims—"He who seeks justice must do it," "One who asks the aid of equity must come into court with clean hands," etc.[20] It remained a guiding light, so that even today a lawyer arguing an "equity case" (meaning one which formerly would have been tried in Chancery) feels less inhibited in talking about justice than when he is arguing a "law case" (meaning one which formerly would have been tried in a court of common law). No similar starting point can be found for the rules of common law.

This is not to imply that precedent does not govern in equity cases or to suggest that judges have uncontrolled discretion to act according to their private notions of right and wrong. They are no more free to disregard previous decisions in such cases than they are in law cases. The difference is that the equity precedents allow them greater freedom of action.

While generally equity supplemented the common law, there were a few areas where that was not true—where the two came into conflict. The Chancellor sometimes presumed to say that a legal remedy was inadequate or improper because the substantive rule upon which it was based was unjust. In particular, he asserted his right to enjoin a litigant from prosecuting an unjust action in a common law court or from enforcing an unjust judgment already recovered. If the defendant violated the injunction, he would be imprisoned for contempt. Thus the equitable remedy of injunction was trenching close to the province of the extraordinary remedies at common law as well as invading part of the area occupied by the ordinary forms of action.

The Chancellor, following his normal method of enforcing decrees and avoiding the appearance of any such direct attack as would have been involved in the use of a writ of prohibition, did not purport to act directly against the common law courts, but only against litigants who resorted to them.[21] Nevertheless, his assertion of power did not go unchallenged by the common law judges. Their spokesman was Coke, Chief Justice of the Court of King's Bench; his adversary, Lord Ellesmere, the Chancellor. Coke said that he would use the writ of habeas corpus to release any person imprisoned by the Chancellor for violating such an injunction. The controversy was bitter and notorious. King James I, anxious to assert his supremacy over all the judges, appointed a committee of distinguished lawyers, including Sir Francis Bacon, to advise him how the dispute should be settled. On the basis of their report, he decided in 1615 in favor of Chancery.[22] Thenceforth, whenever an equity rule conflicted with a common law rule, the equity rule prevailed.[23]

Cases of conflict, however, were not common. For the most part, equity came into being not to destroy the common law but to supplement it.[24]

## A Common Misconception

Because of its history and name, there is a widespread misconception of the nature of equity. Few topics engender so much confusion and misunderstanding in the minds of law students. They tend to believe that equity is not really law at all, but some vague concept of morality giving judges license to decide cases according to their personal predilections. They infer from the principle that equity would not act where there was an adequate remedy at common law, the peculiar notion that equity would grant a remedy merely because the common law courts would not—a startling non sequitur. They think that whenever a litigant is blocked by a rule of law, he can "go into equity" and get what his heart desires.

These ideas are false and should be discarded. Equity had a limited scope just as the common law did. Equity operated according to rules no less binding than those which prevailed at common law.[25] A judge today, administering both law and equity, is no more immunized against reversal on appeal when he is dealing with an "equity case" than when he is dealing with a "law case."

## The Scope of Equity

We now turn to a more specific description of the scope of equity jurisdiction. In doing so, we shall attempt a rough classification of the activities of Chancery, without any effort to indicate the chronological order of development. A catalog of miscellaneous disconnected rules might be more accurate, but it would leave the subject unnecessarily amorphous.

### New Remedies for Old Rights

One major category of equity jurisdiction was concerned with granting new remedies for old rights. Many of the rights recognized at common law were also recognized by equity in accordance with the same substantive rules. All that equity did was devise new remedies for vindicating those rights without quarreling with or questioning their common law basis.[26]

The best known and most drastic of such remedies was the injunction. It was used to prevent future wrongs rather than to redress past wrongs.[27] If A persisted in travelling over a portion of B's land without permission, equity would enjoin him from continuing. If A disobeyed, the equity court would find him guilty of contempt of court and punish him by fine or imprisonment.[28] If A proposed to cut down timber on a tract of land belonging to B, equity would enjoin him.

In neither of these cases was equity recognizing any right or duty not already recognized at common law and capable of some sort of enforcement in an appropriate form of action. The difficulty was that the common law remedy was inadequate. In the first case it was difficult, if not impossible, for the plaintiff to prove damages. The plaintiff might be able to establish his title and the fact that the defendant was trespassing without permission, but he would end up with a hollow victory, for he could prove only nominal (trivial) damages. In the second case it might be possible to prove actual damages if the timber were cut down, but the plaintiff had a right to a grove of standing trees instead of a sum of money representing a jury's idea of their value.[29]

The usual form of an injunction was negative—that is, it commanded the defendant not to do something. Sometimes that was inadequate.[30] For example, if the defendant had arranged his drainage system so as to empty onto the plaintiff's land, an order to stop would be of little use. Stop what? The only effective remedy in such a situation was a positive command to the defendant to do some affirmative act. For a time, equity balked at granting such positive orders, or at least at granting them in explicit terms. There was a tendency to grant positive injunctions in negative terms, i.e., the defendant would be ordered to cease to allow his drainage system to exist.[31] Gradually, however it was recognized that positive as well as negative injunctions were proper. The positive commands, ordering the defendant to perform some affirmative act, came to be known as "mandatory" injunctions.[32]

We have talked only of injunctions against torts. Could they be used also in connection with breaches of contract? Suppose, for example, that the defendant, having sold a shoe shop in a small town to the plaintiff and having promised not to compete for a period of two years, disregarded his contract and opened up a shoe store across the street from the plaintiff. Could the plaintiff sue in equity for an injunction? Yes, because his remedy at law was inadequate. It would be almost impossible to prove the damage caused by the defendant's wrongful conduct, and furthermore, it would be unjust to make the plaintiff wait until the expiration of the two year period before bringing action.[33]

The injunction was an extremely flexible remedy. It could be used to fit almost any situation, for the defendant could be ordered to do whatever was just or to refrain from doing whatever was unjust. It was also an extremely effective remedy, for judges enforced it by putting the defendant in jail until he complied with the court's order.[34]

Whether an injunction would be granted depended upon whether the plaintiff had an adequate remedy at law.[35] That gave the judge wide discretion. The factors which he considered were the difficulty of proving damages, the adequacy of damages if provable, the impracticability of legal remedies, the possibility of avoiding a multiplicity of law suits, and the overall justice of the plaintiff's claim in the circumstances of the particular case.[36]

Closely akin to the injunction was the equitable remedy of specific performance. A decree for specific performance was, indeed, only a particular species of mandatory injunction, limited to contract cases.[37]

Such a decree would not be granted to require the performance of any contract, but only if there were no adequate remedy at law.[38] If, for example, the plaintiff lent the defendant £1000 to be repaid in two months and the defendant failed to pay, the plaintiff could not go into equity asking specific performance. He had an adequate remedy at common law in the action of assumpsit. Similarly, if the defendant agreed to sell a carload of wheat and then refused to deliver, the plaintiff had no standing in equity to compel specific performance. By the action of assumpsit, he could recover the difference between the contract price for the wheat and the market price at the time and place fixed for delivery.[39]

If, on the other hand, the defendant had contracted to sell a piece of real estate or a unique chattel, the equity court would grant specific performance.[40] Every parcel of real estate was considered unique, and some chattels were too, like paintings and rare vases.[41] The buyer of such an article was not required to forego his rights to it and be satisfied with damages. Equity would compel the defendant to perform.[42]

The criterion for granting specific performance was the same as for granting an injunction: whether there was an adequate remedy at common law; and, if not, whether the equitable remedy would be appropriate and just in the circumstances of the particular case. This was a highly discretionary matter. The judge was required not only to decide whether the plaintiff had a right which the defendant had violated, as in a common law case (where the remedy followed the right as a matter of course), but also the further and distinct question of whether he ought to give an equitable remedy in the circumstances of the particular case.[43]

The line dividing jurisdiction between Chancery and the common law courts was necessarily hazy because of the discretion exercised in granting remedies.[44] Many a plaintiff chose the wrong court and after proving his case discovered that he would have to start all over again in the other court.[45] That is not to say that there were no rules as to when injunctions or decrees for specific performance would be granted. Some situations evolved definite rules,[46] but in many others it was nearly impossible to know in advance whether equity would act.

Often the plaintiff had a choice between remedies. He could sue either in equity or at common law. If, for example, the defendant had agreed to convey to the plaintiff a certain parcel of real estate, the plaintiff might sue for specific performance in equity, or he might sue in assumpsit at common law for damages.[47] If he chose the latter alternative, the question of whether a contract was made and whether it was breached would be decided by a jury. If he decided to sue in equity the identical questions would be decided by the court alone without a jury.[48]

It must not be supposed that either the common law courts or Chancery or both combined gave an adequate remedy for every legal wrong.[49] Sometimes (and this is true today) the plaintiff's legal right was violated but he could find no real redress in any court. If, for example, he agreed to buy a standard article at list price and the seller refused to go through with the deal, the plaintiff's right would be violated, but he could prove nothing but nominal damages. Furthermore, there was no sufficient reason for equity to intervene, for the plaintiff could go on the market and buy the identical article for the same price.

## New Rights and New Remedies

Another broad category of equity jurisdiction was concerned with devising new rules in place of common law rules which were thought to be unjust. Accompanying the new rules were new remedies.

The common law courts dealt with some situations in a manner that the Chancellor did not like, particularly in contract law. The common law courts had a hard time deciding whether to enforce contracts, but once having decided they would, they enforced them with a vengeance, according to their literal terms. They did not hesitate to exact severe penalties and forfeitures so long as they were provided in writing.[50]

The Chancellor, considering words less important than intentions, devised two common and important remedies to avoid the rigors of the common law in the field of contracts.

One was reformation. If A agreed orally to sell a house for £10,000 but wrote down "£1,000," Chancery would entertain an action to make the writing express the actual agreement of the parties. Then and only then could the contract be enforced.[51]

The other remedy was recision. It was used when fraud or mistake was involved in the negotiation of a contract rather than in reducing it to written form.[52] If a jeweler falsely appraised a rare gem worth £5,000 at one shilling and agreed to buy it at that figure, the seller could go into equity and have the contract "rescinded."[53] That is, the Chancellor would set the agreement at naught, and the seller would be relieved of his bargain.

The remedies of recision and reformation still exist today after the merger of law and equity.[54] The facts which justify them, however, are more frequently used as the basis for affirmative defenses than as the basis for independent actions. Thus if the plaintiff sues the defendant for breach of contract, the defendant will allege grounds for reformation or recision because of fraud or mistake in his answer. In such a case a question is presented as to the mode of trial, because the plaintiff is suing on a cause of action "at law," and the defendant defending on the basis of what previously would have been a suit in equity. In that situation, as explained in Chapters 5 and 13, the judge submits the legal issues to the jury, and determines the equitable issues by himself.

In addition to interfering with ordinary contracts, equity also moved into the extremely important field of mortgage contracts.[55] The old form of mortgage was a conveyance of property subject to a condition subsequent. The condition was that the debtor could redeem by paying the amount of the debt.[56] But if he did not pay by the very minute of the very hour of the very day specified, he lost the property forever. Mortgages were treated at common law as in the old-fashioned melodrama. The mortgagee, if he were a black-hearted, technical minded fellow, could insist on the mortgagor losing his home and turning his poor children out on the streets.[57]

The Chancellor did not like the ending, and undertook to rewrite it. He allowed the mortgagor to come into the court of equity after his legal period of redemption—that specified in the contract—had expired, and still redeem the payment. Thus the mortgagor acquired a right to an extension of time, which came to be known as his "equity of redemption."[58]

But now the mortgagee was in trouble. He could never be sure where he stood after enforcing his legal rights. The mortgagor could always run to equity. So equity now undertook to help the mortgagee too.[59] It allowed him to come into equity and "foreclose" the mortgage. That is, the equity court would fix a definite period—whatever it considered just in the circumstances of the particular case—for the mortgagor to redeem. If he failed to do so within the time allowed, the mortgagee acquired good title to the property. Later the procedure was modified to require foreclosure by sale of the property. The proceeds were used to pay the debt and after paying court costs, any remainder was returned to the mortgagor.[60]

In all of the situations discussed in this section, the equity rules were in conflict with the common law rules. The common law courts said that contracts would be enforced as written. Equity said no. As we saw earlier, the equity rules prevailed as a result of King James I's decision in the Coke-Ellesmere controversy.

## New Fields of Law

A third portion of equity jurisdiction concerned areas of conduct not dealt with by the common law courts at all. Two great areas had been left almost untouched: trusts and estates.

A trust is a device whereby one person holds property for the benefit of another. If A conveys land to B with instructions that he is to apply the rents and income for the support of A's children, a trust is created. B is the trustee, and A's children the beneficiaries. The common law courts gave effect to the conveyance of land from A to B, but not to the duties imposed upon B. If a third person injured or stole the trust property, the trustee would be allowed to sue at law to recover damages. Therefore he was said to have "legal title." But if the trustee violated his duties and pocketed the income from the land, the beneficiaries were not allowed to maintain any action against him in a common law court. They could, however, sue in equity to compel him to give an account of his stewardship and to surrender ill-gotten gains. For this reason, the beneficiaries were said to have "equitable" interests in the subject matter of the trust.[61]

Precisely why the common law courts did not enforce trusts is difficult to say. Very likely it is because no form of action was equal to the job until the development of general assumpsit. The rationale of that action was broad enough, but its procedure was ill-adapted to the task of continuing supervision over administration. Besides, by the time that assumpsit developed, equity had already preempted the field.[62]

Trusts frequently are created by will, but that is not the entire explanation of Chancery's jurisdiction over the administration of estates. At one time, ecclesiastical courts attended to the matter, but they were elbowed out of the field by Chancery at the time of the Reformation.[63] Thereafter, its jurisdiction was undisputed over the administration of the estates not only of decedents but also of minors and incompetents.[64] The common law courts, with their rigid forms of action and rigid procedures, were quite unable to cope with collecting the assets of a deceased or incompetent person, paying his past debts and distributing the balance to heirs, or with matters involving guardianships, family settlements, complicated accounts and long drawn out administration.[65] Equity procedure was flexible and better adapted to the task.[66] This was a large and important field of legal work, and equity's imprint is still very evident in modern probate practice.[67]

Chancery's flexible procedure also explains its jurisdiction to handle accounts other than those arising in connection with trusts or the administration of estates. At one time, the common law courts, by the ancient action of "account," attempted to deal with such matters, but because of their use of juries and the inflexibility of their procedure, the attempt was abandoned in favor of Chancery's power.[68] Thus partnership accounts and other accounts arising out of complicated commercial transactions came under the head of equity jurisdiction.

The foregoing description does not purport to be a complete catalog of Chancery's activities. All that has been attempted is a picture of the scope of equity jurisdiction, to be placed alongside of the picture previously presented of the scope of common law jurisdiction.

## Equity Procedure

Some contrasts between equity procedure and that which prevailed at common law have already been mentioned, notably the absence of the jury in equity, the fact that equity was free of the curse of the forms of action, and the fact that equity acted in personam, issuing direct commands to litigants. Other contrasts also merit consideration.

Largely because it was not confined to forms of action, equity could deal more effectively with complex litigation than could the common law courts. At common law, arbitrary rules prevailed. The plaintiff could join unrelated trespasses in a single lawsuit because they fitted under a single form of action, but he could not join a claim of trespass with a claim of case, even though both were based on the same factual situation, because each required a different form of action.[69] The rules as to joining parties were similarly inflexible.[70] If the interests of potential litigants were joint (as in the case of joint promisees or joint obligors), they were not only permitted but compelled to join as plaintiffs or defendants. If their interests were not joint (as in the case of several unrelated persons injured by a single negligent act of the defendant), they could not be joined, however much sense that might make from the point of view of saving time and expense and avoiding duplicate litigation.[71]

Equity followed a different philosophy. Its goal was to avoid a multiplicity of lawsuits by allowing and sometimes compelling closely related claims and parties to be joined.[72] Equity would not act where there was an adequate remedy at common law, but once having acquired jurisdiction over a claim properly cognizable in equity—for example, for an injunction against a future tort—the court would go on to deal with other related claims between the parties—for example, awarding damages for past torts of the same nature (which if pursued alone would have been solely within the jurisdiction of the common law courts).[73] The policy of avoiding piecemeal litigation led also to treating some persons as necessary or indispensable parties even though their interests were not joint.[74] The distinction between "necessary" and "indispensable" parties was "loose and ambiguous in its expression and uncertain in its application" as an American court remarked.[75] Nevertheless, equity's basic idea of permitting and encouraging joinder of both parties and claims has been adopted in modern procedural codes in preference to the narrow, restrictive rules that prevailed at common law.[76]

Equity also invented new kinds of actions to deal with complex situations. An example was the action of interpleader, whereby a stakeholder threatened or actually beset by conflicting claims from rival claimants could sue as plaintiff in a court of equity, naming the rival claimants as defendants, and forcing them to fight out their differences between themselves while the stakeholder retreated to the sidelines.[77] Also notable was the class action, whereby one or a few persons of a large group afflicted by a common grievance were allowed to sue not only on behalf of themselves but also on behalf of all others similarly situated.[78] Both of these devices have been incorporated into modern procedural codes,[79] but since their subject matter overlapped that cognizable in the common law courts, difficult problems as to the right of trial by jury have arisen. These are discussed in Chapter 13.

While common law procedure was primarily oral, equity procedure relied heavily on the written word.[80] The equity equivalent of a modern complaint or a common law declaration was called a "petition."[81] It stated the plaintiff's version of the facts, avoiding the fictionalized and stereotyped forms found at common law, but in an almost equally objectionable manner because so much detail was given that the document tended to become unduly lengthy and verbose (lawyers were sometimes paid by the word). Part of the petition consisted of a demand that the defendant provide under oath detailed written responses to the plaintiff's allegations.[82] This sowed the seeds for two modern procedural devices—discovery and verification. They are now markedly different from the equity concepts, but still historically identifiable as their descendants. Equity gave evidential effect to the defendant's responses to the plaintiff's allegations.[83] If they took the form of admissions, they might well destroy all or part of the defense, but if they took the form of denials, they had to be overcome by the testimony of two witnesses for the plaintiff or one such witness plus circumstantial evidence of equal value.[84] If the defendant failed either to admit or deny the plaintiff's allegations, as he might do if he demurred, or "disclaimed" (showing that he should not be retained as a party to the suit), or submitted a special plea alleging new matter not contradicting the plaintiff's allegations (similar to the common law plea of confession and avoidance), the plaintiff was required to prove his allegations. This rule was the opposite of that which prevailed at common law, where an allegation not denied was deemed admitted.[85] The common law rule is the one that prevails today. Furthermore, we no longer automatically assign evidential value to pretrial statements made either in pleadings or discovery procedures, which are now distinct and separate from the pleadings. Our basic reliance today is on oral testimony given in open court, just as at common law.

Equity discovery in its early stages was not only cumbersome, but also narrow and one-sided. It operated only in favor of the plaintiff and only for the purpose of proving his own case, not for the purpose of allowing him to pry into the other side's case.[86] Subsequent developments broadened its scope. A "Bill of Discovery" was invented to aid the defendant. In effect, it initiated a new lawsuit designed to do nothing more than compel the plaintiff to answer questions put by the defendant.[87] But still questions and answers were in written form, and the questioner—now the defendant—was restricted to seeking information to prove his own case.[88] Neither side was allowed to explore his opponent's case. This restriction was rooted in the fear that litigants might manufacture false evidence if they knew in advance what the other side's evidence was going to be.[89] Another extension of discovery was in aid of actions in the common law courts where no parallel procedures could be found. If either plaintiff or defendant in a common law action needed information to establish his own case, he was allowed to bring a suit in equity for the sole purpose of acquiring such information.[90] Questions and answers were in written form, and the same restrictions on prying into the other side's case applied. The procedures just described, though cumbersome and primitive, contained the seminal ideas which underlie discovery today.

Because of its heavy emphasis on the written word, the Court of Chancery became mired in paperwork. Its proceedings tended to drag on interminably and become ruinously expensive to litigants—defects dramatically detailed by Dickens in *Bleak House*. At the end of the 18th Century, reform was needed for equity procedure no less than for that which prevailed at common law.

## Chapter 13

## REFORM AND THE MODERN JUDICIAL SYSTEM

As the English legal system matured, it became rigid, not in the sense that substantive law stagnated, but rather in the sense that procedure became unduly stiff. Fictions flourished, expanding and improving the substantive law; and statutes were enacted in ever increasing volume to keep the law abreast of the times. But form was exalted over substance. A prospective plaintiff had to choose the right court and the right writ at all costs. If he entered the wrong court, he was thrown out, even though the law considered as a whole entitled him to a remedy on the facts. He might even enter the right court by the wrong door, and suffer the same treatment. There were no interconnecting passages between Chancery and the common law courts, or within the common law courts themselves. Each form of action was a separate corridor with a special entrance (the appropriate writ) and a special exit (a particular remedy). Each had its own procedure, quite apart from any necessary difference arising from the facts involved or the remedy sought. Chancery was no more immune to the stiffening process than the common law courts. Moreover, it was almost hopelessly bogged down in paper work.

The system as a whole caused litigants to waste time, energy and money. Mistakes were easy to make, for the lines separating the forms of action and dividing the jurisdiction of Chancery from that of the common law courts were hazy, subtle and shifting. Lawyers' mistakes were magnified out of all proportion to their importance.

### Reception of English Law

That was the situation during the period when the American colonies were being established. Since most of the early colonists were Englishmen who knew only what prevailed at home, it was natural that they should initially adopt the

English legal system. Sometimes the adoption was formal, as by this statutory enactment in Virginia:[1]

> And be it further ordained, That the common law of England, all statutes or acts of parliament made in aid of the common law prior to the fourth year of the reign of king James the first, and which are of a general nature, not local to that kingdom, together with the several acts of the general assembly of this colony now in force, so far as the same may consist with the several ordinances, declarations, and resolutions of the general convention, shall be the rule of decision, and shall be considered as in full force, until the same shall be altered by the legislative power of this colony.

Sometimes the "reception" of English law was more informal and reluctant, particularly because of resistance in some localities to equity with its connotations of arbitrary sovereignty.[2] Nevertheless the law of England, including that developed in the court of equity as well as that developed in the courts of common law, was "received" in the first American colonies along the Eastern seaboard.[3] As the nation grew, English legal institutions accompanied the settlers in their westward migrations. Thus Congress in 1789 provided in the ordinance for the Northwest Territory that judicial proceedings should be conducted "according to the course of the common law."[4] The term "common law" was understood in its broad sense to mean judge-made law—not only that developed in the common law courts but also that originating in equity.[5] Ultimately this body of law spread throughout the nation, even into California, Texas and Louisiana, which, having been settled by persons other than Englishmen, had started with legal institutions derived from other cultures.[6]

The law so imported into America was not embalmed permanently in the form it was originally received. Because of the principle of stare decisis with its implicit recognition that law could develop and change through judicial decision, judge-made law contained within itself the seeds for future growth. Equally important, judge-made law was subject to being supplemented and altered by legislation.

## The Character of the Changes

Reform of procedure was in the offing, and it came primarily through constitutional and legislative enactment. There were two main steps in the reform, each supplemented by gradual development and refinement.

One was the merger of the law and equity courts. There was no sense in having one set of courts administering legal remedies, and another administering equitable remedies. The line separating their respective jurisdictions was too indistinct and too productive of wasteful, unnecessary litigation to be continued. Accordingly, it became customary to provide, as in many state constitutions, that judicial power "both as to matters of law and equity" should be vested in certain named courts.[7] The United States Constitution (art. III) contained this provision governing the federal courts:

> The judicial power of the United States, shall be vested in one supreme court, and in such inferior courts as the Congress may from time to time ordain and establish.
>
> . . . The judicial power shall extend to all cases, in law and equity, arising under this constitution, the laws of the United States, and treaties made, or which shall be made, under their authority . . .

Today as a result, the same courts administer both law and equity. Each judge is vested with both legal and equitable powers, using either or both as the circumstances of the particular case require. The rules of equity are as binding as the rules of common law. Hence he enforces contracts by money judgments in some situations and by specific performance in others. He grants damages for past torts and injunctions against future torts. He enforces trusts and mortgages as well as ordinary contracts.

The second step was a procedural change. Had the reform stopped at the jurisdictional merger, the single resulting court would have had to administer the rules of common law according to common law procedure and the rules of equity according to equity procedure.[8] What was done, therefore, was to institute a single form of civil action in place of the multifarious forms of action previously existing. The

223

New York provision of 1848, prototype of them all, was as follows:

> The distinction between actions at law and suits at equity, and the forms of all such actions and suits heretofore existing, are abolished; and, there shall be in this state, hereafter, but one form of action, for the enforcement and protection of private rights and the redress of private wrongs, which shall be denominated a civil action.[9]

A new procedure had to be created which could be used for any type of lawsuit, whether formerly triable at common law or in equity. The old models of procedure had to be discarded, but not in their entirety. The best features of each could be and were retained, but with modifications and improvements.[10]

The heart of the reform was in pleading. The new rules required the complaint to contain "a plain and concise statement of the facts constituting a cause of action, without unnecessary repetition."[11] Instead of the fictions and conclusions of common law pleadings or the verbosity of equity pleadings, the plaintiff was to state in his complaint what happened between him and the defendant in plain, simple language.[12] The defendant, instead of hiding behind an ambiguous plea of general issue at common law or stating his defense in evidential detail as in equity, was required to respond with straightforward denials and admissions, or if he relied on what we today call affirmative defenses, he had to plead the new facts in plain language.[13] On the whole, greater borrowings were made from equity procedure than from common law procedure, partly because the former was never cursed with the separate forms of action, partly because equity allowed freer joinder of claims and parties in its effort to avoid a multiplicity of actions, and partly because it insisted upon more ample pretrial disclosure through the rudiments of what we now call discovery.

In some states, the jurisdictional merger and the procedural reform took place simultaneously, or almost so.[14] In others, a considerable interval elapsed between them.[15] In the Federal court system, where the merger of legal and equitable jurisdiction had been accepted from the very beginning (1789), the institution of a single form of action was delayed for 150 years—until the promulgation of the Federal Rules of Civil Procedure in 1938.[16]

## The Federal Pattern

Until 1938, law and equity had not been fully merged in the federal courts. Equity cases were governed by a uniform set of federal rules, but procedure in common law cases was required to conform to the procedure of the state in which the federal court trying the case was sitting.[17] In 1934, Congress, recognizing the urgent need for federal procedural reform, abandoned the idea embodied in the New York Code of 1848 that procedure ought to be regulated by legislative enactment, and reverted—at least partially—to the idea that it should be regulated by the courts themselves. It vested in the Supreme Court of the United States the power to promulgate rules of procedure for the federal district courts but was careful to reserve a veto power for itself and to provide that the Supreme Court's rules should not "abridge, enlarge, or modify the substantive rights of any litigant" and further that the "right of trial by jury as at common law and as declared by the Seventh Amendment to the Constitution shall be preserved to the parties inviolate."[18] The Supreme Court appointed an Advisory Committee consisting of judges, practicing lawyers, and law professors to draft an appropriate set of the uniform rules covering both equity and common law actions.[19] The Committee worked diligently for about three years, choosing the best procedural ideas it could find in the various states, consulting broadly with the bench and bar of the United States and finally producing what has become a model set of rules.

The Supreme Court adopted the rules recommended by the Advisory Committee,[20] which became effective after they had been submitted to Congress. Since 1938, the rules have been amended several times following basically the same method of operation as was used in their original drafting and promulgation. At the present time, there is an Advisory Committee on civil rules charged with responsibility for carrying on a continuous study of the rules in operation and proposing needed amendments and additions. This specialized committee functions under the aegis of a general committee on rules of practice and procedure. The Supreme Court now has broader rule-making power than was originally delegated to it, under which it has promulgated rules of criminal procedure, appellate procedure, bankruptcy procedure, evidence, etc. The general committee in turn operates under the supervision of the Judicial Conference of the United States, a body of federal judges drawn from all eleven circuits. The Judicial Conference makes final recommendations to the Supreme Court. The ultimate power to promulgate rules, subject only to the reserved power of Congress to prevent or postpone their taking effect, resides in the Supreme Court.[21]

The Federal Rules have a significance extending beyond the fact that they govern procedure in the Federal Courts. They have been widely copied as models for state court procedure, having been adopted in whole or in part by more than half the states.[22] Almost inevitably today when state procedural reform is contemplated, the starting point is to compare existing state procedure with the federal rules. Moreover, there is a strong tendency to copy not only the substance of the Federal Rules, but also the method by which they were originally promulgated and subsequently amended.[23] In other words, the current pattern is to vest procedural rule-making power in the courts themselves with the hope of securing expertness in draftsmanship, a broad consensus of the legal profession, continuing attention to the way rules work in practice, and flexibility to meet changing needs in the light of experience. Should the legal profession shirk its responsibility, become mired in technicalities and forget that courts exist not for lawyers or judges, but for litigants, the general public could again inaugurate radical reform through legislative action in the tradition of the New York Code of 1848.

The main improvements made by the Federal Rules over the New York Code of 1848 (apart from the manner in which they came into being), may be summarized as follows:

1. Pleading was further simplified. The command of the New York Code to plead "facts" had proved troublesome in operation.[24] Lawyers had wrangled endlessly over such questions as whether the averment that a promise was made "for a valuable consideration" was a proper allegation of fact or an improper conclusion of law and whether an averment that an act was done "negligently" was or was not a sufficient pleading. The federal rules virtually put an end to such futile, metaphysical speculations by substituting for the "fact-cause of action" formula a requirement that a complaint should contain "a short and plain statement of the claim showing that the pleader is entitled to relief."[25] The new formula was backed up by officially authorized forms of pleading for recurring fact situations, which forms were stated also to be illustrative for other situations of the simplicity and brevity of statement which rules contemplate.[26] Similar improvements were made with respect to defensive pleading, general denials being substantially outlawed in favor of specific denials fairly meeting "the substance of the averments denied"[27] in good faith.

Difficulties which had been encountered in allocating the burdens of pleading between plaintiff and defendant were largely solved by a specific enumeration of the matters that had to be pleaded as affirmative defenses in the answer, thus by implication relieving the plaintiff of the necessity of dealing with those matters in complaint.[28]

Amendments to pleadings were freely authorized so that cases could be decided on their merits rather than on the basis of time consuming and justice defeating technicalities.[29] More generally, the rules stated that they should be construed "to secure the just, speedy, and inexpensive determination of every action."[30]

2. Pleading was not only simplified by the federal rules. It was also de-emphasized in favor of what was believed to be an improved method of enabling the parties to prepare for trial—namely, discovery.[31] An extensive array of discovery tools was created, with minimal restrictions on their use and minimal judicial supervision.[32]

3. Procedures for handling complicated litigation were consolidated and liberalized, allowing almost unlimited joinder of claims and parties.[33] The idea of avoiding a multiplicity of actions when one could accomplish all that needed to be done was brought closer to realization.[34]

4. Miscellaneous procedural devices such as motions for summary judgment,[35] motions addressed to the face of the pleadings,[36] and the pre-trial conference were improved and made broadly available.[37]

Not all states have followed the lead of the federal rules, and there are some states that have not even fully adopted the ideas of the New York Code of 1848.[38] It is fair to say, however, that there is no state where the influence of these two great landmarks of procedural reform has not been felt.[39] The consequences of procedural mistakes are not as drastic as formerly; equitable defenses can be interposed in actions at law; cases can be transferred from one court to another, rather than dismissed.

Lawsuits today are determined on the basis of the whole law rather than the law of trespass or the law of assumpsit or the law of specific performance. Procedure is distinguished from substantive law and put in its proper place, as merely a means for finding facts and applying substantive law to them in order to determine whether any judicial remedy should be granted. If the plaintiff pleads and proves facts which entitle him to *any* remedy, he will get it, even though he may have asked for a different one, to which he was not entitled.[40] If the facts are such as to relieve the defendant from liability under any rule of law, whether developed at common law or in equity, he will succeed.[41]

The reforms, where adopted, were not achieved without effort. Resistance and inertia had to be overcome, and habits of thought changed slowly. It has taken a long time for bench and bar to appreciate the scope of the changes wrought, and even today in some jurisdictions which have embraced the reforms there are throwbacks to ancient technicalities.

## Vestiges of History

Despite the merger of the law and equity courts and the abolition of the forms of action, two important remnants of the old system persist. It is mainly because of them that our brief excursion into history has been necessary.

The first relates to the mode of trial. Trial by jury is available only in those cases which formerly were triable at common law. In cases formerly triable in equity, the judge alone decides the issues of fact as well as of law.[42] In a particular case, it is perfectly possible that he will be deciding exactly the same kind of issues as would be submitted to a jury in another type of case. In other words, there is no rational or purely logical explanation of the right to trial by jury. The only explanation is historical.[43]

Why is trial by jury available today in an auto accident case, or an action for assault and battery, or false imprisonment, or slander or libel? Only because those actions grew out of trespass and case at common law. Why is that mode of trial not available if the plaintiff is asking for an injunction? Only because injunctive relief had to be sought in equity. Why should there be a jury trial if the plaintiff is asking damages for the defendant's breach of a contract to sell real estate, but not if he is demanding specific performance of that contract? Again only because of history: specific performance was a remedy available only in equity, whereas damages could be had in an action of assumpsit at common law. Why are juries not used in probate courts? Why not in actions to foreclose mortgages on real estate? Why not in suits by beneficiaries of trusts to impose liability on trustees? Why not in partnership accountings? Why not in suits to reform or rescind contracts? Always the answer is the same: history.

The distinction between actions at law and suits in equity for purposes of jury trial is a firm one, not likely to be uprooted within the foreseeable future.[44] It is embodied in the state and federal constitutions. The federal provision (the Seventh Amendment), which is typical, reads: "In suits at common law, where the value in controversy shall exceed twenty dollars, the right of trial by jury shall be preserved . . ." In other words, the right is preserved in those cases where it formerly existed, but not extended to all cases.[45]

If a case today involves both types of issues, the legal issues of fact may be submitted to a jury and the equitable issues of fact determined by the judge alone (although in practice it sometimes happens that a judge submits all issues to the jury, and treats the verdict as advisory only with respect to the equitable issues). Thus, if a man sues to have a contract reformed and to recover a money judgment on it as reformed, the factual issues involved in determining whether reformation is justified will be decided by the judge; the other issues, including the amount of damages, will be submitted to a jury. Many modern cases involve both types of issues. The plaintiff is allowed to join legal and equitable causes of action in a single complaint, and the defendant is allowed to interpose all the defenses and counterclaims he has, whether legal or equitable or both.[46]

In recent years, the Supreme Court of the United States has somewhat blurred the distinction between law and equity in its interpretation of the Seventh Amendment's guarantee of the right to trial by jury. Instead of patiently trying to discover how the issues in a modern law suit would have been handled prior to the merger of law and equity, it has considered issues in isolation rather than in context, and decreed that if a particular issue could under any circumstances have been tried in a common law court it must be tried by jury today. For example, in *Roth v. Bernhard*[47] which was a derivative stockholders' action, the court held that the judge alone should try the question of whether the stockholder could sue in behalf of the corporation but that the jury should try the claim against directors and third parties for mismanaging corporate funds. Prior to the merger of law and equity, equity would have tried the entire case on the theory that once having assumed jurisdiction it would go on to give complete relief.[48]

The Supreme Court has also held that if an issue of fact is common to and determinative of both a legal and an equitable claim or defense, it must be tried by jury.[49] The earlier view had been that a judge had discretion whether to try the equitable claim or the legal claim first.[50] The Supreme Court, however, held that one party's right to trial by jury, being guaranteed by the Constitution, must prevail over the other party's right, not guaranteed by the Constitution, to have the issue tried by the judge alone. Prior determination of the issue by the judge alone might otherwise control the result by way of res judicata or collateral estoppel.

The Supreme Court's approach is not binding on state courts in interpreting their own state constitutional guarantees of trial by jury because the Seventh Amendment is binding only on the federal courts. It has not been extended to the state courts.[51] State courts remain free to follow the older practice of determining the right to trial by jury on the basis of how the various issues—viewed in context, not isolation—would have been handled prior to the merger of law and equity.

The other exception to the uniform treatment of cases formerly triable at common law or in equity lies in the matter of remedies and their enforcement. Equitable remedies are available today only for the same reasons which Chancery insisted upon when it was a separate court. If a plaintiff wants an injunction or some other equitable remedy, he must still plead and prove facts which show that his "legal" remedy is inadequate.[52] Similarly, legal remedies are available today only for the same reasons which justified them at common law. Ejectment in an assault and battery case would be as inappropriate and unthinkable today as in 1776. Remedies are a part of substantive law, and that was not changed by the developments we have been considering. As to enforcement, equitable remedies are enforced today in substantially the same way as formerly—by personal constraint on the defendant—whereas legal remedies are also enforced as before—by the sheriff.[53] But again, as pointed out in a previous chapter, the methods of enforcing the two kinds of judgments have tended to coalesce.

## Continuing Difficulties

Great as has been the change effected by the merger of the law and equity courts and the abolition of the forms of action, the job of simplifying jurisdiction and procedure is not finished. The jurisdictional line between law and equity is gone in most states, but in some of them other jurisdictional lines, equally arbitrary, have been created. A multitude of special courts and administrative agencies have been established to do special jobs, each with limited jurisdiction and special procedure.[54]

In some states—for example, California—there are courts of truly general jurisdiction, possessing both legal and equitable powers and empowered to handle all types of cases—civil, criminal, probate, matrimonial, juvenile, etc.[55] These approach the ideal. In other states, jurisdiction is fragmented among many courts, one handling serious criminal cases, another minor criminal cases, another large civil cases, another small civil cases, another probate cases, and so forth. Not infrequently special statutory courts for particular cities or counties are in existence, no two of which may be alike, even though going under the same name.[56] Jurisdiction and procedure may vary enormously from one to another.

Supplementing the mass of courts is a network of administrative agencies, many of which are performing judicial functions in a limited field.[57] Industrial commissions, for example, deal with industrial accidents—formerly within the province of ordinary courts.[58] Each administrative agency, like each court, is likely to follow a procedure peculiar to itself.

Superimposed upon the judicial systems of the states is a federal judicial system, again with difficult jurisdictional lines.[59] And the federal court system is supplemented by a very extensive federal administrative system.

Though modern jurisdictional lines are different from the one which formerly separated law and equity, they are not necessarily more defensible. A common distinction today allocates cases between different courts upon the basis of the amount in controversy[60]—as if a poor person with a small case should have a different brand of justice than a rich person with a big case, or as if the legal problems involved were essentially different. Whatever the basis, the fact that such jurisdictional lines are being drawn is itself disturbing. The consequences of overstepping or mistaking them are scarcely less serious than were the consequences in 1776 of going into a common law court with an equity case, or vice versa.[61]

In addition to jurisdictional lines drawn according to subject matter, there are jurisdictional lines based upon geographical boundaries. The power of a court normally runs only to the borders of the state in which it is sitting.[62] This is true even for the federal courts.[63] The result is that a prospective plaintiff must worry not only about whether the court he chooses will have power to handle the type of action brought, but also whether it will have power to subject the defendant to its commands.

Contemplating the variety of tribunals functioning in this country, one cannot help wondering whether the jurisdictional and procedural difficulties of today are less troublesome than those which existed before the merger of the law and equity courts and the abolition of the forms of action. Have we really improved the administration of justice, or merely changed it? Is the path of the citizen seeking to vindicate his legal rights any better illuminated or less rocky than it was two centuries ago?

# Part IV

# LITIGATION IN CONTEXT

## Chapter 14

### COURTS IN PERSPECTIVE

The preceding chapters of this book, tracing the successive stages of litigation, may have given the reader a lopsided impression of the law, as if it revolved mainly around bringing, trying and deciding lawsuits. That impression is likely to have been further distorted by exposure to the case method of instruction used in most law schools. Under that method, attention is devoted primarily to cases that have been decided by appellate courts.

It is the purpose of this chapter to try to correct such distortions by putting litigation into clearer perspective.

How typical of the whole law are the appellate opinions found in casebooks, particularly those decided in the Supreme Court of the United States, which are the ones most prized for inclusion in casebooks? How typical is the process by which these opinions came into being? Not typical at all. Almost by definition, the situations and events recorded in them are unusual. If not, they would never have given rise to lawsuits, and if not very unusual they would never have reached the appellate courts, certainly not the Supreme Court of the United States.

In every state, even the smallest, people enter into and terminate millions upon millions of transactions (sales, loans, property transfers, etc.) and relationships (marriage, employment, tenancy, etc.) in the course of a year. How many of them result in disputes? Not very many. How many of the disputes ripen into lawsuits? Still fewer. How many of the lawsuits go to trial? Fewer still. How many of the cases tried are appealed? Very few indeed.

Most citizens have never been involved in a lawsuit and hope never to be.[1] They try to avoid legal controversy. Many would rather submit to an unjust demand or give up a just claim (provided the amounts involved are not too staggering) than incur the trouble and expense of getting involved in litigation or even consulting a lawyer. They would rather forego their rights and suffer in silence than go to court. If involved in a legal controversy that cannot be ignored or avoided, they seek and often find alternative means of disposing of it.

## Settlement

Settlement is always a possibility, with or without the help of lawyers. Many thousands of claims are made annually against insurance companies for personal injuries and property damage, for medical expenses, for losses by theft or fire, etc. The overwhelming bulk of them are settled without filing lawsuits. Additional thousands of disputes arise annually between merchants and their customers, between landlords and tenants, between husbands and wives, indeed between people in general, but again very few of them ever reach court.[2] Each side gives a little, and a compromise is reached.

## Arbitration

If settlement cannot be reached, another possibility is arbitration.[3] This is a method of resolving disputes without judges or juries. Traditionally it is a voluntary proceeding to which both sides must agree. They may do so after a dispute has arisen or may have done so in advance in anticipation of disputes arising in the future. An individual who stands impartial between the parties is agreed upon as arbitrator. Although he is not a judicial officer, he performs basically the same functions, generally with greater speed and less formality. He fixes a time and place for hearing the parties and their witnesses. The hearing is held without advance pleadings or motions and without the necessity of complying with the formal rules of evidence.

When the arbitrator notifies the parties of his decision, it is final and non-appealable if the arbitration was properly conducted. Most labor-management disputes today are resolved by arbitration, and it is becoming increasingly common for building contracts and commercial contracts of all sorts to provide that disputes arising under them will be submitted to arbitration.[4] Arbitration is even being used to resolve "human relations" disputes, as where groups of citizens are vying with each other as to where a playground should be located or how a school should be run.[5] Surprisingly, a few states have made arbitration compulsory, not voluntary, for court-commenced auto accident cases which the courts are too busy to handle in the usual way.[6] A party dissatisfied with an arbitrator's decision in such a case has a right to a retrial in court, but this right is seldom exercised because of the reluctance of most citizens to become involved in litigation.[7]

## Administrative Proceedings

Some disputes cannot be brought to court, at least initially. They go instead to a variety of administrative agencies, which are charged with basic responsibility for adjusting many of the legal rights, duties and relationships that individuals and corporations have in relation to federal, state and local governments and in relation to each other.[8] The vast majority of factual and legal questions relating to federal taxes are finally resolved within the Internal Revenue Service. Similarly, social security questions are for the most part finally resolved within the Social Security Administration; welfare questions within the Department of Health, Education and Welfare; labor relations questions within the National Labor Relations Board; and so on.[9] These federal administrative agencies have state and local counterparts, sometimes dealing in the first instance with questions that ultimately may have to be dealt with in Washington (for example, local welfare offices), sometimes dealing in a more final way with state and local matters not subject to federal control (for example, state public utility commissions and municipal zoning boards).[10] Many administrative agencies, state, local

237

and federal, have elaborate procedures for resolving these questions—hearings before trial examiners (roughly equivalent to trial judges) followed by review in a hierarchy of review boards (roughly equivalent to appellate courts).[11] Some of the questions with which they deal are exclusively concerned with an individual's relationship to some unit of government—his entitlement to welfare benefits, for example, or the amount of taxes owing from him. Others concern also his relationship to other individuals or groups. When the Federal Communications Commission grants a television or radio broadcasting license, for example, it is determining not only the rights of the applicant for that license *vis a vis* the government, but also the rights of competitors who oppose the application and also possibly those of public interest groups seeking certain types of programming. Finally, some questions resolved by administrative agencies do not directly concern the government at all, but primarily, if not solely, the rights of individuals and groups in relation to each other. For example, when the National Labor Relations Board certifies a labor union as the appropriate bargaining agent for the employees of a certain corporation, it is determining the rights and duties of the employer, the employees, the union and possibly rival unions. Another example is found in the activities of workmen's compensation boards, which have been established in almost all states to take over what previously was a major part of the work of traditional courts in dealing with industrial injuries.[12] When an award of compensation is made to a person injured while on his job and within the scope of his employment, it represents a determination of his rights and the duties of his employer and the employer's insurance carrier.[13]

Some of the controversies decided by administrative agencies involve many millions of dollars, others trifling amounts. In this respect, administrative agencies do not differ greatly from traditional courts, which also handle small as well as large cases. No generalization is possible that courts handle more important controversies than administrative agencies, or vice versa.

Ultimately some of the questions decided by administrative agencies find their way into the courts, for no way has yet been devised to completely insulate administrative decisions from judicial review.[14] When courts intervene, they do so only to keep the agencies within their proper jurisdictional boundaries and to insure that the procedures they follow are consistent with due process of law. Courts are not empowered to substitute their own judgments for those of administrative agencies acting properly within their jurisdiction. Intervention is by way of review only, much in the manner of appellate courts reviewing the judgments of trial courts.[15] Judicial review of administrative action is relatively uncommon, with only a handful of the questions decided by administrative agencies ever reaching the courts.[16] Most of the persons involved are not disposed to carry their disputes beyond the agencies.

## Uncontested Court Proceedings

Of the cases that go to court initially, many are there not because there is any dispute to be resolved, but because the stamp of judicial approval is necessary to accomplish what all interested parties want. There are some proceedings over which the courts have been granted monopoly control because of the real or presumed public interest in what would otherwise be regarded as private matters.

Divorce is an example. A husband and wife cannot privately dissolve their marriage or submit the matter to arbitration; and there is no administrative agency to which they can resort. Hence they must go to court regardless of whether there is any controversy as to the wisdom of dissolving their marriage, the financial arrangements between them or the custody of their children.[17] If there are areas of dispute, of course the court will resolve them; but today, with "no-fault" divorces becoming increasingly common, the court seldom has any function beyond seeing that both parties are aware of what they are doing.[18]

Another type of court proceeding that seldom involves controversy concerns the administration of estates.[19] When a person dies, someone must collect his assets, pay his debts,

239

and distribute the remainder of his property to those entitled to inherit. If he left a will, this work is done by the "executor" named in it under the supervision of the appropriate court; if not, it is done by an "administrator" appointed by the court, who also operates under its general supervision and in accordance with the laws of "intestacy" (governing the distribution of property of a person who dies without a will). When nobody questions the way the estate is being handled, the role of the court is mainly to make sure that all interested parties have adequate notice of what is going on and an opportunity to object. If a party objects, full-scale and even bitter controversy may develop, to be resolved by the court. Generally speaking, however, the administration of estates proceeds smoothly without contest.[20]

Among other cases which must be processed in court but which seldom develop into contests are those dealing with adoptions, guardianships and the administration of estates of those incapable of managing their own affairs—minors and incompetents.

Many cases are brought to court which might have been, but were not, privately settled or submitted to arbitration. Prominent among these are actions to collect routine bills. Filing a suit serves as a catalyst to induce the overwhelming majority of debtors to pay their just debts, possibly on installment plans worked out between them and their creditors after the commencement of suit.[21] Many other types of claims, notably those seeking damages for personal injuries, are filed not with the expectation of trial, but rather in the hope of settlement. The hope turns out to be justified in the great majority of cases, leaving relatively few to be fully litigated.[22]

## Law Practice

The generally non-litigious nature of law is underscored and confirmed by the prevailing character of law practice. Most law offices practice "preventive law,"[23] with the object of avoiding litigation as far as possible. Many lawyers who rarely if ever go to court serve their clients well. Their time is devoted to drafting contracts, leases and wills, forming partnerships and corporations, arranging mortgages, advising on taxes, administering estates and the like. They attempt to anticipate difficulties and prevent disputes from arising. When disputes do arise, they attempt to settle them without litigation. It is true, of course, that in advising their clients, they are acutely conscious of the possibility of full-scale lawsuits and of how they might turn out, but they do not relish the prospect of courtroom battle and they try hard, and usually successfully, to avoid it.

## Why the Courts Keep Busy

In view of what has been said thus far in this chapter, one might assume that courts have little to do. The opposite is the truth. Many courts, particularly those in metropolitan areas, are not keeping up with their work. Huge backlogs of cases await trial.[24] It is not uncommon for litigants to wait three or four years before their cases can be heard.[25]

The chores imposed on judges in handling uncontested matters of the type already discussed take a great deal of time. Much more time is consumed in cases that are hard fought. The procedural steps that must be taken to dispose of a fully contested case are numerous and complicated as Parts I and II of this book demonstrate. A single case may require dozens, even hundreds, of judicial rulings, most of which are subject to review on appeal, and may drag on for years.

Nevertheless, ordinary civil work does not fully account for the delay and congestion that characterize our judicial system today. Still to be considered are criminal cases and civil cases of an extraordinary nature.

## Criminal Cases

Although criminal cases are generally beyond the purview of this book, their impact on the handling of civil cases cannot be ignored. Few courts handle civil cases exclusively. The typical pattern both at the trial and appellate levels is for a single court to be vested with jurisdiction over criminal as well as civil cases.[26]

Criminal cases are like divorce cases in the sense that only courts can dispose of them. They cannot be privately settled,[27] arbitrated or brought before an administrative agency. They compete with civil cases for the time and attention of the judges and they are entitled to priority. A person accused of crime is constitutionally guaranteed the right to a speedy trial.[28] At one time, the constitutional guarantee was not taken very seriously, with the result that men and women sometimes languished in jail for unconscionable periods of time before their cases were heard. In recent years, however, laws have been passed and court rules promulgated mandating the release of accused persons unless they are brought to trial within a specified number of days.[29] The result in some courts has been that the processing of civil cases has been suspended for weeks or months at a time while judges devote all their time to criminal cases.[30]

The criminal law is the dumping ground for many unsolved social problems—gambling, prostitution, pornography, alcoholism, homosexuality, vagrancy, drug abuse and the like. Unlike crimes which result in injury or death to clearly identified victims, these so-called "victimless crimes" result in injury mainly, if not exclusively, to the individuals who commit them. Society nevertheless is offended by their conduct and tries to put a stop to it by declaring it criminal. The effort is usually futile because criminal sanctions are unequal to solving the underlying problems. Until better solutions are found, however, the courts are forced to spend an inordinate amount of time dealing with the prosecutions that result. Offenders are brought to court, usually given a small fine or short jail sentence, and soon released back into society to continue their way of life.[31]

Criminal prosecutions are also relied upon to enforce a wide variety of other social regulations that do not fit the pattern of those defining classic crimes like murder, robbery and burglary. Criminal penalties are scattered throughout the statute books, dealing with such diverse subjects as parking and traffic, billboard advertising, the pollution of air and water, sanitary food processing and practices that restrain competition and foster monopolies.

Most criminal cases, like most civil cases, are uncontested. They result in pleas of guilty, many entered after "plea bargaining." This term describes the process by which the prosecuting attorney and the defense attorney agree to a plea of guilty to a lesser charge than the one originally filed. The prosecutor wants to avoid the uncertainty of a jury verdict while at the same time conserving his resources to deal with the backlog of other cases for which he is responsible; and the accused counts on receiving a less severe sentence than would be imposed if he were found guilty of the original charge after a trial. A guilty plea saves judicial time, but not as much as might be expected. The defendant must still be informed in open court of the charges against him, advised of his rights, and ultimately sentenced.[32]

When a plea of not guilty is entered, a trial becomes necessary, usually before a jury. Some criminal trials take only a few minutes, an hour or a day, but others, particularly those that have political overtones or that have been widely publicized, are likely to go on for weeks or months.[33] The selection of a jury alone may drag on for weeks.[34]

Two factors combine to make criminal proceedings lengthy and complicated. One is the fact that indigent persons accused of serious crime are furnished counsel free of charge.[35] Most criminal defendants are indigent and they freely avail themselves of the services of lawyers paid out of public funds. These lawyers, commonly called "public defenders" must and do represent their clients zealously. This often involves taking advantage of what laymen call "technicalities." No matter how guilty a man may be, no matter how vicious or depraved, he is entitled to vigorous legal representation. Defending him is approved and applauded, not condemned, in the ethical rules governing lawyers.[36]

The second factor making criminal proceedings lengthy and complicated is the nature of the rules by which they must be conducted. A criminal case today is less likely to be a simple and straightforward inquiry into guilt or innocence than a series of tangential inquiries into whether the constitutional rights of the accused were protected and whether the police acted properly in apprehending, arresting and detaining him and in collecting evidence against him. If the accused confessed, was he warned of his rights beforehand and given or offered the assistance of counsel? When his home was searched for fruits of the crime, had a search warrant been duly issued? Such questions must be dealt with whenever they are raised, and they consume much judicial time not only at trial but also on appeal.[37] Review of criminal cases is very common, partly because the accused has nothing to lose by appeal (it is subsidized if he is indigent) and partly because an additional procedure to obtain review is available. Commonly called a habeas corpus proceeding or a post-conviction remedy, it enables the defendant to attack his conviction on the ground that his constitutional rights were violated in the earlier proceeding.[38] Many of the questions raised in such collateral proceedings or an appeal are frivolous,[39] but since they all must be carefully considered, they consume a large share of judicial time.

## Extraordinary Civil Cases

In view of the reluctance of most persons to go or be dragged into court, it seems paradoxical that some types of civil litigation are burgeoning. They grow out of social problems that formerly would have been dealt with—if officially dealt with at all—by legislative bodies.[40] Now courts are becoming involved in such problems as racial and sexual discrimination,[41] school busing,[42] school financing,[43] abortion,[44] birth control,[45] equal voting rights,[46] consumer protection[47] and ecology.[48] Mainly because they possess the power to invalidate legislation on constitutional grounds and to exercise some measure of control over the executive branch of the government, courts are increasingly being regarded as agencies capable of effectuating basic social change. They are often called upon to act when legislators cannot or will not respond.[49]

Cases presenting such problems for adjudication do not fit easily into traditional litigation molds. Some are class actions or multiparty cases,[50] but even if not, they are seldom two-sided private disputes about past events, governed by recog-

244

nized legal rules. Instead they tend to be many-sided, continuing controversies, in which many competing interests have to be reconciled and for which existing legal principles and rules furnish little or no guidance.[51] The job of solving such problems is vastly different from the job of deciding two-sided disputes, and is more truly legislative in nature than judicial. Yet the courts called upon to perform it do not have the facilities for collecting relevant information. They have no staffs to investigate the "legislative facts" and no committees to hold public hearings.[52] Understandably, therefore, such cases are unusually difficult and they place a heavy drain on the main resource that courts have—the energy of their judges.

A decision of the Supreme Court of the United States will suffice to illustrate the kind of controversies now under consideration and their impact on the judicial system. In *Brown v. Board of Education*[53] the Supreme Court outlawed racial segregation in public schools. In order for its decree to become effective, the public schools had to be integrated under judicial supervision. Old school systems had to be dismantled and new ones created, boundaries of school districts had to be redrawn, pupils, teachers and administrators had to be transferred from school to school, busing had to be arranged and so forth, amid continuing controversy within each affected community as to how and when the various steps needed to accomplish integration should be taken. Lower federal courts and state courts, all bound by the Supreme Court decision, were plunged headlong into these problems, and they have continued deeply immersed in them for over twenty years—ever since the decision was announced in 1954.[54]

## Chapter 15

## PERSONNEL AND THE ADMINISTRATION
## OF JUSTICE

Earlier chapters of this book have dealt with the machinery of justice (court structure, state and federal, trial and appellate), the rules for starting, running and stopping it (procedure), the raw materials fed into it (cases and controversies of various kinds), and the products that emerge from it (decisions and opinions). Not yet considered adequately are the people who operate the machinery, upon whom the quality of justice ultimately depends. They are the subject of this concluding chapter.

Until the early part of this century, hardly any systematic study was devoted to the persons in and around the courts or to the administration of justice in its broader aspects. Judges, lawyers and law professors were so preoccupied with substantive and procedural rules that they paid little attention to the matrix in which the law operated. They became aware from time to time that a particular judge might be corrupt or incompetent, or that a certain court was unduly slow in disposing of its cases, or that some lawyers and judges were overworked while others had little or nothing to do, but they tended to regard such problems as isolated, aberrational and relatively unimportant. It did not occur to them that the overall functioning of the judicial system and the people in it required sustained and thoughtful attention. Political scientists also avoided the subject. Believing that the courts were the special preserve of the legal profession, they concentrated their concern on the executive and legislative branches of government and neglected the judicial branch. This left judicial administration to politician-legislators. Without the benefit of disinterested study or empirical data and without being fully conscious of the importance of the concerns with which they were dealing, they created new judgeships, prescribed how judges were to be selected, appropriated money for the judicial branch of government, etc.

Today the situation is changed, largely because of the stimulus provided by Roscoe Pound and Arthur T. Vanderbilt. In 1906, Pound (then a young, obscure lawyer from Nebraska, later destined to become the famous Dean of the Harvard Law School) delivered a speech to the American Bar Association entitled, "The Causes of Popular Dissatisfaction with the Administration of Justice."[1] The title alone was shocking to his generally complacent audience, and his analysis of judicial waste, inefficiency and delay even more so. Nevertheless, his ideas kindled interest in the minds of the few of his listeners, who over the next quarter century became leading members of the Bar.[2] In 1937 when Arthur T. Vanderbilt became President of the American Bar Association, he made it his main goal and one of the major goals of the Association to improve the administration of justice. In that year, the Association came out publicly against the popular election of judges[3] and undertook to formulate minimum standards of judicial administration, promulgated the following year.[4] Vanderbilt (who later reorganized the judicial system of New Jersey and became its Chief Justice) summed up his long-standing determination to improve judicial administration and the frustrations he encountered in that endeavor in an often quoted remark: "Judicial reform is no sport for the short winded."[5] The impetus provided by Pound and Vanderbilt has continued. In 1962 the American Bar Association promulgated a model judicial article for state constitutions.[6] Beginning in 1964 it promulgated standards of criminal justice,[7] and as of 1977 it is working on the standards of juvenile justice[8] as well as reformulating standards of judicial administration.[9] In addition to the American Bar Association, many other organizations are now enlisted in the continuing struggle to improve the courts. Prominent among them are the National Center for State Courts,[10] the Federal Judicial Center,[11] the Institute of Judicial Administration,[12] and the American Judicature Society.[13] Others will be mentioned in the ensuing discussion.

Although the science (or is it an art?) of judicial administration deals not only with the personnel of the courts, but also with the institutional framework in which they operate and the procedures they follow, we shall concentrate here on personnel. The other subjects have been dealt with in earlier parts of this book.[14]

## Judges

*Qualifications for Office*

It is often taken for granted that every judge must be legally trained, but this is not universally true. In the rural areas of many states, justices of the peace are empowered to handle minor cases. They need not be and frequently are not lawyers. Too often they bring to their judicial work only the political skills and loyalties that brought them to office and little or no knowledge of the law. They ordinarily serve part-time, devoting the major share of their attention and energy to their primary means of earning a livelihood—for example, farming, selling real estate, running a filling station or barbering.[15]

In some states, justices of the peace, organized on a highly local basis, serving every town, village and hamlet, have been replaced by full-time, professionally trained judges serving larger geographical areas.[16] In others, reform movements to reach the same objective are underway, or, where it is not feasible to accomplish so substantial a change, to disqualify laymen from serving or at least to require them as a condition of retaining office to attend training programs designed to acquaint them with their powers and duties.[17]

Above the justice of the peace level, judges are required, sometimes by constitutional provision or statute, sometimes only by tradition, to be professionally trained and in some states to have served a specified length of time at the bar.[18] Beyond such requirements, it becomes almost impossible to define by law the qualities that are needed in a judge.[19] The only protection against unfit persons being elevated to the bench must be sought in the method by which judges are chosen.

*Selection*

There are four different ways of selecting judges in effect in various jurisdictions in the United States.

The least common method, used only in a few states, is legislative election of judges. A lawyer who has never been a legislator or a relative or close friend of a legislator is not likely to have much chance of becoming a judge. Apart from unduly restricting the field from which judges are drawn, this method tends to emphasize party politics over merit as the chief criterion of selection.[20]

The most common method of selecting judges, scarcely less political, is popular election. Persons seeking judicial office must run against rival candidates, sometimes on party tickets. They attend church suppers, extol their own virtues over radio and television and otherwise participate in the rituals of politics. Voters seldom have much interest in judicial contests or knowledge about the candidates, being content to leave the choice to the political leaders who nominate them.[21] The claimed strength of this method is that judges are more responsive to the popular will if elected rather than chosen in some other manner. This argument is easily ridiculed,[22] but there is something to it. Judges on appellate courts are constantly making choices among social and economic alternatives, and even at the trial level the philosophy and background of the judge may determine how he reacts to disputes between members of competing social groups— landlords against tenants, for example, or consumers against merchants. Perhaps this explains why citizens in many states have refused to give up the popular election of judges for allegedly better methods of choosing them.[23]

The third method of choosing judges, used in the federal system and in some state courts, is appointive. The Chief Executive—the President of the United States, the governor of a state or the mayor of a city, as the case may be—appoints judges subject to their being confirmed by the legislature. This concentrates responsibility for judicial selection and makes the process more visible than popular election, but it does not eliminate politics either from the initial appointment or from the confirmation.[24]

The fourth method is relatively new and growing in popularity. Called the "Missouri Plan" because Missouri was the first state in which it became operative, it attempts to retain the virtues and eliminate the deficiencies of both the elective and appointive methods. Its essence is that when a judicial vacancy occurs, several persons are nominated by a non-partisan or bipartisan commission; then their names are submitted to the governor or other appointing authority who must make his appointment from the list provided; then the individual appointed serves for a probationary period; and finally he stands for reelection on his record. He does not run against any other candidate. On the ballot the voters are called upon only to decide whether or not the judge should be retained in office.[25] Enthusiasts for the Missouri Plan claim that it eliminates politics and transforms the process of selecting judges into one based solely upon merit. The claim seems extravagant, for political considerations may be simply transferred from political clubhouses to bar associations. Nevertheless, the Missouri Plan is widely believed to be superior to other methods of judicial selection.[26] It eliminates undignified political campaigning and the embarrassments that sometimes prevent qualified lawyers from seeking judicial office; it preserves ultimate popular control; and it eliminates clearly unqualified candidates by making it impossible for them to be appointed by the chief executive or elected popularly.[27] The Missouri Plan need not be made applicable to all judicial offices[28] or formally established by law. In some places where the appointive system is in effect, executives having the power of appointment have voluntarily established nonpartisan judicial nominating commissions and thus relinquished some of their authority.[29] Another form of self-limitation upon the appointing authority found in the federal system and some states entails the submission of names of prospective judicial appointees to bar associations for their nonbinding recommendations.[30] Such developments, while they are voluntary and while they do not completely eliminate politics from the process of selecting judges, represent forward steps in judicial administration.

## Tenure, Compensation, Retirement, and Removal

Getting good judges does not depend solely upon the methods by which they are selected. It depends also upon the attractiveness of judicial office. One of the factors to be considered is tenure. In the federal courts and those of a few states, judges hold office for life during good behavior. In most states, however, their tenure is limited, requiring that they be reappointed or reelected periodically.[31] If they had not already become politicians in order to reach the bench, they may have to become politicians in order to remain, even to the point of currying favor by avoiding unpopular decisions.[32] The trend today is to prolong tenure in an effort to remove judges from politics, in some cases by adopting the tenure aspects of the Missouri Plan. The fact that under that plan a judge does not have to compete against other candidates for reelection or reappointment tends to prolong his tenure indefinitely. A sitting judge is seldom removed when there is no obvious alternative. The tenure aspect of the Missouri Plan is separable from its selection aspect, as has been demonstrated in Illinois. When a new judicial article for the state constitution was adopted, the elective system of selection was retained, but judges were required to run for reelection only on their records, not against rival candidates.[33]

Another factor affecting the attractiveness of judicial office is compensation. Although grumbling is heard from time to time from judges that their salaries are inadequate to attract highly qualified persons to office, judicial salaries are high compared to those of most government officials and have been increasing rapidly. Since World War II, the salaries of federal district judges have increased more than threefold, going from $15,000 in 1946 to $54,000 in 1977.[34] There are wide variations in the judicial salaries paid in the various states. Some are higher than federal salaries while others are considerably lower.[35]

As important as getting the right persons on the bench in the first place is getting rid of those whose powers have failed or who have demonstrated by their conduct that they are not fit to hold judicial office. Retirement plans, varying widely from state to state, go a long way toward taking care of the problems posed by overage judges or those suffering from physical or mental disabilities.[36] However, if those suffering from such disabilities are unwilling to recognize them and cooperate by accepting retirement, they must be forced into mandatory retirement after a fair investigation of their claimed incompetency, as is done in California.[37] Judges who turn out to be corrupt, habitually drunk, neglectful of their duties or grossly lacking in judicial temperament pose different problems. If they have short tenure, they can be eliminated by the simple expedient of refusing to reelect or reappoint them; but if they have long tenure, some other method of removal is necessary.

The traditional method of getting rid of unfit judges is impeachment, involving legislative accusation and trial. It is unsatisfactory for a number of reasons: first, the procedure is cumbersome, consuming an undue amount of time of legislators whose attention and energy should be directed elsewhere; second, the grounds for impeachment are either excessively narrow, reaching only specified misconduct, or excessively broad, putting the accused judge at the mercy of his judges; and third, the only sanction is the drastic one of removal with no possibility of any milder form of discipline such as suspension from office or reprimand.[38] Because of such defects, there is a trend to supplant or supplement impeachment by other techniques for the discipline of judges. The most promising development has taken place in California, where a commission was established to investigate charges of willful misconduct in office, persistent failure to perform judicial duties or habitual intemperance and to recommend the discipline of judges found guilty of such charges. The final decision on its recommendations is up to the Supreme Court of the state.[39] The California plan is being widely copied in other states.[40]

*Judicial Education*

In some nations law graduates at an early age choose between becoming judges or practicing lawyers, with those who become judges receiving special training for their jobs and regular promotions through the hierarchy of courts.[41] We have no such career judiciary in the United States. Here judges are ordinarily chosen from the members of the bar at a mature age—usually their forties or fifties—and they assume office without specialized training. For this reason, and because those who have been on the bench for a considerable period of time sometimes need help in orienting themselves to new developments, training programs for judges have become accepted and even popular within the last quarter century.[42] The pioneer program was the appellate judges seminar at New York University, inaugurated in 1956 by the Institute of Judicial Administration and still going strong. It runs for two weeks each summer and is attended by 20 to 25 appellate judges drawn from state supreme courts and United States courts of appeal. During their two week session, they study and discuss such subjects as opinion writing, appellate control of the judge-jury relationship, and new trends in the law. Their discussions, guided by experienced appellate judges who are assisted by a sprinkling of law professors, are conducted on a seminar basis with a free interchange of ideas around the table.[43] The success of these seminars led to the establishment of similar educational opportunities for other judges. The most prominent of these is administered by the National College of the State Judiciary, which offers an extensive program of courses, usually one month in duration, to state trial judges, especially those newly appointed or elected. There are also refresher programs for judges of greater seniority.[44] Scarcely any group of judges is neglected today. There are seminars for federal judges, juvenile court judges, traffic court judges, even justices of the peace. Some are on a local basis, some on a state, regional or national basis.[45]

*The Number of Judges*

A final factor affecting the quality of the judiciary is the number of judges. Unless there are enough of them to carry the caseload, they may be forced to do their work hastily, or their cases may be unduly delayed, or both. In attempting to deal with the chronic problem of delay, the tendency in recent years has been to emphasize judicial reform and increased efficiency and to be skeptical of the need for more judges.[46] Perhaps the emphasis on judicial reform has been overdone. Litigation has been increasing at an even faster pace than the population.[47] For reasons suggested in the preceding chapter, the problems facing the courts are multiplying. Whether the number of judges has expanded sufficiently to take care of new business after taking into account the increased efficiency that reasonably can be demanded is a question that must be approached with an open mind. If additional judges are really needed, refusing to provide them may bring on more drastic measures, ones which would radically alter the character of our legal system. Currently under discussion are proposals to eliminate trial by jury in civil cases.[48] Other proposals, long advocated and now going into effect in various states, call for the creation of no-fault insurance to deal with auto accident cases and no-fault divorce to deal with matrimonial troubles.[49] Such proposals may or may not be wise, but they ought to be considered on their merits, not solely in the narrow perspective of calendar congestion. If additional judges are genuinely needed but not provided, those in office may be forced, in a desperate effort to clear their calendars, to apply undue pressure for settlements in civil cases and for pleas of guilty in criminal cases.

## Parajudicial Personnel

Judges do not work alone. They are assisted by a variety of functionaries, some of whom furnish technical supporting services (court reporters, bailiffs, clerks, etc.) and others who perform work closely akin to that done by the judges themselves. We are concerned here with the latter group.

Law clerks are used in virtually all appellate courts and in a few trial courts. Most of them are young persons fresh out of law school with high academic records, who are chosen by and who serve individual judges rather than the court as a whole. They serve for a year or two and then pass on to other careers, being replaced by more recent graduates. Their duties are mainly to do legal research, but sometimes to prepare drafts of opinions, depending upon the wishes of the particular judges for whom they work.[50]

Central staff attorneys are beginning to be used in appellate courts to supplement the work done by law clerks. These are more mature lawyers who serve the court as a whole and who enjoy indefinite tenure. Typically they deal with routine cases, recommending the disposition to be made of them and drafting opinions to that end, subject to the approval of the judges acting collectively.[51] They can also be used to monitor and expedite the procedural steps necessary to perfect an appeal,[52] and to conduct pre-argument conferences with a view to settling cases on appeal, or, when that is not possible, streamlining the issues to be heard by the judges.[53]

At the trial court level are found persons who may fairly be described as assistant or second-class judges. They go by a variety of names in different jurisdictions, the most common being "referees," "masters," "commissioners" and "magistrates." Under the supervision (real or theoretical) of the regular judges and subject to the terms of the statutory and constitutional provisions governing their offices, they hold hearings, take testimony, make reports, write opinions and in general perform duties scarcely distinguishable from those performed by the judges themselves. Usually, however, because of a widespread belief that a wholesale delegation of judicial authority is dangerous, unwise and unwarranted, the ultimate decision-making power remains with the regular judges.[54] These subordinate, quasi-judicial officials are used on a regular basis in some courts to process a large volume of routine cases (juvenile delinquency, petty offenses, for example)[55] and sporadically in other courts to deal with cases that require unusually prolonged and complicated fact-finding.[56]

The individuals described thus far assist judges in their primary function of disposing of cases. Another group of individuals assists them in more generalized functions. They are called "court administrators" and their concern is with court management. The need for them was expressed by Arthur T. Vanderbilt when he was Chief Justice of New Jersey as follows:

> The Chief Justice and the other justices of the Supreme Court who are charged with responsibility for the proper administration of the courts are all busy people preoccupied with their extensive judicial duties. If they are to be able adequately to discharge their administrative responsibilities it is essential that they have assistance. That is where an administrative office of the courts comes in. Its function is to supply the Supreme Court and the Chief Justice with the information that they need to decide intelligently what administrative action is to be taken and then to assist in carrying their decisions into effect.[57]

Any court system, even the smallest, is a large enterprise which each year employs thousands of people, processes hundreds of thousands of cases, costs the taxpayers millions of dollars and produces revenue from filing fees, fines and penalties in an even greater amount. Business-like management is clearly needed to keep such an enterprise operating efficiently and economically. Statistics must be kept to ensure an orderly flow of cases and to see that judges, jurors, court reporters, etc. are available when and where needed; budgets must be prepared; liaison must be maintained with the legislative and executive branches of government and between the courts within the system; citizen complaints must be investigated; supporting personnel must be recruited and supervised; and physical facilities must be provided and maintained. Such are the tasks performed by court administrators.

The first system-wide administrative machinery was developed for the federal courts in 1939 in the form of the Administrative Office of the United States Courts.[58] It proved so successful that the pattern has been copied in many states.[59]

Important as centralized administration of a judicial system at the highest level is, it is not always enough to make courts operate efficiently. Administrative personnel and machinery at lower levels may be needed as well. In the federal system, at the urging of Chief Justice Warren Burger, the office of "Circuit Executive" was established in 1971 for each of the eleven federal circuits,[60] and the Institute for Court Management was created to train persons to fill these posts.[61] The posts were quickly filled, but the Institute continues. Its primary mission now is to train administrators for state courts.[62] In metropolitan areas like Los Angeles and New York, where the volume of litigation is so heavy that hundreds of judges are involved, local court administrators are needed. They are highly respected and highly paid, for their work rivals in difficulty and importance that of the judges themselves.[63]

## Jurors

The civil jury has virtually disappeared in England,[64] the nation from whom we derived the institution, but in the United States it still flourishes. It is one of the main avenues for citizen participation in the work of the courts, especially since lay justices of the peace are fast being replaced by professionally trained judges. Nevertheless, there are persistent suggestions that the jury ought to be eliminated in civil cases. Such suggestions are based in part upon the hotly debated claim that juries are deficient as fact-finding bodies,[65] and in part upon the proposition that they consume an undue amount of time and money.[66] There can be little doubt that jury trials take longer than court trials—in the view of some experienced judges, three times as long. Apart from the time of judges and lawyers, the time of many citizens is consumed as they await their turn at jury service while other cases are being settled. Critics of the civil jury point out that not only in England but also in Louisiana, where the civil jury is also virtually unknown, court calendars are reasonably up to date.[67]

While the complete abolition of civil juries seems unlikely within the foreseeable future, especially in view of the fact

258

that this would require amendments to the federal and state constitutions, changes are being made to reduce the time and expense occasioned by their use. Juries of six rather than 12 persons are becoming increasingly common, as are less-than-unanimous verdicts.[68] New ways of dealing with issues traditionally tried by juries are being devised—no-fault divorce, no-fault auto accident insurance and compulsory arbitration, for example.[69]

Efforts are also being made to expedite[70] and improve the method of selecting jurors. One goal is to secure more intelligent and better educated jurors.[71] Another, sometimes working at cross purposes with the first, is to secure jurors who are fairly representative of the whole community, with special emphasis on ethnic and other minority groups.[72]

### Lawyers

One of the recurring themes of this book is that the proper functioning of the courts depends not alone upon judges, jurors, and court administrators, but also upon the performance of the bar. If lawyers are capable, conscientious and responsible, the quality of justice is likely to be good; if not, it is likely to be poor. The adversary system is predicated upon lawyers presenting to the court the raw materials, both factual and legal, which will govern decision. Indeed a court has been likened to a three-legged stool: one leg is the judge, another the lawyer for the plaintiff (or prosecution), and the third the lawyer for the defense. It will topple if any one of the legs is missing or so weak that it collapses.[73]

In many respects, the quality of legal representation has improved in recent years. Lawyers today are better educated than ever before. Formerly an important avenue of admission to the bar was through studying law in the office of some practitioner and then hanging out a shingle.[74] Today the training of lawyers is entrusted almost exclusively to law schools and the apprenticeship method of training has virtually disappeared. Law schools have become formidable institutions of higher learning with high standards of admission and even higher standards for graduation.[75] Programs of

259

continuing legal education for lawyers already admitted to
the bar also have become a feature of the American scene.
They are so numerous and diverse as to defy description.
Some are for new lawyers to help them bridge the gap
between law school and practice, others for older lawyers
to keep them abreast of the growth of the law; some are for
general practitioners, others for specialists. The subjects
covered are as varied as the problems lawyers are called upon
to handle for their clients.[76]

Standards for admission to the bar have also risen. An
applicant must ordinarily pass a difficult written examination
and then be screened by a committee of lawyers as to his
general character and fitness for the profession before he
can practice. The examination is locally prepared, administered and graded, and the lawyers are local practitioners.
Despite the fact that the practice of law is becoming increasingly national in nature, with a lawyer from state A not
infrequently advising his clients not only with respect to
local law, but also the law of states B, C, and D,[77] a successful
applicant is not admitted to practice in the United States as a
whole, but only to practice in a particular state, and then
only in the state courts.[78] If he wishes to practice in the
federal courts of his home state, he must go through an
additional admission procedure. This tends to be a formality,
involving nothing more than submission of papers to prove
his admission to practice in the state courts.[79] If, however,
he wishes to practice in the courts of another state except
ad hoc for a single case,[80] admission is more than a formality;
unless he has practiced for a considerable period of time,
and sometimes even then, he must go through the same
motions that a person fresh out of law school must follow
and also satisfy stringent residence requirements.[81] This is
sometimes thought to be one of the consequences of having
a federal government with 51 judicial systems instead of
one, but perhaps better explanations may be found elsewhere.
Lawyers tend to be traditionalists, prizing the familiar past
over the unknown future, and some of them, enjoying lucra-
tive practices, are not anxious to invite competition from
afar. Whatever the reasons, the legal profession has not

moved as fast or as far as have the professions of medicine, accountancy and architecture in the direction of national standards for admission to practice.[82] Tentatively and very cautiously, the legal profession may be moving in that direction through the development and use of "multi-state" questions in local bar examinations.[83]

Despite improved legal education and higher standards for admission to the bar, judges frequently complain that they are not given the assistance they should receive from the lawyers who appear before them, claiming that a major cause of delay in the courts is that there are too few lawyers equipped to handle the cases.[84] For this reason, some courts are beginning to insist that lawyers must take certain courses in law school or after its completion before they are permitted to appear as courtroom advocates.[85]

Ethical standards for the legal profession are troublesome (although probably no more or less so than for other professions). The bar has a long-standing tradition of policing itself,[86] but the results are not entirely satisfactory to all segments of the profession or to the public at large. Rules of conduct are prescribed in the Code of Professional Responsibility, drafted by the American Bar Association and put into effect in each state by local statute or rule of court, sometimes with local variations.[87] The rules, although always phrased in terms of the public interest, are in fact partly in the selfish interest of the profession—to restrain outside competition— or of certain groups within it—to justify and preserve their special privileges. The Supreme Court of the United States recently invalidated two well established professional practices—the maintenance of minimum fee schedules[88] and the banning of advertising by lawyers—as not being in the public interest.[89]

The machinery of bar discipline also needs improvement. Like the machinery for admission to the bar, it is locally, not nationally, controlled. A lawyer disbarred, suspended or reprimanded in one state may continue to practice elsewhere in state and federal courts to which he has been admitted until those courts act independently to restrain him.[90] Occasionally a lawyer can flout the best traditions of his profession with total immunity because bar discipline is so cumbersome and slow moving and because many lawyers and even judges are reluctant to act against members of their own fraternity.[91] Primary responsibility for bar discipline rests upon the supreme court of the lawyer's home state. If the state bar there is "integrated" (by which in this context is meant that paid membership is mandatory for all lawyers admitted to practice), the court may delegate to it the power to conduct preliminary hearings and make recommendations. If the bar is not integrated, the court ordinarily appoints its own committee of lawyers (usually drawn from voluntary bar associations) to perform those functions.

The fact that legal ethics is now the subject of a required course in many law schools does not ensure that high ethical principles will be absorbed by the students or carried into practice in their professional lives, but it is certainly a step in the right direction.[92] Perhaps another step in the same direction is the growth of actions for legal malpractice, paralleling actions for medical malpractice against doctors.[93]

One of the central ethical ideals of the profession is to make legal services available to all who need them.[94] This ideal is reinforced by self-interest on the part of lawyers, many of whom are worried about the overcrowding of the bar and the possibility that there may not be enough legal work to go around, and by the insistence of the Supreme Court of the United States that equal protection of the laws requires that indigents be furnished legal representation in serious criminal cases free of charge to themselves.[95] Such representation today is commonly provided at government expense through "public defender" offices, manned by salaried lawyers paid out of the public treasury in the same manner that their opposite numbers, prosecuting attorneys, are paid.[96] At present there is no constitutional requirement that free legal representation be given to indigents who become involved in civil litigation. Nevertheless, under the leadership of the profession, legal aid societies (manned by salaried lawyers paid from charitable contributions, many of which come from lawyers in private practice) and neighborhood law offices (manned by salaried lawyers paid from public funds) have been and are being established in many communities to assist indigents in civil matters as well as criminal.[97] In addition, it is not uncommon for public-spirited lawyers in private practice to devote part of their time to representing indigents in both civil and criminal matters outside of the framework of public defender offices, neighborhood law offices and legal aid societies.[98]

As for people who are economically above the poverty level though still of modest means, they too may need professional representation more than they realize, particularly if they are going to venture into court. It is beginning to be made available to them through prepaid group legal service plans, administered by labor unions and similar organizations employing or retaining lawyers to serve their membership.[99]

Improved and expanded methods of delivering legal services benefit not only the recipients of such services, but also the lawyers rendering them, who otherwise might be unemployed. They also improve the functioning of the courts. Ill-equipped to deal with litigants in person, courts are largely dependent upon the help given them by lawyers. Without such help, the machinery of justice might grind to a halt.

### Paraprofessionals

Just as judges are assisted by parajudicial personnel, some lawyers enjoy the help of paraprofessionals in their offices. These are persons who have not had the full training that lawyers have had and who have not run the gauntlet of admission to practice. Nevertheless, they have had sufficient specialized training or experience to be able to perform recurring tasks—in the administration of estates, real estate closings, uncontested divorces, etc.—as effectively as their employers, sometimes more effectively. Furthermore, since they are paid relatively modest salaries compared to the earnings of lawyers, they can perform such tasks more economically, thus potentially reducing the cost of legal services to the ultimate consumers of them, the clients. Although they must work under the supervision of lawyers, theirs is an emerging and honorable profession.[100]

## Epilogue

Capable judges, lawyers, jurors, court administrators and their helpers can make even a poor judicial system work tolerably well, whereas incompetent people are not likely to achieve satisfactory results even in a good system.

Alexander Pope said:

> For Forms of Government let fools contest; whate'er is best administered is best . . .[101]

The view that people are at least as important as the structural framework in which they operate and the procedures they follow was shared by Roscoe Pound and Arthur T. Vanderbilt. Pound applied it to the judicial branch of government as follows:

> Whether or not men count in the law as set forth in the books, they count powerfully in the law in action . . . . [The practising lawyer knows] how much depends on the particular judge on whose list his case chances to be; he understands well how much depends upon who argues a case before a given tribunal; he appreciates how much the result hangs upon the personnel of the appellate tribunal before which a decisive battle of the law chances to be waged . . . .[102]

Vanderbilt listed as essentials of a sound judicial system:

> 1. . . . a simple system of courts, for the work of the best bench and bar may be greatly handicapped by a multiplicity of courts with overlapping jurisdictions . . .
>
> 2. . . . a corps of judges, each of them utterly independent and beholden only to the law and to the Constitution, thoroughly grounded in his knowledge of the law and of human nature including its political manifestations, experienced at the bar in either trial or appellate work and preferably in both, of such temperament that he can hear both sides of a case before making up his mind, devoted to the law and justice, industrious, and, above all, honest and believed to be honest . . .
>
> 3. Honest and intelligent juries, representing a cross-section of the honest and intelligent citizenry of a county . . .

4. . . . honorable, well educated lawyers, and an effective organization of the bar. It is too much to expect that the work of judges or of juries will often rise much above the level of the work of the lawyers appearing in the cases the judges and juries decide . . .

5. We must have competent court clerks, stenographic reporters, and bailiffs, but above all we need an administrative judge and his alter ego, an administrative director of the courts working under him, to supervise the judicial system and to see that it functions effectively as a business organization . . .[103]

# NOTES

## Chapter 1

### THE SUMMONS

1. Relatively few controversies reach the stage of litigation and fewer still reach the point of trial. *See* Part IV *infra*.

2. This is adapted from Form 1 in the Appendix of Forms accompanying the Federal Rules of Civil Procedure. These forms, according to Rule 84, are intended not only "to indicate the simplicity and brevity of statement which the rules contemplate" but also are stated to be "sufficient under the rules."

3. Faretta v. California, 422 U.S. 806 (1975). This case dealt with criminal proceedings, but the same principle would seem to apply even more clearly in civil cases.

4. *Id.*

5. The summons may also be left at his "dwelling house or usual house of abode" or delivered to "an agent authorized . . . to receive service of process." FED. R. CIV. P. 4(d). *See also* Chapter 9 *infra*.

6. This is now thought to be unsatisfactory, in the light of the increasing complexity of legal problems. The 1971 National Conference on the Judiciary made its sentiments on the subject clear in its "Consensus": "Judges should be full-time officials, professionally trained in the law . . ." L.E.A.A., JUSTICE IN THE STATES, 266 (1971). Also, in its STANDARDS RELATING TO COURT ORGANIZATION (1974), the American Bar Association lent its support to the same line of thinking: "[Judges] should be professionally qualified as lawyers so that they can interpret and apply the law competently." (p. 43.) *See also* Chapter 15 *infra*.

7. This is a most unfortunate, though commonly used, description. It tends to become a self-fulfilling prophesy. Chief Justice Vanderbilt of New Jersey had this to say about such courts:

> . . . [I]t must be apparent to all who consider the matter that the local courts of first instance are the very foundation of the enforcement of the criminal law. On them rests the primary responsibility for the maintenance of peace in the various communities of the state, for safety on our streets and highways, and, most important of all, for the development of respect for law on the part of our citizenry, on which, in the last analysis, all of our democratic institutions depend. This is the underlying reason why I have repeatedly called the municipal courts the

most important in our state. Not only is the work of the municipal court fundamental to the preservation of the social order, but . . . it comes in direct contact with thousands where the other trial courts only reach hundreds, and where the appellate courts reach very few indeed. It is obvious that the use in the Constitution of New Jersey of the term "inferior courts" is a phrase, however it may be justified historically, which should never be applied to the municipal courts. It is a court of first impression with limited jurisdiction, but it is in no respect an inferior court.

Vanderbilt, *The Municipal Court*, 10 RUTGERS L. REV. 647, 650 (1956).

8. 6 MARTINDALE-HUBBEL LAW DIRECTORY 199, 465 (1977).

9. *Id.* at 1727.

10. Adam v. Saenger, 303 U.S. 59 (1938).

11. *E.g.*, FED. R. CIV. P. 4(d)(1), (f).

12. Pennoyer v. Neff, 95 U.S. 714 (1877).

13. *Id.*

14. *E.g.*, FED. R. CIV. P. 4(c).

15. *E.g.*, N.Y. CIV. PRAC. LAW § 2103 (2a) (McKinney 1976).

16. A case showing that even trickery may be used to effectuate service of process is Gumperz v. Hofmann, 245 App. Div. 662, 283 N.Y.S. 823 (1935), where a private process server falsely posed as a messenger with a letter from the New York City Medical Society when serving a summons on a doctor from Buenos Aires. The service was held valid, as the deception was "practiced for the purpose, and had only the effect, of inducing the defendant to do that which in any event he should voluntarily have done."

However, if trickery is used to induce the defendant to enter a state for the purpose of obtaining jurisdiction over him, such service is fraudulent and invalid. Wyman v. Newhouse, 93 F.2d 313 (2d Cir. 1937).

17. RESTATEMENT OF JUDGMENTS § 14 (1942).

18. For a case exploring the relationship between statutes of limitation and the commencement of an action, *see* Burnett v. New York Cent. R.R., 380 U.S. 424 (1965); *cf. also*, American Pipe and Constr. Co. v. Utah, 414 U.S. 538 (1974).

19. RESTATEMENT OF JUDGMENTS §§ 19, 20 (1942); *cf.*, United States v. Balanovsky, 236 F.2d 298 (2d Cir. 1956), *cert. denied*, 352 U.S. 968 (1957).

20. *E.g.*, FED. R. CIV. P. 55.

21. Christensen v. Forst, 153 Cal. App. 2d 465, 314 P.2d 746 (1957).

22. Stevens, *Venue Statutes: Diagnosis and Proposed Cure*, 49 MICH. L. REV. 307 (1951) (a comparative study of state venue provisions).

23. Olberding v. Illinois C.R.R., 346 U.S. 338 (1953); Paige v. Sinclair, 237 Mass. 482, 130 N.E. 177 (1921); FED. R. CIV. P. 12(b)(3), 12(g), 12(h).

# Chapter 2

# THE COMPLAINT

1. FED. FORM 9.

2. FED. R. CIV. P. 11.

3. FIRST REPORT OF HER MAJESTY'S COMMISSIONERS FOR INQUIRING INTO THE PROCESS, PRACTICE, AND SYSTEM OF PLEADING IN THE SUPERIOR COURTS OF COMMON LAW 11-16 (1851).

4. For discussions of the lawyer's job in preliminarily investigating the facts, *see* Conboy, *The Preparation of a Case for Trial*, 11 A.B.A.J. 310 (1925); Hornaday, *Some Suggestions on the Investigation of Facts*, 15 IND. L. J. 498 (1940); F. WELLMAN, SUCCESS IN COURT (1941); Bowman, *How To Make an Investigation*, 21 OKLA. B. A. J. 1346 (1950); GOLDSTEIN & LANE, TRIAL TECHNIQUE § 2.48 (2d ed. 1969); A. MORRILL, TRIAL DIPLOMACY (2d ed. 1972).

5. Tag v. Linder, 87 Ohio App. 302, 94 N.E.2d 383 (1949); State v. Hardy, 218 Ind. App. 279, 30 N.E.2d 974 (1941); Maylender v. Fulton County Gas & Elec. Co., 131 Misc. 514, 227 N.Y.S. 209 (1928); C. CLARK, HANDBOOK OF THE LAW OF CODE PLEADING 225 (2d ed. 1947) [hereinafter cited as CLARK]; BLISS, TREATISE ON CODE PLEADING § 38 (3d ed. 1894).

6. *See, e.g.*, B. SHIPMAN, HANDBOOK OF COMMON LAW PLEADING, 230-31 (1923); CLARK, *supra* note 5, at 225.

7. 1848 N.Y. Laws, c. 379, § 120(2); 9. The system of pleading which developed in the N.Y. Code of 1848 is commonly referred to as code pleading.

8. Cook, *Statements of Fact in Pleading Under the Codes*, 21 COLUM. L. REV. 416 (1921) [hereinafter cited as Cook]; CLARK, *supra* note 5, at 231-36.

9. Morris, *Law & Fact*, 55 HARV. L. REV. 1303 (1942) [hereinafter cited as Morris].

10. CLARK, *supra* note 5, at §§ 45, 47; Morris, *supra* note 9; Cook, *supra* note 8.

11. Act of June 19, 1934, c. 651, 48 Stat. 1064. The current text of the Enabling Act appears in 28 U.S.C. § 2072 (1970).

12. FED. R. CIV. P. 8(a).

13. By an amendment to FED. R. CIV. P. 84 in 1948.

14. FED. R. CIV. P. 9.

15. C. WRIGHT, LAW OF FEDERAL COURTS 294 (3d ed. 1976).

16. Clark v. Chicago, M. & St. P. Ry., 28 Minn. 69, 71, 9 N.W. 75 (1881).

17. *See* MCCORMICK, EVIDENCE § 335 (2d ed. 1972) [hereinafter cited as MCCORMICK], discussing "judicial notice" of the law.

18. ". . . the plaintiff need not set forth matters of defense, that is, matters which legally should come from the other side." CLARK, *supra* note 5, at 250-51.

19. CLARK, *supra* note 5, at 606-07.

20. MCCORMICK, *supra* note 17, at § 337.

21. W. PROSSER, LAW OF TORTS 139 (4th ed. 1971) [hereinafter cited as PROSSER].

22. PROSSER, *supra* note 21, at 416-17.

23. CLARK, *supra* note 5, at 303-07.

24. A. CORBIN, CONTRACTS 980. (One Volume ed. 1952).

25. CLARK, *supra* note 5, at § 45; 27 MINN. L. REV. 318 (1943).

26. CLARK, *supra* note 5, at 607.

27. *Id.* at § 36.

28. *Id.* at 215.

29. FED. R. CIV. P. 11.

30. American Auto. Ass'n v. Rothman, 104 F. Supp. 655 (E.D.N.Y. 1952); Freeman v. Kirby, 27 F.R.D. 395 (S.D.N.Y. 1961); FED. R. CIV. P. 11.

31. Sometimes it is the intended result, as where punitive damages are allowed. D. DOBBS, REMEDIES 204 (1973).

32. FED. R. CIV. P. 8(a).

33. Garland v. Garland, 165 F.2d 131 (10th Cir. 1947); Fink v. Fink, 173 Kan. 82, 244 P.2d 184 (1952); FED. R. CIV. P. 54(c).

34. Dewey, *Logical Method and Law*, 10 CORNELL L. Q. 17 (1924).

35. *E.g.*, Bartolotta v. United States, 276 F. Supp. 66 (D. Conn. 1967).

36. *Cf.* ABA CODE OF PROFESSIONAL RESPONSIBILITY DR 7-102(A-2); *see also* Erie R.R. v. Tompkins, 304 U.S. 64 (1938).

37. *See* Chapter 7 *infra.*

NOTES

# Chapter 3

## THE DEFENDANT'S RESPONSE

1. *E.g.*, FED. R. CIV. P. 54(c).

2. The term "common law," as here used, refers to a system which prevailed in some courts in England at an earlier time. *See* Chapter 12 *infra;* C. CLARK, HANDBOOK OF THE LAW OF CODE PLEADING 502, 505 n. 15 (2d ed. 1947) [hereinafter cited as CLARK].

3. FED. R. CIV. P. 12(b).

4. Anderson & Brown Co. v. Anderson, 161 F.2d 974 (7th Cir. 1947); FED. R. CIV. P. 12(h)(2); 2A MOORE, FEDERAL PRACTICE 2455 (2d ed. 1975) [hereinafter cited as MOORE].

5. Township of Lincoln v. Cambria Iron Co., 103 U.S. 412 (1880) (as to verdict); Underwriters Salvage Co. v. Davis & Shaw Furn. Co., 198 F.2d 450 (10th Cir. 1952) (as to evidence); Lientz v. Wheeler, 113 F.2d 767 (8th Cir. 1940) (as to answer); CLARK, *supra* note 2, at §§ 119, 120.

6. FED. R. CIV. P. 56. Service on a lawyer can be and frequently is made by mail.

7. Adapted from FED. FORM 19.

8. FED. R. CIV. P. 6(d).

9. Chicago & N.W. Ry. v. First Nat'l Bank, 200 F.2d 383 (7th Cir. 1952).

10. Kahan v. Rosentiel, 424 F.2d 161 (3d Cir. 1970); Norwalk CORE v. Norwalk Redev. Agency, 395 F.2d 920 (2d Cir. 1968); Blazer v. Black, 196 F.2d 139 (10th Cir. 1952).

11. Gardner v. Toilet Goods Ass'n, 387 U.S. 167 (1967); Leimer v. State Mut. Life Assur. Co., 108 F.2d 302 (8th Cir. 1940).

12. CLARK, *supra* note 2, at 514.

13. FED. R. CIV. P. 12(b). Summary judgment will be considered in Chapter 4 *infra*.

14. FED. R. CIV. P. 56.

15. CLARK, *supra* note 2, at 92.

16. FED. R. CIV. P. 12(b).

17. 1935 N.Y. Laws, c. 263, §§ 61(b), 61(d).

18. C. MCCORMICK, HANDBOOK OF THE LAW OF EVIDENCE 776 (2d ed. 1972) [hereinafter cited as MCCORMICK].

19. Foman v. Davis, 371 U.S. 178 (1962).

20. Chapman v. Sheridan-Wyoming Coal Co., 338 U.S. 621 (1950); Grombach v. Oerlikon Tool and Arms Corp. of America, 276 F.2d 155

(4th Cir. 1960); Hohensee v. Akron Beacon Journal Publishing Co., 174 F. Supp. 450 (N.D. Ohio 1959), aff'd, 277 F.2d 359 (6th Cir. 1960), cert. denied, 364 U.S. 914 (1960); Scott v. Statesville Plywood and Veneer Co., 240 N.C. 73, 81 S.E.2d 146 (1954).

21. CLARK, supra note 2, at 80, 82.

22. Id. §§ 36, 93 at 593.

23. E.g., FED. R. CIV. P. 8(d).

24. Sovereign Bank of Canada v. Stanley, 176 F. 743 (2d Cir. 1910); Lopez v. Resort Airlines, 18 F.R.D. 37 (S.D.N.Y. 1955); CLARK, supra note 2, at 591-92.

25. For example, if the complaint alleges "the defendant maliciously hit the plaintiff on the head with a baseball bat on February 1, 1977 in Williamsburg, Virginia" and if the answer reads—"The defendant denies that he maliciously hit the plaintiff on the head with a baseball bat on February 1, 1977 in Williamsburg, Virginia," no one knows whether he is just denying the date or place or if he is denying that he hit the plaintiff at all. See Freedom Nat'l Bank v. Northern Ill. Corp., 202 F.2d 601 (7th Cir. 1953); Frank v. Soloman, 94 Ariz. 55, 381 P.2d 591 (1963); 2A MOORE, supra note 4, at § 8.24.

26. 2A MOORE, supra note 4 §§ 8.24, 8.25.

27. Mahanor v. United States, 192 F.2d 873 (1st Cir. 1951); Porto Transport, Inc. v. Consolidated Diesel Elec. Corp., 20 F.R.D. 1 (S.D.N.Y. 1956); Ice Plant Equip. Co. v. Martocello, 43 F. Supp. 281 (E.D. Pa. 1941); Schnibbe v. Glenz, 245 N.Y. 388, 157 N.E. 504 (1927).

28. E.g., FED. R. CIV. P. 8(b).

29. National Millwork Corp. v. Preferred Mut. Fire Ins. Co., 28 F. Supp. 952 (E.D.N.Y. 1939); CLARK, supra note 2, at § 93.

30. CLARK, supra note 2, at 597-99.

31. Id. at 599.

32. Omaha & Repub. Ry. v. Wright, 49 Neb. 456, 68 N.W. 618 (1896).

33. CLARK, supra note 2, at 606-7.

34. Id. at 687-88.

35. E.g., FED. R. CIV. P. 8(d).

36. E.g., FED. R. CIV. P. 7(a).

37. E.g., FED. R. CIV. P. 8(e)(2).

38. E.g., FED. R. CIV. P. 12(c).

39. CLARK, supra note 2, at 524.

40. E.g., FED. R. CIV. P. 12(f).

41. Wyatt v. Pennsylvania R.R., 154 F. Supp. 143 (D. Del. 1957).

42. FED. R. CIV. P. 12(e).

43. Conley v. Gibson, 355 U.S. 41 (1957); Mitchell v. E-Z Way Towers, Inc., 269 F.2d 126 (5th Cir. 1959).

44. CLARK, *supra* note 2, at §§ 54, 87.

45. Adapted from FED. FORM 20.

46. McCORMICK, *supra* note 18, at § 184; FED. R. EVID. 402.

47. Foman v. Davis, 371 U.S. 178 (1962); *E.g.*, FED. R. CIV. P. 15(a).

48. Emich Motors Corp. v. General Motors Corp., 229 F.2d 714 (7th Cir. 1956).

49. Green v. Walsh, 21 F.R.D. 15 (E.D. Wis. 1957); FED. R. CIV. P. 15(c).

50. Wasnik v. Borg, 423 F.2d 44 (2d Cir. 1970); FED. R. CIV. P. 15(b).

51. *E.g.*, FED. R. CIV. P. 15(d).

52. *Cf.* Garrison v. Baltimore & O.R.R., 20 F.R.D. 190 (W.D. Pa. 1957).

# Chapter 4

# PROCEDURE BEFORE TRIAL

1. Derived historically from Equity. *See* Chapter 12 *infra;* and for a fuller account, *see* D. KARLEN, PROCEDURE BEFORE TRIAL IN A NUTSHELL 177-183 (1972).

2. *E.g.*, FED. R. CIV. P. 45. If the person to be examined is an adverse party, no subpoena is necessary. Notice is enough. FED. R. CIV. P. 37(d).

3. Although a lawyer may object to the taking of a deposition in the office of the opposing lawyer or before an employee of that lawyer, frequently the objection is waived by stipulation. *E.g.*, FED. R. CIV. P. 29.

4. *See* Chapter 5 *infra.*

5. *E.g.*, FED. R. CIV. P. 32(b). C. McCORMICK, HANDBOOK OF THE LAW OF EVIDENCE 114 (2d ed. 1972) [hereinafter cited as McCORMICK]. If an objection relates to form only, so that it could be obviated by a rephrasing of the question, it must be placed on the record during the taking of the deposition. *E.g.*, FED. R. CIV. P. 32(d)(3). If it concerns evidential questions of substance, it is enough if the objection is made at the time of trial when the deposition is being read into evidence.

6. *E.g.*, FED. R. CIV. P. 26(b)(1). "Relevancy" for purposes of discovery is a broader concept than "relevancy" for purposes of trial.

7. *Id. See* McCORMICK, *supra* note 5, at 151.

8. *E.g.*, FED. R. CIV. P. 26(b)(3); *see also* Hickman v. Taylor, 329 U.S. 495 (1945). The lawyer's work product is not absolutely inviolate. It can be obtained by discovery if the party seeking the information

convinces the court that he cannot otherwise obtain it without undue hardship.

9. *E.g.*, FED. R. CIV. P. 37(a).

10. *E.g.*, FED. R. CIV. P. 37(b).

11. *E.g.*, FED. R. CIV. P. 30(e).

12. *E.g.*, FED. R. CIV. P. 32(a)(2).

13. *E.g.*, FED. R. CIV. P. 32(a)(3).

14. Another reason for requiring the deponent to testify at the trial if he is available is the fact that the lawyers for both sides should then have a fuller understanding of all issues in the case than they had weeks or months earlier when the deposition was taken.

15. *E.g.*, FED. R. CIV. P. 32(a)(1).

16. *E.g.*, FED. R. CIV. P. 31.

17. *E.g.*, FED. R. CIV. P. 33.

18. *E.g.*, FED. R. CIV. P. 34.

19. Courts have broad power to enter protective orders to prevent discovery procedures from being used to annoy, embarrass, oppress or unduly burden any party or other person. *E.g.*, FED. R. CIV. P. 26(c).

20. *E.g.*, FED. R. CIV. P. 35.

21. The parties are allowed broad power to modify discovery procedures by stipulation. *E.g.*, FED. R. CIV. P. 29.

22. *E.g.*, FED. R. CIV. P. 37.

23. *E.g.*, FED. R. CIV. P. 36, 37(b)(2)(A).

24. *E.g.*, FED. R. CIV. P. 37(c).

25. Alyeska Pipeline Serv. Co. v. Wilderness Soc'y, 421 U.S. 240 (1975).

26. *E.g.*, FED. R. CIV. P. 56(c); 6 MOORE, FEDERAL PRACTICE 197-201 (2d ed. 1976) [hereinafter cited as MOORE].

27. *E.g.*, FED. R. CIV. P. 56(c).

28. *See* Chapter 3 *supra*.

29. *E.g.*, FED. R. CIV. P. 56(c), 6 MOORE, *supra* note 26, at 197.

30. *E.g.*, FED. R. CIV. P. 56(e); Robin Constr. Co. v. United States, 345 F.2d 610 (3d Cir. 1965); 6 MOORE, *supra* note 26, at 1303.

31. *E.g.*, FED. R. CIV. P. 56(e).

32. *E.g.*, FED. R. CIV. P. 56(a), (b).

33. *E.g.*, FED. R. CIV. P. 56; Bland v. Norfolk and S. R.R., 406 F.2d 863 (4th Cir. 1969).

34. *E.g.*, FED. R. CIV. P. 56(d).

35. *E.g.*, FED. R. CIV. P. 56(c); Incorporated Soc'y v. Lorusso, 5 Misc. 2d 551, 161 N.Y.S. 2d 483 (Sup. Ct. 1957).

36. Arnstein v. Porter, 154 F.2d 464 (2d Cir. 1946).

37. Dwan v. Massarene, 199 App. Div. 872, 192 N.Y.S. 577 (Sup. Ct. 1922).

38. Galloway v. United States, 319 U.S. 372 (1943).

39. Dwan v. Massarene, 199 App. Div. 872, 192 N.Y.S. 577 (Sup. Ct. 1922).

40. *E.g.*, FED. R. CIV. P. 12(c).

41. *E.g.*, FED. R. CIV. P. 16.

42. *Id.*

43. *See generally* M. ROSENBERG, THE PRETRIAL CONFERENCE AND EFFECTIVE JUSTICE (1964) [hereinafter cited as ROSENBERG] especially Chapter 1; Karlen, Book Review, 20 RECORD OF THE ASS'N OF THE BAR OF CITY OF N.Y. 299 (May 1965).

44. Link v. Wabash R.R., 370 U.S. 626 (1962).

45. Padovani v. Bruchhausen, 293 F.2d 546 (2d Cir. 1961).

46. *Cf.* Lynn v. Smith, 281 F.2d 501 (3d Cir. 1960).

47. A pretrial order is sometimes lengthy. For example, *see* 36 MINN. L. REV. 663, 669 (1952).

48. *E.g.*, FED. R. CIV. P. 16; Globe Cereal Mills v. Scrivener, 240 F.2d 330 (10th Cir. 1956).

49. The decision whether to settle or try a case belongs to the client, not to the lawyer—ABA CODE OF PROFESSIONAL RESPONSIBILITY EC 7-7.

50. *See generally*, ROSENBERG, *supra* note 43. This study was commissioned by the Supreme Court of New Jersey. *See also* ZEISEL, KALVEN & BUCHHOLZ, DELAY IN THE COURT (1959).

## Chapter 5

## TRIAL

1. *See* note 2 in Chapter 14 *infra*. Judicial Statistics compiled by the Administrative Office of the U.S. Courts and by equivalent agencies in many states confirm the relative infrequency of trials compared to settlements.

2. C. MCCORMICK, HANDBOOK OF THE LAW OF EVIDENCE § 185 (2d ed. 1972) [hereinafter cited as MCCORMICK]; J. THAYER, A PRELIMINARY TREATISE ON EVIDENCE AT THE COMMON LAW §§ 264-66 (1898).

3. FED. R. CIV. P. 15(b).

4. FED. R. CIV. P. 42(b).

5. N.Y. CIV. PRAC. LAW, § 3402 (McKinney 1970).

6. N.Y. CIV. PRAC. LAW, § 3216 (McKinney 1970).

7. *Cf.* FED. R. CIV. P. 40.

8. For a comprehensive overview of delay in civil cases, *see* J. FRANK, AMERICAN LAW: THE CASE FOR RADICAL REFORM (1969) and D. KARLEN, JUDICIAL ADMINISTRATION: THE AMERICAN EXPERIENCE (1970).

9. *Cf.* H. ZEISEL, H. KALVEN & B. BUCHHOLZ, DELAY IN THE COURT, Chapter 3 (1959).

10. *Id.* at 287.

11. Marovitz, *Calendar Control—Civil and Criminal,* 68 F.R.D. 251 (1975); Sykes & Isbell, *Court Congestion and Crash Programs: A Case Study,* 44 DEN. L. J. 377 (1967); Watkins, *Remedies to Court Congestion,* 19 SYRACUSE L. REV. 714 (1968).

12. Washburn v. Allen, 77 Me. 344 (1884).

13. *E.g.,* FED. R. CIV. P. 41.

14. *Id.*

15. ALAS. CONST. art. I, § 16.

16. A leading case discussing the restricted application of the Seventh Amendment to the U.S. Constitution is Minneapolis & St. L. R.R. v. Bombolis, 241 U.S. 211 (1916).

17. Baldwin v. New York, 399 U.S. 66 (1970); Duncan v. Louisiana, 391 U.S. 145 (1968); Bloom v. Illinois, 391 U.S. 194 (1968).

18. Devitt, *Federal Civil Jury Trials Should Be Abolished,* 60 A.B.A.J. 570 (1974); Janata, *Federal Civil Jury Trials Should Not Be Abolished,* 60 A.B.A.J. 934 (1974); *The Symposium: Jury Trial on Trial,* 28 N.Y. St. B. BULL. 322 (1956).

19. *See* Williams v. Florida, 399 U.S. 78 (1970), discussing the Florida provisions in criminal cases; *see also* FLA. CONST. art. I, § 22 on civil cases.

20. Because of the merger of law and equity and because most modern procedural rules freely allow the assertion of numerous claims, counterclaims, crossclaims and defenses, a single case today may include issues which formerly would have had to be tried in separate actions at law and in equity. When such is the case, the right to trial by jury is not determined for the case as a whole, but for particular issues in it. Thus a jury might be empaneled to decide the plaintiff's claim for damages arising out of an auto accident, while the judge alone would decide the defendant's counterclaim for specific performance of a contract. The right to trial by jury is further discussed in Part III, Chapter 13 *infra.*

21. Brady v. Place, 41 Idaho 747, 242 P. 314 (1925). Deciding when a "new" right and remedy has been created is not easy; *compare* NLRB v. Jones and Laughlin Steel Corp., 301 U.S. 1 (1937) (no right to trial

by jury when employee seeks back pay because of alleged wrongful discharge for union membership) *with* Curtis v. Loether, 415 U.S. 189 (1974) (jury trial required in case involving injunction and damages for alleged racial discrimination in housing under Civil Rights Act.)

22. *See* Wiggins v. Williams, 36 Fla. 637, 18 So. 859 (1896); *but see* Cassel v. Gregori, 28 Cal. App. 2d Supp. 769, 70 P.2d 721 (1937).

23. *E.g.*, FED. R. CIV. P. 39.

24. Capital Traction Co. v. Hof., 174 U.S. 1 (1899).

25. Colgrove v. Battin, 413 U.S. 149 (1973) (upholding as constitutional a local District Court rule reducing the size of a jury from twelve to six in civil cases).

26. *E.g.*, FED. R. CIV. P. 39.

27. FED. R. CIV. P. 38(d); Wilson v. Corning Glass Works, 195 F.2d 825 (9th Cir. 1952). Some states require the party demanding a jury to deposit in advance the expenses which will be entailed in paying fees and mileage for persons chosen to serve as jurors. *See* CALIF. CIV. PROC. CODE § 631 (West 1976); N.M. STAT. ANN. §§ 21-1-1, 21-8-14 (1953).

28. Carter v. Jury Comm'n, 396 U.S. 320 (1969).

29. *Id.*

30. A modern statute dealing with jury qualifications, exemptions, and excuses is the Federal Jury Selection and Service Act of 1968, 28 U.S.C. § 1861 *et seq.* (1970).

31. Taylor v. Louisiana, 419 U.S. 522 (1975).

32. Thiel v. Southern Pac. Co., 328 U.S. 217 (1946); Moore v. Navassa Guano Co., 130 N.C. 229, 41 S.E. 293 (1902).

33. *E.g.*, FED. R. CIV. P. 47(a).

34. Babcock, *Voir Dire; Preserving "It's Wonderful Power,"* 27 STAN. L. REV. 545 (1975); Levit, Nelson, Ball & Chernick, *Expediting Voir Dire: An Empirical Study*, 44 S. CAL. L. REV. 916 (1971).

35. On the problem of pretrial publicity leaked by lawyers to the news media, *see* ABA CODE OF PROFESSIONAL RESPONSIBILITY DR 7-107.

36. Sutton v. Fox, 55 Wis. 531, 13 N.W. 477 (1882).

37. *Cf.* Swain v. Alabama, 380 U.S. 202 (1965).

38. F. JAMES & G. HAZARD, CIVIL PROCEDURE § 7.2 (2d ed. 1977) [hereinafter cited as JAMES & HAZARD].

39. On jury handbooks, *see* United States v. Gordon, 253 F.2d 177 (7th Cir. 1958). On timing of instructions to the jury, *see* Prettyman, *Jury Instructions—First or Last?*, 46 A.B.A.J. 1066 (1960).

40. WICKER, FLORIDA CIVIL TRIAL PRACTICE §§ 4.2, 4.3 (2d ed. 1970).

41. Maggio v. Cleveland, 151 Ohio St. 136, 84 N.E.2d 912 (1949).

42. The fact that a witness is also a party or otherwise has an interest in the outcome of the action does not disqualify him. MCCORMICK,

*supra* note 2, at § 65; FED. R. EVID. 601. It may, however, have an important bearing on the weight to be given to his testimony. McCORMICK, *supra* note 2, at § 65.

43. McCORMICK, *supra* note 2, at §§ 31, 245.

44. *Id.* at §§ 6, 25.

45. *See* Chapter 4 *supra*.

46. *E.g.*, FED. R. CIV. P. 50(a). In some states a rough equivalent to the federal motion for a directed verdict at the end of the plaintiff's case is the motion for a "non-suit." If such a motion is granted, the decision is not considered to be "on the merits," meaning that the plaintiff is not barred from bringing a new action on the same claim. In the federal courts and in state courts which use the directed verdict, the granting of such a motion is regarded as a decision on the merits, finally determining the case in favor of the defendant and barring the plaintiff from starting again. *See* Gummer v. Trustees of Omro, 50 Wis. 247, 6 N.W. 885 (1880) on the nonsuit motion.

47. *E.g.*, FED. R. CIV. P. 50(a), 58.

48. Globe Indemnity Co. v. Daviess, 243 Ky. 356, 47 S.W.2d 990 (1932).

49. *See* Chapter 4 *supra* for discussion of discovery.

50. *Id.*

51. McCORMICK, *supra* note 2, at § 246.

52. *Id.* at § 245.

53. *Id.* at § 297.

54. *Id.* at § 262.

55. Note, *Major Changes Under the Proposed Federal Rules of Evidence*, 37 TENN. L. REV. 556, 759 (1970); Swartz, *The Proposed Federal Rules of Evidence: An Introduction and Critique*, 38 U. CIN. L. REV. 449 (1969); Estes, *The Need for Uniform Rules of Evidence in Federal Courts*, 24 F.R.D. 331 (1960); Joiner, *The Rule Making Power and the Exertion of Judicial Leadership in the Field of Evidence Reform*, 26 INS. COUNSEL J. 57 (1959).

56. FED. R. EVID. 802, 803; Note, *Hearsay and the Proposed Federal Rules of Evidence*, 17 N.Y.L.F. 241 (1971); Falknor, *Hearsay*, 1969 LAW AND THE SOC. ORDER 591.

57. McCORMICK, *supra* note 2, at § 12.

58. *Id.* at § 11.

59. *Id.* at § 13.

60. Myers, *The Battle of the Experts: A New Approach to an Old Problem in Medical Testimony*, 44 NEB. L. REV. 539 (1965); Levy, *Impartial Medical Testimony*, PA. B.A.Q. 348 (1959); Friedman, *Expert Testimony: Its Abuse and Reform*, 19 YALE L.J. 247 (1910).

61. ASSOCIATION OF THE BAR OF THE CITY OF NEW YORK, IMPARTIAL MEDICAL TESTIMONY: A REPORT BY A SPECIAL COMMITTEE ON THE MEDI-

NOTES

CAL EXPERT TESTIMONY PROJECT (1956); Martin, *The Impartial Medical Testimony Project*, 28 INS. COUNSEL J. 612 (1961).

62. MCCORMICK, *supra* note 2, at § 230.

63. Other formulae are sometimes used: the jury must decide the case if there is a "scintilla" of evidence in favor of the party against whom the motion is made; or "any" evidence in his favor; or "substantial" evidence in his favor, etc. All such tests, however, are vague and highly subjective and tend to boil down to the same criteria. *See* Galloway v. United States, 319 U.S. 372 (1943).

64. *Id.*

65. Gunning v. Cooley, 281 U.S. 90 (1930).

66. Globe Indem. Co. v. Daviess, 243 Ky. 356, 47 S.W.2d 990 (1932).

67. Dick v. New York Life Ins. Co., 359 U.S. 437 (1959).

68. *E.g.*, Lohmann v. Wabash R.R., 364 Mo. 910, 269 S.W.2d 885 (1954).

69. *Cf.* Railroad Co. v. Stout, 84 U.S. 657 (1873).

70. *Cf.* Inman v. Baltimore & O. R.R., 361 U.S. 138 (1959); Pokora v. Wabash Ry., 292 U.S. 98 (1934).

71. For the permissible bounds of summations, *see* Conn v. Seaboard Air Line Ry., 201 N.C. 157, 159 S.E. 331 (1931).

72. Carmody v. Kolocheski, 181 Wis. 394, 194 N.W. 584 (1923).

73. *E.g.*, FED. R. CIV. P. 51.

74. Withers v. Lane, 144 N.C. 184, 56 S.E. 855 (1907).

75. Chicago & E. I. R. Co. v. Burridge, 211 Ill. 9, 71 N.E. 838 (1904).

76. Withers v. Lane, 144 N.C. 184, 56 S.E. 855 (1907).

77. Virginia Ry. v. Armentrout, 166 F.2d 400 (4th Cir. 1948).

78. Quercia v. United States, 289 U.S. 466 (1933).

79. 3 AM. JUR. PL. & PR. 917, Form #1464 (1966); FED. R. CIV. P. 51. In many jurisdictions "pattern" instructions are available in book form. *See* R. MCBRIDGE, THE ART OF INSTRUCTING THE JURY (1969); E. DEVITT & C. BLACKMAR, FEDERAL JURY PRACTICE AND INSTRUCTIONS (3d ed. 1977); Note, *Jury Instructions*, 98 U. PA. L. REV. 223 (1949).

80. *E.g.*, FED. R. CIV. P. 49.

81. *See, e.g.*, WIS. STAT. § 270.27.

82. Sunderland, *Verdicts, General and Special*, 29 YALE L.J. 253 (1920).

83. *See* 374 U.S. 865, 867-68 (1963) (remarks by Justices Black and Douglas).

84. *E.g.*, FED. R. CIV. P. 49(b).

85. Delaware, Lackawanna and W. R.R. v. Converse, 139 U.S. 469 (1891).

86. MCCORMICK, *supra* note 2, at 435.

87. Winans v. Attorney General, [1904] A.C. 287, 289.

88. McCORMICK, *supra* note 2, at § 342.

89. *See* note 83 *supra*.

90. ULMAN, A JUDGE TAKES THE STAND, 21-34 (1933).

91. McDonald v. Pless, 238 U.S. 264 (1915); *but see generally* Maher v. Isthmian S.S. Co., 253 F.2d 414 (2d Cir. 1958); JAMES & HAZARD, *supra* note 38, at § 7.19; 8 WIGMORE, EVIDENCE § 2345 (3d ed. 1940); Note, *Chance & Quotient Verdicts*, 37 VA. L. REV. 849 (1951). Comment, *Impeachment of Jury Verdicts*, 25 U. CHI. L. REV. 360, 366-72 (1958).

92. *See* Rich v. Finley, 325 Mass. 99, 89 N.E.2d 213 (1949); Smith v. Wisconsin, 51 Wis. 615, 8 N.W. 410 (1881).

93. JAMES & HAZARD, *supra* note 38, at § 7.4.

94. *E.g.*, FED. R. CIV. P. 59.

95. Aetna Cas. and Sur. Co. v. Yeatts, 122 F.2d 350 (4th Cir. 1941); *but see* Lind v. Schenley Indus., 278 F.2d 79 (3d Cir. 1960).

96. *Cf.* Virginia Ry. v. Armentrout, 166 F.2d 400 (4th Cir. 1948).

97. *Cf.* THAYER, PRELIMINARY TREATISE ON EVIDENCE 183-85 (1898); O. HOLMES, THE HOLMES POLLOCK LETTERS 84 (1961); A. HERBERT, MISLEADING CASES IN THE COMMON LAW 10 (1930).

98. McCORMICK, *supra* note 2, at § 60.

99. *E.g.*, FED. R. CIV. P. 52.

100. *Cf.* Ray v. Foreman, 441 F.2d 1266 (6th Cir. 1971).


# Chapter 6

# JUDGMENT AND EXECUTION

1. *E.g.*, FED. R. CIV. P. 58.

2. *Id.*

3. *E.g.*, FED. R. CIV. P. 49(b).

4. *E.g.*, FED. R. CIV. P. 52.

5. *E.g.*, FED. FORM 31.

6. *Id.*

7. *E.g.*, FED. R. CIV. P. 54(c).

8. *Id.*

9. Alyeska Pipeline Serv. Co. v. Wilderness Soc'y, 421 U.S. 240 (1975). For a general discussion of costs and their assessment, *see* WRIGHT & MILLER, FEDERAL PRACTICE AND PROCEDURE, 2665-2679 (1973).

10. *See* Chapters 11 and 12 *infra*.

11. *See generally* on execution, D. EPSTEIN, DEBTOR-CREDITOR RELATIONS IN A NUTSHELL (1973) [hereinafter cited as EPSTEIN].

12. *See generally* on enforcement of equitable decrees D. Dobbs, Remedies 91 (1973).

13. *See* on writ of assistance, W. Walsh, Equity 47-8 (1930).

14. On modern statutory practice, *see* Garfein v. McInnis, 248 N.Y. 261, 162 N.E. 73 (N.Y. 1928).

15. *See* Epstein, *supra* note 11, at 17-18 (on Sheriff's bonds).

16. On contempt in supplementary proceedings, *see* Reeves v. Crownshield, 274 N.Y. 74, 8 N.E.2d 283 (1937).

17. *See* Epstein, *supra* note 11, at 55-56 (on supplementary proceedings).

18. Karlen, *Exemptions from Executions,* 22 Bus. Law. 1167 (1967).

19. Fauntleroy v. Lum, 210 U.S. 230 (1908).

20. *See* Enforcement of Foreign Judgments Act (rev. 1964); for a similar procedure for registering a federal judgment in another federal district, *see* 28 U.S.C. § 1963.

21. For a discussion of the policy reasons underlying the doctrine of res judicata, *see* Durfee v. Duke, 375 U.S. 106 (1963).

22. *See* Chapter 7 *infra.*

23. *E.g.,* Fed. R. Civ. P. 60.

24. New York Life Ins. Co. v. Nashville Trust Co., 200 Tenn. 513, 292 S.W.2d 749 (1956).

25. Dearden v. Hay, 304 Mass. 659, 24 N.E.2d 644 (1939).

26. *Cf.* Jones v. Morris Plan Bank, 168 Va. 284, 191 S.E. 608 (1937).

27. Secor v. Sturgis, 16 N.Y. 548 (1858).

28. *See generally,* R. Casad, Res Judicata in a Nutshell (1976).

29. Restatement (Second) of Judgments § 47 (Tent. Draft No. 1, 1973).

30. Fauntleroy v. Lum, 210 U.S. 230 (1908).

31. Durfee v. Duke, 375 U.S. 106 (1963).

32. For a discussion of the concept, *see* Bruszewski v. U. S., 181 F.2d 419 (3d Cir. 1950).

33. Restatement (Second) of Judgments § 107.1 (Tent. Draft No. 3, 1976).

34. Restatement (Second) of Judgments § 89 (Tent. Draft No. 3, 1976).

35. Schwalich v. Guenther, 282 Minn. 504, 166 N.W.2d 74 (1969).

36. For a general discussion, *see* Casad, *supra* note 28, at 202 *et seq.*

37. *See generally* Bernhard v. Bank of America, 19 Cal. 2d 807, 122 P.2d 892 (1942).

38. *Id.; see also* Blonder-Tongue Labs. v. University of Ill. Foundation, 402 U.S. 313 (1971).

39. *Cf.* United States v. United Air Lines, 216 F. Supp. 709 (D. Nev. 1962); *also* Casad, *supra* note 28, at 212 *et seq.*

Chapter 7

# APPEALS

1. P. Carrington, *A Statistical Analysis of the Workload of the United States Courts of Appeals*, in 1 APPELLATE JUSTICE, 44 (1975); P. Carrington, *Crowded Dockets and the Courts of Appeals: The Threat To The Function of Review and the National Law*, 82 HARV. L. REV. 542 (1969).

2. *Id.*

3. P. CARRINGTON, D. MEADOR & M. ROSENBERG, JUSTICE ON APPEAL 1-12 (1976) [hereinafter cited as CARRINGTON]; D. MEADOR, APPELLATE COURTS: STAFF AND PROCESS IN THE CRISIS OF VOLUME (1974).

4. *Id.*

5. A. VANDERBILT, MINIMUM STANDARDS OF JUDICIAL ADMINISTRATION 389-395 (1949); *cf.* Capital Traction Co. v. Hof., 174 U.S. 1 (1899).

6. *Cf.* Ulmer, Hintze & Kirklosky, *The Decision to Grant or Deny Certiorari: Further Consideration of Cue Theory*, 6 L. AND SOC'Y REV. 637 (1972); Hanus, *Denial of Certiorari and Supreme Court Policy-Making*, 17 AM. U. L. REV. 41 (1967); Clark & Stone, *Findings of Fact*, 4 U. CHI. L. REV. 190 (1937).

7. Douglas v. California, 372 U.S. 353 (1963); Griffin v. Illinois, 351 U.S. 12 (1956); McKane v. Durston, 153 U.S. 684 (1894); *Ex parte* McCardle, 74 U.S. (7 Wall.) 506 (1868).

8. Victor Talking Mach. Co. v. George, 105 F.2d 697 (3d Cir. 1939).

9. Sturm v. Chicago & N. W. Ry., 157 F.2d 407 (8th Cir. 1946); 28 U.S.C. § 2111.

10. The concept of harmless error is discussed generally in R. TRAYNOR, THE RIDDLE OF HARMLESS ERROR (1970).

11. Skidmore v. Baltimore & O. R., 167 F.2d 54 (2d Cir. 1948).

12. Aetna Cas. and Sur. Co. v. Yeatts, 133 F.2d 350 (4th Cir. 1941); *but cf.* Lind v. Schenley Indus., 278 F.2d 79 (3d Cir. 1960).

13. *Cf.* Moller v. Avirom, 384 F.2d 319 (D.C. Cir. 1967); Keen v. Overseas Tankship Corp., 194 F.2d 515 (2d Cir. 1952); FED. R. CIV. P. 46.

14. *E.g.*, FED. R. CIV. P. 12 (h)(3); *cf.* Taylor v. Sommers Bros. Match Co., 35 Idaho 30, 204 P. 472 (1922); Paige v. Sinclair, 237 Mass. 482, 130 N.E. 177 (1921).

15. Wagner v. N. Y. Life Ins. Co., 123 F.2d 28, 37 (8th Cir. 1942).

16. Twentieth Century Fox Film Corp. v. Goldwyn, 328 F.2d 190 (9th Cir. 1964); FED. R. CIV. P. 52(a).

17. NLRB v. International Van Lines, 409 U.S. 48, 52 n. 4 (1972); NLRB v. Express Publishing Co., 312 U.S. 426, 431-32 (1941).

18. *Cf.* Galloway v. United States, 319 U.S. 372 (1943); Dyer v. McDougall, 201 F.2d 265 (2d Cir. 1952); Globe Indem. Co. v. Daviess, 243 Ky. 356, 475 S.W.2d 990 (1932).

19. *Cf.* Louisville & N.R. Co. v. Chambers, 165 Ky. 703, 178 S.W. 1041 (1915) (on the "scintilla" rule).

20. Gunning v. Cooley, 281 U.S. 90 (1930).

21. Johnson v. Aetna Life Ins. Co., 158 Wis. 56, 147 N.W. 32 (1914); Agen v. Metropolitan Life Ins. Co., 105 Wis. 217, 80 N.W. 1020 (1899).

22. Adapted from FED. R. APP. P. FORM 1.

23. Hanley v. Hanley, 23 Cal. 2d 120, 142 P.2d 423 (1943).

24. *E.g.,* FED. R. APP. P. 7.

25. *E.g.,* FED. R. APP. P. 8.

26. *E.g.,* FED. R. APP. P. 10a.

27. *E.g.,* FED. R. APP. P. 10b.

28. *E.g.,* Willcox, Karlen, & Roemer, *Justice Lost—By What Appellate Papers Cost,* 33 N.Y.U. L. REV. 934 (1958) [hereinafter cited as *Justice Lost*].

29. *E.g.,* FED. R. APP. P. 10e.

30. *E.g.,* FED. R. APP. P. 11.

31. *Justice Lost, supra* note 28.

32. *E.g.,* FED. R. APP. P. 30.

33. *E.g.,* FED. R. APP. P. 30b.

34. *E.g.,* FED. R. APP. P. 28.

35. *E.g.,* FED. R. APP. P. 31.

36. FED. R. APP. P. 31, 26.

37. *E.g.,* AUSTRIAN CODE OF CIVIL PROCEDURE, § 509.

38. Karlen, *Appeals in England and the United States,* 78 L. Q. REV. 371 (1962), *reprinted in* D. KARLEN, APPELLATE COURTS IN THE UNITED STATES AND ENGLAND (1963) [hereinafter cited as KARLEN].

39. FED. R. APP. P. 34.

40. *Id.*

41. KARLEN, *supra* note 38.

42. CARRINGTON, *supra* note 3, at 32-41.

43. *E.g.,* FED. R. APP. P. 41.

44. Hawkins v. Perry, 123 Utah 16, 253 P.2d 372, 377 (1953).

45. CARRINGTON, *supra* note 3, at 35.

46. McCaffey v. Lake, 234 Wis. 251, 290 N.W. 283, 284 (1940); Hardwick v. Harris, 22 N.M. 394, 163 P. 253 (1917).

47. Webster v. Fall, 266 U.S. 507, 511 (1925).

48. *E.g.,* Pennoyer v. Neff, 95 U.S. 714 (1877), discussed in Chapter 9 *infra.*

**49.** Green v. United States, 356 U.S. 165 (1958); B. WITKIN, MANUAL ON APPELLATE COURT OPINIONS, § 93 (1977); Wolfgang, *Limits of Judicial Lawmaking and Prospective Overruling*, 29 MOD. L. REV. 593 (1966).

**50.** *See generally* Green v. United States, 356 U.S. 165 (1958) *supra*; Burnet v. Coronado Oil & Gas Co., 285 U.S. 393 (1932); R. Jackson, *Decisional Law and Stare Decisis*, 30 A.B.A.J. 334 (1944).

**51.** CARRINGTON, *supra* note 3, at 132-33, 135-36.

**52.** Lynch v. N. Y. *ex rel.* Pierson, 293 U.S. 52 (1934); 28 U.S.C. § 1257.

**53.** *Cf.* Li v. Yellow Cab Co., 13 Cal. 3d 804, 532 P.2d 1226 (1975).

**54.** Dept. of Mental Hygiene v. Kirchner, 380 U.S. 194 (1965).

**55.** 28 U.S.C. § 1257.

**56.** Brest, *The Supreme Court 1975 Term*, 90 HARV. L. REV. 1 (1976).

# Chapter 8

# THE DUAL SYSTEM OF STATE AND FEDERAL COURTS

1. This broad statement is necessarily an oversimplification of a large and complex area of law, beyond the scope of this book. Rules as to choice of law and jurisdiction of courts are covered in detail in courses and texts on "Conflict of Laws." Each state has its own body of conflict of law rules. *See* ALI, RESTATEMENT (SECOND) OF CONFLICT OF LAWS.

2. In the early history of English law, all actions were considered local. Partly this was because most people lived and died in the place they were born, and therefore few claims arose except in the locality where the parties resided. Partly it was because of the nature of the fact-finding process in early days. Juries were composed of "neighbor-witnesses"—persons who decided on the basis of their own personal knowledge of the events in controversy. As English civilization developed, social and commercial intercourse between persons in different localities and even in different nations expanded. Meanwhile the jury system was changing. Jurors, instead of relying on their own information, heard the testimony of others having direct knowledge of the facts, resolved any conflicts in such testimony, and based their decisions on the evidence presented to them. These two developments in combination caused English judges to abandon the idea that all actions were local. They came to realize that a person who committed a wrong in one place might move away from the locality; and since he could not be sued there, the injured party was left without redress. At first the judges were hesitant about enforcing any claims other than local

NOTES

ones, so they proceeded to change the law, as was their wont, through an elaborate fiction. The plaintiff would allege the facts giving rise to his claim, stating the locality in which they had taken place ("Amsterdam," for example) but adding the words, "to wit, in the County of Middlesex." The defendant, served locally with process (for he could be sued wherever he was found) was not allowed to deny or dispute that the locality where the events had taken place was located in the County of Middlesex. By means of this fiction (which was abandoned after it had served its purpose) most common law actions came to be considered "transitory" rather than local, meaning that they could be brought wherever the defendant could be found and served with process.

3. Taylor v. Sommers Bros. Match Co., 35 Idaho 30, 204 P. 472 (1922); Livingston v. Jefferson, 1 Brock 203 (C.C.D. Va. 1811).

4. Little v. Chicago, St. P., M & O Ry., 65 Minn. 48, 67 N.W. 846 (1896).

5. C. WRIGHT, HANDBOOK OF THE LAW OF FEDERAL COURTS 26 (3d ed. 1976) [hereinafter cited as WRIGHT].

6. Second Employers' Liability Cases, 223 U.S. 1 (1911); Terry v. Kolski, 254 N.W.2d 704 (Wis. 1977).

7. Generally, the defendant may remove a case from a state court to a federal district court if it would have had original jurisdiction had the case been brought there by the plaintiff. 28 U.S.C. §§ 1331, 1332, 1441.

8. 28 U.S.C. §§ 1331, 1332.

9. U.S. CONST. art. III, § 2.

10. This is not easy to accomplish, as President Franklin D. Roosevelt discovered when he attempted unsuccessfully to "pack" the court in 1937.

11. See generally U.S. CONST. art. III. The organization of the federal courts is regulated by Title 28, United States Code.

12. There are also specialized courts, such as the Court of Claims, the Customs Court and the Court of Military Appeals, which Congress has established under either Article III or Article I of the Constitution. See WRIGHT, supra note 5, at § 11.

13. There is one minor exception to this rule: the District Court for the District of Wyoming includes all of that state and such portions of Yellowstone National Park as are within Montana and Idaho. WRIGHT, supra note 5, at 7. See generally 28 U.S.C. §§ 81-131 (1970).

14. 28 U.S.C. §§ 1441. 1446. See WRIGHT, supra note 5, at 160.

15. When there are multiple parties, diversity must be "complete," meaning that adverse parties cannot be from the same state. Strawbridge v. Curtiss, 7 U.S. (3 Cranch) 267 (1806). Therefore, if a party from North Carolina and a party from Virginia bring a joint action against two defendants, there will be no diversity of citizenship if either of the defendants is a citizen of Virginia or North Carolina.

There is one exception to this rule. In interpleader cases the federal statute calls for only "two or more adverse claimants of diverse citizenship." *See* WRIGHT, *supra* note 5, at §§ 24, 27.

16. 28 U.S.C. § 1441.

17. WRIGHT, *supra* note 5, at 289-90.

18. Swift v. Tyson, 41 U.S. (16 Pet.) 1, 18 (1842). The Judiciary Act of 1789 dictated that the federal courts were to follow the laws of the state tribunals in all cases to which they applied. The Supreme Court interpreted the word "laws" to mean statutes promulgated by the legislative authority of the state and not the decisions of the courts within the state. The latter were held to be only evidence of what the law was, and not the law itself. This interpretation permitted the federal courts to determine the common law independent of state court decisions.

19. Act of June 19, 1934, c. 651, 48 Stat. 1064; WRIGHT, *supra* note 5, at 292. The Enabling Act, as subsequently revised, is now 28 U.S.C. § 2072.

20. 304 U.S. 64 (1938).

21. Black & White Taxicab & Transf. Co. v. Brown & Yellow Taxicab & Transf. Co., 276 U.S. 518 (1928).

22. Klaxon Co. v. Stentor Elec. Mfg. Co., 313 U.S. 487 (1941).

23. In the next chapter we shall see that a plaintiff often has a choice between suing in one state or another. If conflict of laws rules were uniform throughout the nation, the choice would make no difference in result, but unfortunately such rules vary from state to state.

24. *See* Lehman Bros. v. Schein, 416 U.S. 386 (1974); *see also* Clark, *State Law in Federal Courts: The Brooding Omnipresence of Erie R.R. v. Tompkins*, 55 YALE L. J. 267 (1946).

25. Initially the choice belongs to the plaintiff, but in some cases if the initial choice is a state court, the defendant can remove the case from a state court to a federal court. *See* note 7 *supra*.

26. The Supreme Court's power of review extends to the highest court of a state in which a decision could be had. Not all cases are subject to review in state supreme courts. In 1960 the Supreme Court of the United States directly reviewed the judgment of a municipal court in Louisville, Ky. A man who had been convicted of disorderly conduct and fined ten dollars claimed that the proceedings violated the due process clause of the Fourteenth Amendment, but under the Kentucky statute, review was not permitted in so seemingly trivial a case in any higher court. In these circumstances, the Supreme Court of the United States granted review and reversed the decision. Thompson v. City of Louisville, 362 U.S. 199 (1960).

27. Direct appeals to the Supreme Court are allowed from decisions of three-judge federal district court decisions invalidating acts of Congress and in a few other special types of cases. *See* 28 U.S.C. §§ 1252,

1253 (1970); 18 U.S.C. § 3731 (1970); 15 U.S.C. §§ 29, 49 (1970); 49 U.S.C. § 45 (1970).

28. 28 U.S.C. §§ 1254, 1257; see WRIGHT, *supra* note 5, at § 107.

29. WRIGHT, *supra* note 5, at § 108.

30. *Id.*

31. CARRINGTON, *supra* note 3 to Chapter 7, at 208, *et seq.*

## Chapter 9

## NONRESIDENTS AND FOREIGN CORPORATIONS

1. *See* Chapter 10 *infra.*

2. 95 U.S. 714 (1877).

3. Durfee v. Duke, 375 U.S. 106 (1963); Fauntleroy v. Lum, 210 U.S. 230 (1908).

4. Darrah v. Watson, 36 Iowa 116 (1872).

5. For cases showing how far the concept of consent has been carried in modern litigation, *see* National Equip. Rental, Ltd. v. Szukent, 375 U.S. 311 (1964); D. H. Overmyer Co. v. Frick Co., 405 U.S. 174 (1972).

6. *See* Chapter 1 *supra.*

7. Jurisdiction in modern divorce and family relations cases (beyond the scope of the present volume) is based on in rem jurisdiction over status. *See* Maynard v. Hill, 125 U.S. 190 (1888).

8. The Court assumed, without having to decide the question, that an in rem action would never have any effect beyond the thing against which it was directed. That turned out to be true when judgment went by default. Later cases, however, have shown that if the defendant contests an in rem proceeding on the merits and loses, he will be collaterally estopped from relitigating the merits in a later in personam action brought to collect the balance of the claim not satisfied by the property originally attached. For this reason, it is held that even in the original in rem action, if the defendant contests the merits he is making a general appearance which subjects him to in personam jurisdiction. Thus, again as if by magic, what was originally an in personam claim is converted to an in rem claim and then reconverted back into an in personam claim. If the defendant wishes to restrict the original proceeding to the property attached, he can do so only by defaulting, thereby forfeiting the property but saving his defense for a later day in another proceeding. *See* United States v. Balanovski, 236 F.2d 298 (2d Cir. 1956), *cert. denied*, 352 U.S. 968 (1977).

9. Mullane v. Central Hanover Bank & Trust Co., 339 U.S. 306 (1950).

10. Milliken v. Meyer, 311 U.S. 457 (1940).

11. Henry L. Doherty & Co. v. Goodman, 294 U.S. 623 (1935); McDonald v. Mabee, 243 U.S. 90 (1917).

12. International Shoe Co. v. Washington, 326 U.S. 310 (1945); Wuchter v. Pizzutti, 274 U.S. 352 (1927).

13. Mullane v. Central Hanover, 339 U.S. 306 (1950).

14. International Shoe Co. v. Washington, 326 U.S. 310 (1945).

15. Milliken v. Meyer, 311 U.S. 457 (1940); McDonald v. Mabee, 243 U.S. 90 (1917).

16. International Shoe Co. v. Washington, 326 U.S. 310 (1945); Doherty v. Goodman, 294 U.S. 623 (1935).

17. Nelson v. Miller, 11 Ill. 2d 378, 143 N.E.2d 673 (1957).

18. McGee v. International Life Ins. Co., 355 U.S. 220 (1957); Jones Enterprises, Inc. v. Atlas Serv. Corp., 442 F.2d 1136 (9th Cir. 1971).

19. Hanson v. Denckla, 357 U.S. 235 (1958); Longines-Wittnauer Watch Co. v. Barnes & Reinecke, Inc., 15 N.Y.2d 443, 209 N.E.2d 68 (1965).

20. Shaffer v. Heitner, 97 S. Ct. 2569 (1977).

21. Perkins v. Benguet Consol. Mining Co., 342 U.S. 437 (1952).

22. The most sweeping type of "long arm statute" is like that found in California. CAL. CIV. PRO. CODE § 410 (West 1973) provides in pertinent part as follows: "A court of this State may exercise jurisdiction on any basis not inconsistent with the Constitution of this State or of these United States."

23. Toomer v. Witsell, 334 U.S. 385 (1948).

24. Gulf Oil Corp. v. Gilbert, 330 U.S. 501 (1947).

25. Erie R.R. v. Tompkins, 304 U.S. 64 (1938).

26. *Supra* Chapter 8.

27. FED. R. CIV. P. 4(f). However, *see* Chapter 10 *infra* for special rules governing service of process in interpleader actions.

28. FED. R. CIV. P. 4(e).

29. *See supra* Chapter 1.

30. 28 U.S.C. § 1391(b).

31. 28 U.S.C. § 1391(a).

32. 28 U.S.C. § 1391(c).

33. 28 U.S.C. §§ 1404, 1406.

34. 28 U.S.C. § 1404.

# Chapter 10

# MULTIPLE CLAIMS AND MULTIPLE PARTIES

1. *E.g.*, FED. R. CIV. P. 18, 20(a). Under traditional codes the rules are less liberal.

2. *E.g.*, FED. R. CIV. P. 20(b), 42(b).

3. United Mine Workers v. Gibbs, 383 U.S. 715 (1966).

4. Mills v. DeWees, 141 W. Va. 782, 93 S.E.2d 484 (1956).

NOTES

5. Secor v. Sturgis, 16 N.Y. 548 (Ct. App. 1858).

6. FED. R. CIV. P. 13(a).

7. Ressequie v. Byers, 52 Wis. 650, 9 N.W. 779 (1882).

8. If the judge anticipates confusion, he can order separate trials of the separate claims. FED. R. CIV. P. 42(b).

9. Chance v. County Bd. of School Trustees, 332 F.2d 971 (7th Cir. 1969).

10. Moore v. New York Cotton Exch., 270 U.S. 593 (1926).

11. *E.g.*, FED. R. CIV. P. 20(a).

12. Hartman Ranch Co. v. Associated Oil Co., 10 Cal. 2d 332, 73 P.2d 1163 (1937).

13. Bank of California Nat'l Ass'n v. Superior Court, 16 Cal. 2d 516, 106 P.2d 879 (1940).

14. FED. R. CIV. P. 19(a), (b).

15. FED. R. CIV. P. 17(a).

16. G. BOGERT, TRUSTS & TRUSTEES §§ 870, 871 (2d ed. 1962).

17. Schwartz v. Horowitz, 131 F.2d 506 (2d Cir. 1942).

18. *E.g.*, FED. R. CIV. P. 14(a), (b).

19. *Id.*

20. *E.g.*, FED. R. CIV. P. 13(g).

21. *E.g.*, FED. R. CIV. P. 24(b).

22. *E.g.*, FED. R. CIV. P. 24(a).

23. *Cf.* Atlantis Dev. Corp. v. United States, 379 F.2d 818 (5th Cir. 1967).

24. *Cf.* Hansberry v. Lee, 311 U.S. 32 (1941).

25. Kalven & Rosenfield, *The Contemporary Function of the Class Suit*, 8 U. CHI. L. REV. 684 (1941).

26. *E.g.*, FED. R. CIV. P. 23.1.

27. *Id.*

28. *E.g.*, FED. R. CIV. P. 23(a).

29. Eisen v. Carlisle & Jacquelin, 417 U.S. 156 (1974); Katz v. Carte Blanche Corp., 496 F.2d 747 (3d Cir. 1974), *cert. denied*, 419 U.S. 885 (1974).

30. *See supra* Chapters 6 and 7.

31. Gordon v. Eastern Airlines (5th Cir. Apr. 4, 1977) (No. 74-2074), noted in Speiser, *From Roosevelt Field to Tenerife*, 82 CASE & COMMENT 3 (1977).

32. *E.g.*, FED. R. CIV. P. 22.

33. *See supra* Chapter 6.

34. Klaber v. Maryland Cas. Co., 69 F.2d 934 (8th Cir. 1934).

35. New York Life Ins. Co. v. Dunlevy, 241 U.S. 518 (1916).

36. 28 U.S.C. §§ 1335, 1397, 2361 (1970).

37. *E.g.*, FED. R. CIV. P. 42.

# Chapter 11

# THE COMMON LAW

1. On feudal law, *see generally* E. JENKS, A SHORT HISTORY OF ENGLISH LAW 26-38 (4th ed. 1928).

2. 1 W. HOLDSWORTH, A HISTORY OF ENGLISH LAW 17-21 (7th ed. 1956) [hereinafter cited as HOLDSWORTH].

3. H. HANBURY, ENGLISH COURTS OF LAW 21 (4th ed. 1967) [hereinafter cited as HANBURY].

4. F. MAITLAND, THE FORMS OF ACTION AT COMMON LAW 14 (1st ed. 1909) (with EQUITY); (first published separately 1936) [hereinafter cited as THE FORMS OF ACTION].

5. *Id.* at 22.

6. 3 T. STREET, THE FOUNDATIONS OF LEGAL LIABILITY 37 (1906) [hereinafter cited as STREET].

7. T. PLUCKNETT, A CONCISE HISTORY OF THE COMMON LAW 353-56 (5th ed. 1956) [hereinafter cited as PLUCKNETT].

8. 1 HOLDSWORTH, *supra* note 2, at 34-41.

9. HANBURY, *supra* note 3, at 31.

10. *Id.* at 64.

11. THE FORMS OF ACTION, *supra* note 4, at 41.

12. PLUCKNETT, *supra* note 7, at 356.

13. THE FORMS OF ACTION, *supra* note 4, at 35-36.

14. HANBURY, *supra* note 3, at 24.

15. *Id.*

16. THE FORMS OF ACTION, *supra* note 4, at 48.

17. HANBURY, *supra* note 3, at 28.

18. THE FORMS OF ACTION, *supra* note 4, at 48.

19. *Id.*

20. 3 STREET, *supra* note 6, at 207.

21. *Id.* at 278.

22. *Id.* at 290-91.

23. *See generally id.* at 207-22.

24. *E.g.*, R. NORDSTROM, LAW OF SALES 481-83 (1970).

25. *See* THE FORMS OF ACTION *supra* note 4, at 35-40.

26. 3 STREET, *supra* note 6, at 248.

27. 1 HOLDSWORTH, *supra* note 2, at 58-59; W. SWINDLER, MAGNA CARTA: LEGEND AND LEGACY, 308-11 (1965).

28. 1 HOLDSWORTH, *supra* note 2, at 47.

29. *Id.*

30. THE FORMS OF ACTION, *supra* note 4, at 51-52.

31. *Id.* at 4.

32. *Id.* at 80-81.

33. MAINE, EARLY LAW AND CUSTOM 389 (1883).

34. THE FORMS OF ACTION, *supra* note 4, at 4-5.

35. HANBURY, *supra* note 3, at 66.

36. THE FORMS OF ACTION, *supra* note 4, at 17.

37. PLUCKNETT, *supra* note 7, at 116-18.

38. HANBURY, *supra* note 3, at 65.

39. *Id.* at 23-24.

40. THE FORMS OF ACTION, *supra* note 4, at 17.

41. *Id.* 18-21.; R. MILLAR, CIVIL PROCEDURE OF THE TRIAL COURT IN HISTORICAL PERSPECTIVE 20 (1952).

42. HANBURY, *supra* note 3, at 88.

43. *Id.* at 29.

44. THE FORMS OF ACTION, *supra* note 4, at 17.

45. PLUCKNETT, *supra* note 7, at 381-82.

46. 2 HOLDSWORTH, *supra* note 2, at 512-13.

47. THE FORMS OF ACTION, *supra* note 4, at 75-76.

48. 3 STREET, *supra* note 6, at 226.

49. THE FORMS OF ACTION, *supra* note 4, at 49.

50. Maitland, *The Forms of Action at Common Law, reprinted in* A. VANDERBILT, CASES AND OTHER MATERIALS ON MODERN PROCEDURE AND JUDICIAL ADMINISTRATION 1327-28 (1952).

51. THE FORMS OF ACTION, *supra* note 9, at 12-13.

52. 2 HOLDSWORTH, *supra* note 2, at 520.

53. THE FORMS OF ACTION, *supra* note 4, at 54.

54. 3 STREET, *supra* note 6, at 229-31.

55. THE FORMS OF ACTION, *supra* note 4, at 53.

56. *Id.* at 49.

57. HANBURY, *supra* note 3, at 46.

58. Scott v. Shepard, 95 Eng. Rep. 1124 (K.B. 1773).

59. *Id.* at 1124-25.

60. W. PROSSER, LAW OF TORTS §§ 27-31 (4th Ed. 1971) [hereinafter cited as PROSSER].

61. *Id.* at 37-43.
62. THE FORMS OF ACTION, *supra* note 4, at 66.
63. HANBURY, *supra* note 3, at 46-47.
64. J. KOFFLER & A. REPPY, COMMON LAW PLEADING 157 (1969) [hereinafter cited as KOFFLER & REPPY].
65. Reynolds v. Clarke, 93 Eng. Rep. 747, 748 (K.B. 1725).
66. THE FORMS OF ACTION, *supra* note 4, at 67.
67. KOFFLER & REPPY, *supra* note 64, at 61.
68. 3 STREET, *supra* note 6, at 264-65.
69. PLUCKNETT, *supra* note 7, at 408.
70. *Id.* at 165-66.
71. KOFFLER & REPPY, *supra* note 64, at 191.
72. *Id.* at 169.
73. THE FORMS OF ACTION, *supra* note 4, at 72.
74. *See generally* 3 STREET, *supra* note 6, at 159-71.
75. KOFFLER & REPPY, *supra* note 64, at 209-10.
76. *E.g.,* PROSSER, *supra* note 60, at 79-97.
77. *Id.* at 97.
78. THE FORMS OF ACTION, *supra* note 4, at 54.
79. *Id.* at 68-69.
80. 3 STREET, *supra* note 6, at 173-74.
81. HANBURY, *supra* note 3, at 66.
82. *Id.* at 28.
83. *Id.*
84. THE FORMS OF ACTION, *supra* note 4, at 69.
85. HANBURY, *supra* note 3, at 67.
86. *Id.*
87. *Id.* at 68.
88. *Id.* at 69.
89. THE FORMS OF ACTION, *supra* note 4, at 38.
90. *Id.* at 69-70.
91. Slade's Case, 76 Eng. Rep. 1073 (K.B. 1602).
92. 3 STREET, *supra* note 6, at 182-88.
93. *Id.* at 189.
94. THE FORMS OF ACTION, *supra* note 4, at 70.
95. 3 STREET *supra* note 6, at 205.
96. THE FORMS OF ACTION, *supra* note 4, at 70.
97. *Id.* at 68.

98. *Compare* KOFFLER & REPPY, *supra* note 64, at 347-60 *with* FED. R. CIV. P. FORMS 3-8.

99. HANBURY, *supra* note 3, at 72.

100. KOFFLER & REPPY, *supra* note 64, at 155.

101. THE FORMS OF ACTION, *supra* note 4, at 53-54.

102. *Id.* at 55.

103. *Id.* at 56.

104. HANBURY, *supra* note 3, at 72.

105. THE FORMS OF ACTION, *supra* note 4, at 57.

106. HANBURY, *supra* note 3, at 24.

107. THE FORMS OF ACTION, *supra* note 4, at 62.

108. PLUCKNETT, *supra* note 7, at 373-74, 389-90.

109. THE FORMS OF ACTION, *supra* note 4, at 57.

110. HANBURY, *supra* note 3, at 72.

111. THE FORMS OF ACTION, *supra* note 4, at 57-58.

112. *See generally* KOFFLER & REPPY, *supra* note 64, at 227-30.

113. THE FORMS OF ACTION, *supra* note 4, at 59-60.

114. *See generally* DeSmith, *The Prerogative Writs*, 11 CAMBRIDGE L. J. 40 (1951); Jenks, *The Prerogative Writs in English Law*, 32 YALE L.J. 523 (1923).

115. THE FORMS OF ACTION, *supra* note 4, at 4.

116. PLUCKNETT, *supra* note 7, at 410.

117. 3 STREET, *supra* note 6, at 166.

118. KOFFLER & REPPY, *supra* note 64, at 207.

119. *See generally id.* at 227-30.

120. *Cf.* KOFFLER & REPPY, *supra* note 64, at 236; PLUCKNETT, *supra* note 7, at 374.

121. *See generally* PLUCKNETT, *supra* note 7, at 414-16.

122. KOFFLER & REPPY, *supra* note 64, at 485-89.

123. *Id.* at 500-01.

124. PLUCKNETT, *supra* note 7, at 415.

125. KOFFLER & REPPY, *supra* note 7, at 508-12.

126. *Id.* at 379-80.

127. PLUCKNETT, *supra* note 7, at 410.

128. *Id.* at 413.

129. KOFFLER & REPPY, *supra* note 7, at 380-81.

## Chapter 12

## EQUITY

1. *See generally* T. PLUCKNETT, A CONCISE HISTORY OF THE COMMON LAW 355 (5th ed. 1956) [hereinafter cited as PLUCKNETT].

2. F. MAITLAND, EQUITY; A COURSE OF LECTURES 15 (1929) [hereinafter cited as EQUITY]; Langdell, *A Summary of Equity Pleading, reprinted in* A. VANDERBILT, CASES AND OTHER MATERIALS ON MODERN PROCEDURE AND JUDICIAL ADMINISTRATION 1337-38 (1952) [hereinafter cited as LANGDELL].

3. D. DOBBS, REMEDIES 365 (1973) [hereinafter cited as DOBBS].

4. PLUCKNETT, *supra* note 1, at 131.

5. EQUITY, *supra* note 2, at 20; LANGDELL, *supra* note 2, at 1340.

6. EQUITY, *supra* note 2, at 3-5.

7. *See generally* PLUCKNETT, *supra* note 1, at 180-81; 187-88.

8. EQUITY, *supra* note 2, at 6, 238.

9. *Id.* at 258.

10. DOBBS, *supra* note 3, at 91-92.

11. 1 & 2 J. STORY, COMMENTARIES ON EQUITY JURISPRUDENCE, AS ADMINISTERED IN ENGLAND AND AMERICA 16-17 (9th ed. 1866) [hereinafter cited as STORY].

12. EQUITY, *supra* note 2, at 8-11; PLUCKNETT, *supra* note 1, at 692.

13. PLUCKNETT, *supra* note 1, at 131, 169.

14. *Id.* at 279-80; *see generally* 1 HOLDSWORTH, A HISTORY OF ENGLISH LAW 619-21 (7th ed. 1956) [hereinafter cited as HOLDSWORTH].

15. *Id.*

16. EQUITY, *supra* note 2, at 5.

17. *Id.*

18. *Id.* at 19-20.

19. *Id.* at 8.

20. 1 STORY, *supra* note 11, at 59-60.

21. EQUITY, *supra* note 2, at 9.

22. *Id.* at 10; 1 HOLDSWORTH, *supra* note 14, at 459-63.

23. EQUITY, *supra* note 2, at 16.

24. *Id.* at 17.

25. 1 STORY, *supra* note 11, at 9.15-19.

26. 1 HOLDSWORTH, *supra* note 14, at 456.

27. 2 STORY, *supra* note 11, at 57-59.

28. EQUITY, *supra* note 2, at 254.

29. *Id.* at 259-62.

30. *Id.* at 256-57.

31. *Id.* at 254.

32. *Id.* at 256-57.

33. *See* 1 HOLDSWORTH, *supra* note 14, at 458.

34. EQUITY, *supra* note 2, at 254.

35. 2 STORY, *supra* note 11, at 59-61.

36. *See generally* EQUITY, *supra* note 2, at 254-65.

37. *Id.* at 263.

38. 1 HOLDSWORTH, *supra* note 14, at 457.

39. DOBBS, *supra* note 3, at 58; *see generally* 3 STREET, THE FOUNDA-TIONS OF LEGAL LIABILITY 272-77 (1906).

40. *Id.*

41. EQUITY, *supra* note 2, at 239.

42. *Id.* at 238.

43. *Id.* at 239-44.

44. 1 STORY, *supra* note 11, at 710-11.

45. *Id.* at 797.

46. EQUITY, *supra* note 2, at 244.

47. *Id.* at 237-38.

48. 1 STORY, *supra* note 11, at 22-23.

49. *Id.* at 52.

50. 1 HOLDSWORTH, *supra* note 14, at 457-58.

51. DOBBS, *supra* note 3, at 746-47.

52. *Id.* at 254-56.

53. *Id.* at 293-94.

54. *Id.* at 294, 753.

55. EQUITY, *supra* note 2, at 266.

56. *Id.* at 267-68.

57. *Id.* at 273-74.

58. 2 STORY, *supra* note 11, at 188-90.

59. *Id.* at 191.

60. DOBBS, *supra* note 3, at 38-40.

61. 1 BOGERT, TRUSTS AND TRUSTEES 1-10 (2d ed. 1955).

62. EQUITY, *supra* note 2 at 28-29, 115-16.

63. *Id.* at 7, 48, 193.

64. 2 STORY, *supra* note 11, at 547-51.

65. EQUITY, *supra* note 2, at 7.

66. *Id.* at 193.

67. *See* T. ATKINSON, LAW OF WILLS 22, 482-83 (2d ed. 1953).

68. 1 STORY, *supra* note 11, at 420-21.

69. F. JAMES & G. HAZARD, CIVIL PROCEDURE § 10.2 (2d ed. 1977) [hereinafter cited as JAMES & HAZARD.]

70. *Id.* at § 10.11.

71. *See* 1 STORY, *supra* note 11, at 20-21.

72. 2 STORY, *supra* note 11, at 746-47.

73. 1 STORY, *supra* note 11, at 432-33.

74. 2 STORY, *supra* note 11, at 746-47.

75. Bank of Cal. Nat'l Assn v. Superior Court, 16 Cal. 2d 516; 106 P.2d 879, 883 (1940).

76. JAMES & HAZARD, *supra* note 69 at § 10.12.

77. 2 STORY, *supra* note 11, at 15-18.

78. W. LILE, THE EQUITY PLEADING AND PRACTICE 45-46 (3d ed. 1952) [hereinafter cited as LILE.]

79. *E.g.,* FED. R. CIV. P. 22, 23.

80. JAMES & HAZARD, *supra* note 69, at §§ 2.3-2.4.

81. EQUITY, *supra* note 2, at .3.

82. 1 HOLDSWORTH, *supra* note 14, at 645-46.

83. 2 STORY, *supra* note 11, at 705.

84. *Id.* at 748.

85. LILE, *supra* note 78, at 132.

86. JAMES & HAZARD, *supra* note 69, at § 6.1.

87. 2 STORY, *supra* note 11, at 703.

88. JAMES & HAZARD, *supra* note 69, at § 6.1.

89. *Id.* at § 6.2.

90. 2 STORY, *supra* note 11, at 704.

# Chapter 13

# REFORM AND THE MODERN JUDICIAL SYSTEM

1. 9 W. HENNING, THE STATUTES AT LARGE: BEING A COLLECTION OF ALL THE LAWS OF VIRGINIA 127 (Richmond, 1821). (Statute passed in May, 1776.)

2. D. DOBBS, REMEDIES 2.6 (1973) [hereinafter cited as DOBBS].

3. F. JAMES & G. HAZARD, CIVIL PROCEDURE § 1.5 (2d ed. 1977) [hereinafter cited as JAMES & HAZARD].

4. 1 R. PETERS, THE PUBLIC STATUTES AT LARGE OF THE UNITED STATES OF AMERICA 51 n. (a) (Boston, 1845).

5. Z. Chafee, Jr., *Colonial Courts and the Common Law,* in ESSAYS IN THE HISTORY OF EARLY AMERICAN LAW 60-61 (1969).

NOTES

6.  J. HURST, THE GROWTH OF AMERICAN LAW 98-99, 224-25 (1950).

7.  1 J. POMEROY, EQUITY JURISPRUDENCE 43 (4th ed. 1918).

8.  *Id.*

9.  1848 N. Y. Laws 497 (NEW YORK CODE § 62) [hereinafter cited as NEW YORK CODE].

10.  JAMES & HAZARD, *supra* note 3, at § 1.6.

11.  NEW YORK CODE § 120.

12.  JAMES & HAZARD, *supra* note 3, at § 2.5.

13.  NEW YORK CODE §§ 128-30.

14.  For example, in New York equity and common law jurisdiction were merged in 1846, N. Y. CONST. of 1846, art. vi, 3, and art. xiv, 5, and the single form of action was adopted by the New York Code of 1848.

15.  In 1912 New Jersey adopted the single form of action, 1912 N. J. Laws 377, while the jurisdictional merger was delayed until 1947. N. J. CONST. of 1947, art. vi, 3 ¶ 2.

16.  C. WRIGHT, LAW OF FEDERAL COURTS 317 (3d ed. 1976) [hereinafter cited as WRIGHT].

17.  JAMES & HAZARD, *supra* note 3, at § 1.7.

18.  28 U.S.C. § 2072.

19.  Appointment of Committee to Draft Unified System of Equity and Law Rules, 295 U.S. 774 (1935).

20.  Orders Re Rules of Procedure, 302 U.S. 783 (1937).

21.  *See generally* WRIGHT, *supra* note 16, at 62.

22.  *Id.* at 294.

23.  A. VANDERBILT, CASES AND MATERIALS ON MODERN PROCEDURE AND JUDICIAL ADMINISTRATION 21 (1952).

24.  JAMES & HAZARD, *supra* note 3, at § 2.6.

25.  FED. R. CIV. P. 8(a).

26.  FED. R. CIV. P. 84.

27.  FED. R. CIV. P. 8(b).

28.  FED. R. CIV. P. 8(c).

29.  FED. R. CIV. P. 15.

30.  FED. R. CIV. P. 1.

31.  WRIGHT, *supra* note 16, at 68.

32.  FED. R. CIV. P. 26-37.

33.  JAMES & HAZARD, *supra* note 3, at § 10.12.

34.  FED. R. CIV. P. 18-24.

35.  FED. R. CIV. P. 56.

36.  FED. R. CIV. P. 12.

37.  FED. R. CIV. P. 16.

38. Delaware still maintains separate courts of chancery and law, with separate rules. DEL. CODE tit. 10, 341, 342, 343, 541 (1974); DEL. CT. C.P.R. 1, 2; DEL. CHAN. CT. R. 1, 2.

39. WRIGHT, *supra* note 16, at 294.

40. 4 WRIGHT & MILLER, FEDERAL PRACTICE AND PROCEDURE 1043 (1969).

41. *Id.* at 1044.

42. JAMES & HAZARD, *supra* note 3, at § 8.1.

43. *Id.* at 8.2.

44. *Id.* at 8.3.

45. WRIGHT, *supra* note 16, at 92.

46. JAMES & HAZARD, *supra* note 3, at §§ 2.5, 8.8.

47. 396 U.S. 531 (1970).

48. WRIGHT, *supra* note 16, at 73.

49. Beacon Theatres v. Westover, 359 U.S. 500 (1959).

50. Fitzpatrick v. Sun Life Assur. Co., 1 F.R.D. 713 (D.N.J. 1941).

51. Minneapolis & St. Louis R.R. v. Bombolis, 241 U.S. 211 (1916).

52. DOBBS, *supra* note 2, at §§ 2.5, 2.6.

53. *Id.* at § 2.6.

54. JAMES & HAZARD, *supra* note 3, at § 1.11.

55. *See* CAL. CONST. art. vi, §§ 5, 11.

56. *See, e.g.,* H. PETERFREUND AND J. MCLAUGHLIN, NEW YORK PRACTICE 11 (2d ed. 1968).

57. K. DAVIS, ADMINISTRATIVE LAW TEXT 1.02 (3d ed. 1972).

58. *Id.* at § 1.05.

59. WRIGHT, *supra* note 16, at §§ 1-5.

60. *E.g.,* FLA. STAT. §§ 26.012, 34.01 (1975).

61. JAMES & HAZARD, *supra* note 3, at § 12.1.

62. *Id.* at § 12.12.

63. FED. R. CIV. P. 4(f).

# Chapter 14

# COURTS IN PERSPECTIVE

1. Even judges and lawyers tend to feel the same way. Judge Learned Hand said: "As a litigant, I should dread a lawsuit beyond almost anything else short of sickness and death." L. HAND, THREE LECTURES ON LEGAL TOPICS, 104-05.

2. A Michigan survey found that proceedings were begun in only 26 percent of claims involving serious personal injury and in only 5

percent of the claims was a trial actually begun. A. CONARD, AUTOMO-
BILE ACCIDENT COSTS AND PAYMENTS: STUDIES IN ECONOMICS OF IN-
JURIES REPARATION, 183-84 (1964). A survey in New York City revealed
that out of 193,000 bodily injury negligence claims made each year 98
percent are terminated without adjudication by a court. M. FRANKLIN,
R. CHANIN & I. MARK, *Accidents, Money and the Law: A Study of the
Economics of Personal Injury Litigation,* in DOLLARS, DELAY AND THE
AUTOMOBILE VICTIM, 38-40 (1968). For a general treatment of the
subject, *see* H. ROSS, SETTLED OUT OF COURT (1970).

3. *See generally* Sturges, *Arbitration—What Is It?,* 35 N.Y.U. L.
REV. 1031 (1960): Lippman, *Arbitration as an Alternative to Judicial
Settlement: Some Selective Perspectives,* 24 ME. L. REV. 215 (1974).

4. Fischer, *The Steel Industry's Expedited Arbitration: A Judgment After Two Years,* 28 ARB. J. 185 (1973) (Arbitration of labor-
management disputes). Aksen, *Resolving Construction Contract Disputes Through Arbitration,* 23 ARB. J. 141 (1968). (Arbitration of
contract disputes.)

5. Straus, *Mediating Environmental, Energy, and Economic Trade-
offs,* 32 ARB. J. 96 (1977).

6. Rosenberg, *Let's Everybody Litigate,* 50 TEX. L. REV. 1349 (1972).

7. The constitutionality of compulsory arbitration was upheld in
Application of Smith, 381 Pa. 223, 112 A.2d 625, *appeal dismissed sub
nom.,* Smith v. Wissler, 350 U.S. 858 (1955). For a general treatment of
the subject, *see* Rosenberg & Schubin, *Trial by Lawyer: Compulsory
Arbitration of Small Claims in Pennsylvania,* 74 HARV. L. REV. 448
(1961).

8. *See generally* B. SCHWARTZ, ADMINISTRATIVE LAW (1976).

9. *Id.* at 5, 6.

10. *Id.* at § 9.

11. *Id.* at §§ 134, 137.

12. LARSON, WORKMAN'S COMPENSATION FOR OCCUPATIONAL INJURIES
AND DEATH, § 5 (1977).

13. *Id.* at § 2.

14. SCHWARTZ & WADE, LEGAL CONTROL OF GOVERNMENT, 205-07
(1972).

15. *Id.* at 212-216.

16. B. SCHWARTZ, ADMINISTRATIVE LAW, § 10 (1976).

17. *See generally* P. CALLAHAN, THE LAW OF SEPARATION AND DIVORCE
(3d ed. 1970).

18. J. Gallagher, *No Fault Divorce in Delaware,* 59 A.B.A.J. 873
(1972).

19. *See generally* ATKINSON, LAW OF WILLS (2d ed. 1953).

20. *Id.* at 28.

21. Ross, Settled Out of Court (1970).

22. *Id.*

23. For a general treatment of the subject, *see* Brown, Preventive Law (1967).

24. Institute of Judicial Administration, State Trial Courts of General Jurisdiction: Calendar Status Studies (beginning in 1953). *See also* J. Frank, American Law: The Case for Radical Reform (1969).

25. More than 50 percent of the motor vehicle accident claims filed in court took more than ten months to become formal legal cases and more than fourteen months thereafter to terminate. From filing to termination the majority of cases required more than two years to be resolved. Variations in this time from one month to eight years were observed in this study. U.S. Dep. of Transportation, Automobile Accident Litigation 7-8 (1970).

26. ABA Standards Relating to Court Organization §§ 1.00-1.13 (1973).

27. A crime is defined as an offense against the sovereign; and a criminal action as one prosecuted by the state against a person charged with a public offense committed in violation of public law. Keefe v. Schmiege, 251 Wis. 79, 28 N.W.2d 345 (1947).

28. U.S. Const. amend. VI provides in pertinent part: "In all criminal prosecutions, the accused shall enjoy the right to a speedy and public trial.'

29. 18 U.S.C. §§ 3161-3174 (1970). *See Speedy Trial Act Time Limits Take Effect,* The Third Branch (1976). For a general treatment of the subject, *see* Lohman, *The Speedy Trial Act of 1974: Defining the Sixth Amendment Right,* 25 Cath. U. L. Rev. 130 (1975).

30. Black, *The Speedy Trial Act—Justice on the Assembly Line,* 8 St. Mary's L. J. 225 (1976).

31. N. Morris & G. Hawkins, The Honest Politicians' Guide to Crime Control (1970).

32. ABA Standards Relating to Pleas of Guilty, approved draft (1968). *See generally* Rosett & Cressey, Justice by Consent: Plea Bargains in the American Courthouse (1976); *see also* R. Kuh, Plea Copping (1967).

33. D. Danelski, *"The Chicago Conspiracy Trial"* in Political Trials (T. Becker ed. 1971).

34. The jury selection process in the Sharon Tate murder trial lasted a month. From June 16 to July 11, 141 prospective jurors were questioned. N. Y. Times, July 11, 1970, at 12, col. 2.

35. Argersinger v. Hamlin, 407 U.S. 25 (1972). Douglas v. California, 372 U.S. 353 (1963); Gideon v. Wainwright, 372 U.S. 335 (1963).

36. ABA CODE OF PROFESSIONAL RESPONSIBILITY, Canon 7. *See also* F. BAILEY, THE DEFENSE NEVER RESTS (1971); E. WILLIAMS, ONE MAN'S FREEDOM (1962).

37. FLEMING, THE PRICE OF PERFECT JUSTICE (1974) [hereinafter cited as FLEMING]. *See* Mapp v. Ohio, 367 U.S. 643 (1961); Miranda v. Arizona, 384 U.S. 436 (1966).

38. FLEMING, *supra* note 37 at 23-36. *See also* Carter, *The Use of Federal Habeas Corpus by State Prisoners*, 4 AM. CRIM. L. Q. 20 (1965).

39. FLEMING, *supra* note 37, at 27, 28.

40. *See* Rosenberg, *Anything Legislatures Can Do, Courts Can Do Better?* 62 A.B.A. J. 587 (1976) [hereinafter cited as Rosenberg]; Chayes, *The Role of the Judge in Public Law Litigation*, 89 HARV. L. REV. 7 (1976); Friendly, *The Gap in Lawmaking—Judges Who Can't and Legislators Who Won't*, 63 COLUM. L. REV. 787 (1963).

41. Brown v. Board of Educ., 347 U.S. 483 (1954) (school desegregation case); Frontiero v. Richardson, 411 U.S. 677 (1973) (sex discrimination case).

42. North Carolina State Bd. of Educ. v. Swann, 402 U.S. 43 (1971).

43. San Antonio Ind. School Dist. v. Rodriguez, 411 U.S. 1 (1973).

44. Roe v. Wade, 410 U.S. 113 (1973).

45. Griswold v. Connecticut, 381 U.S. 479 (1965).

46. Reynolds v. Sims, 377 U.S. 533 (1964).

47. Greenman v. Yuba Power Prods., Inc., 59 Cal. 2d 57, 377 P.2d 897, 27 Cal. Rptr. 697 (1962).

48. American Can Co. v. Oregon Liquor Control Comm'n, 517 P.2d 691 (Ore. App. 1973).

49. Rosenberg, *supra* note 40.

50. *See* Chapter 10 *supra*.

51. *See* note 40 *supra*.

52. *Id.*

53. 347 U.S. 483 (1954).

54. *See* Goodman, *De Facto School Segregation: A Constitutional and Empirical Analysis*, 70 CALIF. L. REV. 275 (1972). *See also* H. HUDGINS, JR., PUBLIC SCHOOL DESEGREGATION: LEGAL ISSUES AND JUDICIAL DECISIONS (1973).

## Chapter 15

# PERSONNEL AND THE ADMINISTRATION OF JUSTICE

1. 29 A.B.A. REP. 395 (1906).

2. Wigmore, *Roscoe Pound's St. Paul Address of 1906—The Spark that Kindled the White Flame of Progress*, 20 J. AM. JUD. SOC'Y 176 (1936).

3.  62 A.B.A. REP. 893-97 (1937).

4.  A. VANDERBILT, MINIMUM STANDARDS OF JUDICIAL ADMINISTRATION (1949).

5.  2 SELECTED WRITINGS OF ARTHUR T. VANDERBILT, 43 (F. Klein & J. Lee, eds. 1967).

6.  JUDICIAL SELECTION AND TENURE: SELECTED READINGS 222 (G. Winters ed. 1973).

7.  A.B.A. STANDARDS RELATING TO THE ADMINISTRATION OF CRIMINAL JUSTICE, COMPILATION (1974).

8.  IJA-ABA STANDARDS RELATING TO JUVENILE JUSTICE, TENTATIVE DRAFTS (1976-77).

9.  ABA STANDARDS RELATING TO COURT ORGANIZATION (1974); ABA STANDARDS RELATING TO TRIAL COURTS (1976); ABA STANDARDS RELATING TO APPELLATE COURTS, TENTATIVE DRAFT (1976).

10.  It publishes the STATE COURT JOURNAL quarterly.

11.  It publishes THE THIRD BRANCH monthly.

12.  Its publications include the quarterly IJA REPORT.

13.  Its publications include JUDICATURE, published monthly except bi-monthly in June-July and August-September.

14.  On court structure, *see* particularly Chapter 8; on procedure, *see* Parts I and II and Chapter 13.

15.  *See generally* on justices of the peace AMERICAN JUDICATURE SOCIETY, COURTS OF LIMITED JURISDICTION: A NATIONAL SURVEY (1977).

16.  *E.g.*, Nassau County, New York.

17.  *See, e.g.*, N. Y. JUD. LAW § 105 (McKinney Supp. 1977); Karlen, *Judicial Education*, 52 A.B.A.J. 1049 (1966).

18.  2 SELECTED WRITINGS OF ARTHUR T. VANDERBILT 112 (F. Klein & J. Lee eds. 1967).

19.  *Id.* at 114.

20.  *See, e.g.*, VA. CONST. art. 6, § 7; Laski, *The Technique of Judicial Appointment*, 24 MICH. L. REV. 529, 532-33 (1926).

21.  McHendrie, *Qualifications, Selection and Tenure of Judges*, 33 ROCKY MTN. L. REV. 449, 458-59 (1961).

22.  D. KARLEN, JUDICIAL ADMINISTRATION: THE AMERICAN EXPERIENCE 25 *et seq.* (1970).

23.  S. ESCOVITZ, JUDICIAL SELECTION AND TENURE 10 (1975).

24.  G. WINTERS & R. ALLARD, JUDICIAL SELECTION AND TENURE IN THE COURTS, THE PUBLIC AND THE LAW EXPLOSION 160-61 (H. Jones ed. 1965) [hereinafter cited as WINTERS & ALLARD].

25.  R. WATSON & R. DOWNING, THE POLITICS OF THE BENCH AND THE BAR 13-14 (1969).

26.  *Id.* at 345; WINTERS & ALLARD, *supra* note 24, at 161-62.

# NOTES

27. *Id.*

28. Lowe, *Voluntary Merit Selection Plans,* 55 J. AM. JUD. SOC'Y 161 (1971).

29. *Id.*

30. Scott, *The Selection of Federal Judges,* 24 W&L L. REV. 205 (1967); Grossman, *The Role of the American Bar Association in the Selection of Federal Judges: Episodic Involvement to Institutionalized Power,* 17 VAND. L. REV. 785 (1964).

31. *See, e.g.,* KAN. CONST. art. III, §§ 2, 8, 9.

32. WINTERS & ALLARD, *supra* note 24, at 162-63.

33. ILL. CONST. art. 6, § 12.

34. 30 J. AM. JUD. SOC'Y 67 (1946); 60 J. AM. JUD. SOC'Y 458 (1977).

35. *Judicial Salaries in Appellate and Trial Courts,* 58 J. AM. JUD. SOC'Y 196 (1974).

36. WINTERS & ALLARD, *supra* note 24, at 166-67.

37. CALIF. CONST. art. 6, § 18; *see also* Frankel, *Removal of Judges: California Tackles an Old Problem,* 49 A.B.A.J. 166 (1960).

38. WINTERS & ALLARD, *supra* note 24, at 167-68.

39. CALIF. CONST. art. 6, § 18.

40. WINTERS & ALLARD, *supra* note 24, at 170.

41. *E.g.,* M. CAPPELLETTI, J. MERRYMAN & J. PERILLO, THE ITALIAN LEGAL SYSTEM 102-08 (1967).

42. Karlen, *Judicial Education,* 52 A.B.A.J. 1049 (1966).

43. Leflar, *The Appellate Judges Seminar,* 21 ARK. L. REV. 190 (1967).

44. Rosenberg, *Judging Goes to College,* 52 A.B.A.J. 342 (1966).

45. Karlen, *Judicial Education,* 52 A.B.A.J. 1045 (1966).

46. *See* J. FRANK, AMERICAN LAW: THE CASE FOR RADICAL REFORM (1969).

47. THE AMERICAN ASSEMBLY, THE COURTS, THE PUBLIC AND THE LAW EXPLOSION 2 (1965).

48. *See* C. JOINER, CIVIL JUSTICE AND THE JURY (1962).

49. *See supra* Chapter 14.

50. Wright, *Observations of an Appellate Judge: The Use of Law Clerks,* 26 VAND. L. REV. 1179 (1973).

51. D. MEADOR, APPELLATE COURTS: STAFF AND PROCESS IN THE CRISIS OF VOLUME, Chapter 3, through 10 (1974).

52. Stecich, *How the Second Circuit is Speeding Up Criminal Appeals,* in 2 APPELLATE PROCEDURE 134 (1975).

53. Kaufman, *The Pre-argument Conference, An Appellate Procedural Reform,* in 2 APPELLATE PROCEDURE 136 (1975).

54. United States Magistrates Act, 28 U.S.C. §§ 631-639 (1970); Wingo v. Wedding, 418 U.S. 461 (1974); Holiday v. Johnson, 313 U.S.

342 (1941). *See also* Curran & Sunderland, *Use of Commissioners, The Organization and Operation of Courts of Review* in THIRD MICHIGAN COUNCIL REPORT, 65-67 (1933).

55. IJA-ABA STANDARDS RELATING TO COURT ORGANIZATION AND ADMINISTRATION, TENTATIVE DRAFT 22-24 (1977).

56. LaBuy v. Howes Leather Co., 352 U.S. 249 (1957); *see also* cases cited note 54 *supra*.

57. Vanderbilt, *Improving the Administration of Justice—Two Decades of Development*, 26 U. CIN. L. REV. 155 (1957).

58. 28 U.S.C. §§ 601-610.

59. A. VANDERBILT, THE CHALLENGE OF LAW REFORM, 8-97 (1976) [hereinafter cited as VANDERBILT].

60. 28 U.S.C. 332.

61. W. Burger, *Annual Report on the State of the Judiciary*, 62 A.B.A.J. 443 (1976).

62. *Id.*

63. Meyer, *Court Administration: The Newest Profession*, 10 DUQ. L. REV. 220 (1971).

64. B. DEVLIN, TRIAL BY JURY, 129-65 (1956).

65. Slater, *The System Works . . . Or Does It?* 2 TRIAL 36 (1975).

66. *See The Six Man Jury, A discussion before the Judicial Conference of the 4th Circuit*, 59 F.R.D. 180 (1972).

67. *Id.*

68. *See* Chapter 5 *supra*.

69. *See* Chapter 14 *supra*.

70. For a discussion of the time consumed in the trial of cases due to unnecessary voir dire questioning of jurors, *see* Rousseau v. West Coast House Movers, 256 Cal. App. 878, 64 Cal. Rptr. 655 (1967).

71. VANDERBILT, *supra* note 60, at 12.

72. Kairys, *Juror Selection: The Law, a Mathematical Method of Analysis, and a Case Study*, 9 AM. CRIM. L. Q. 771 (1972); *see also* 41 MO. L. REV. 446 (1976).

73. Burger, *Counsel for the Prosecution and Defense—Their Roles Under the Minimum Standards*, 8 AM. CRIM. L. Q. 2 (1969).

74. Lyman, *A Tradition Dies in Connecticut: Law Office Preparation for the Bar is Abolished*, 36 A.B.A.J. 21 (1950).

75. *See* Redmount, *Conceptual View of the Legal Education Process*, 24 J. LEGAL EDUC. 129 (1972); *see also* Ruud, *That Burgeoning Law School Enrollment is Portia*, 60 A.B.A.J. 182 (1974).

76. Heroux, *Responsible Lawyer's Responsibility: Continuing Legal Education*, 51 CHI. B. REC. 155 (1969).

77. Martindale, *Attorney's Liability in Non-client and Foreign Law Situations*, 14 CLEV. MAR. L. REV. 44 (1965); Spencer, *The House Counsel and the Unauthorized Practice of Law*, 33 UNAUTH. PR. NEWS 20 (1967).

78. Goodsby, *Study of the Criteria for Legal Education and Admission to the Bar*, 20 J. OF LEGAL EDUC. 175 (1968); Ehrlich, *A Critique of the Proposed New Admission Rule for the District Courts in the Second Circuit*, 61 A.B.A.J. 1385 (1975); Kaufman, *A Response to the Objections to the Second Circuit's Proposed District Court Admission Rules*, 61 A.B.A.J. 1514 (1975).

79. *Id.*

80. Annot., 45 A.L.R. 2d 1065 (1956).

81. *See* Comment, *Residency Requirement as a Prerequisite to Take the State Bar Examination*, 1 TEX. SO. L. REV. 231 (1971); *see also* Comment, *The Power of the State to Deny an Individual a License to Practice Law*, 25 OKLA. L. REV. 559 (1972).

82. *See* Note, *Easing Multistate Practice-Restrictions—'Good Cause' Based Limited Admissions*, 29 RUTGERS L. REV. 1182 (1976).

83. Covington & Eckler, *New Multistate Bar Exam*, 57 A.B.A.J. 1117 (1971).

84. Burger, *The Special Skills of Advocacy: Are Specialized Training and Certification of Advocates Essential to Our System of Justice*, 42 FORDHAM L. REV. 227 (1973).

85. *New Admission Rules for Federal District Courts*, 61 A.B.A.J. 945 (1975).

86. *See* ABA CODE OF PROFESSIONAL RESPONSIBILITY, preamble and preliminary statement; *see also* Arkin, *Self Regulation and Approaches to Maintaining Standards of Professional Integrity*, 30 U. MIAMI L. REV. 803 (1976).

87. Wright, CODE OF PROFESSIONAL RESPONSIBILITY, 14 ST. LOUIS U. L. J. 643 (1970); *see* PHILLIPS & P. McCOY, CONDUCT OF JUDGES AND LAWYERS, 7-20 (1952).

88. Goldfarb v. Virginia State Bar, 421 U.S. 773 (1975).

89. Bates v. State Bar of Ariz., — U.S. —, 97 S. Ct. 2691 (1977).

90. A.B.A. SPECIAL COMMITTEE ON EVALUATION OF DISCIPLINARY ENFORCEMENT, PROBLEMS AND RECOMMENDATIONS IN DISCIPLINARY ENFORCEMENT (1970). This Committee was headed by former Supreme Court Justice Tom C. Clark.

91. *Id.*

92. Hood, *Renewed Emphasis on Professional Responsibility*, 35 ALA. L. REV. 719 (1975); McKay, *Legal Education: Law, Lawyers, and Ethics*, 23 DEPAUL L. REV. 64 (1974).

93. Blain, *Professional Liability Claims: An Increasing Concern for Lawyers*, 59 ILL. B. J. 302 (1970).

94.  ABA CODE OF PROFESSIONAL RESPONSIBILITY EC 2-25. *See also* Marks, *Lawyer's Duty to Take all Comers and Many Who Do Not Come,* 30 U. MIAMI L. REV. 915 (1976).

95.  Argersinger v. Hamlin, 407 U.S. 25 (1972).

96.  Wice & Suwack, *Current Realities of Public Defender Programs: A National Survey and Analysis,* 10 CRIM. L. BULL. 161 (1974).

97.  Metzger, *Legal Clinics: Getting into the Routine,* 12 TRIAL 32 (1976).

98.  Marks, *Lawyer's Duty to Take all Comers and Many Who Do Not Come,* 30 U. MIAMI L. REV. 915 (1976).

99.  Comment, *Group and Other Legal Services for the Middle Class,* 10 SAN DIEGO L. REV. 333 (1973); Murphy, *Prepaid Taking Root,* 12 TRIAL 14 (1976).

100.  Brown, *Paralegal Profession,* 19 HOW. L. J. 117 (1976); Watermaker, *Impact of the Legal Assistant on the Delivery of Legal Services,* 10 J. BEVERLY HILL B. A. 22 (1976).

101.  A. POPE, ESSAY ON MAN.

102.  R. POUND, INTERPRETATIONS OF LEGAL HISTORY (1923).

103.  Vanderbilt, *The Essentials of a Sound Judicial System,* 48 NW. U. L. REV. 1 (1953).

# INDEX

References are to page numbers.

# INDEX

References are to page numbers.

Domicile, 155.
Dual system of courts, 135-47, 232.

**E**

Ejectment, 24, 108, 193-95, 198-99.
Ellesmere, controversy with Coke, 208.
Equity, 68-70, 108-09, 175, 203-20.
Erie R.R. v. Tompkins, 142-43.
Estates, 216, 239-40.
Evidence, 80-83.
Execution, 107-10.
Ex parte application, 44.
Extraordinary remedies, 195-98.

**F**

Federal courts, 140-47, 157.
Federal Judicial Center, 248.
Federal Rules of Civil Procedure, 17-18, 225-29.
Findings of fact, 101-02.
Foreclosure, 214-15.
Foreign corporations, jurisdiction over, 149-58.
Forms of action, 183-201, 217.
Forum non conveniens, 156.
Full faith and credit, 111, 137.

**G**

Garnishment, 110.
General issue plea, 200-01.
General verdict, 103-04.

**H**

Habeas corpus, 196, 244.
Harmless error, 120.
Hearsay, 80-81.
Hung jury, 94.

**I**

Impeaching verdict, 96.
Impeachment, 253.
Impleader, 166-67.
Indispensable parties, 165-66.
Inference, 90-91.

Injunction, 24, 43-45, 52, 209-11.
Institute of Judicial Administration, 248.
Instructions, 86-87.
Interpleader, 171-73, 201, 218.
Interrogatories, 51-52.
Intervention, 167-68.
Interviews with clients, 14.
Issue preclusion, 114-16.

**J**

Joinder,
  Claims, 161, 201, 217-18.
  Parties, 164-66, 201, 217-18.
Judges, 249-55.
  Education, 254.
  Qualifications, 249.
  Removal, 253.
  Selection, 250-52.
  Tenure, 252-53.
Judgment, 97-98, 103-16.
Judicial administration, 247-65.
Jurisdiction,
  General, 4-7.
  Over parties, 7-9.
  Subject matter, 4-7.
Jury, 66-74, 182, 203, 229-31, 258-59.

**L**

Law Clerks, 255-56.
Lawyers, 3, 183, 240-41, 259-63.
Legal Aid, 262.
Lien of judgment, 107.
Local actions, 136-38.

**M**

Magistrates, 256.
Mandamus, 195-96.
Masters, 256.
Merger of law and equity, 221-32.
Minimum contacts, 154-55.
Mixed law and fact questions, 94-96.
Mortgage, 214-15.
Motions, 27-35, 40-44.

308

# INDEX

References are to page numbers.

## N

National Center for State Courts, 148.
National law, 147.
Necessary parties, 165-66.
Negative pregnant, 37.
New trial, 98-100.
N. Y. Code of 1848, 224.
Nonresidents, jurisdiction over, 149-58.
Note of issue, 63-64.
Notice,
    Appeal, 122.
    Class action, 170.
    Trial, 63-64.

## O

Oath, 75.
Opening statements, 74.
Opinion evidence, 81-82.
Opinions, 126-27.
Oral argument, 125.
Orders, 34, 42-45.

## P

Parajudicial personnel, 255-58.
Paraprofessionals, 263.
Particulars, bill of, 91.
Parties, 164-73.
Pennoyer v. Neff, 149-58.
Peremptory challenge, 73.
Physical examination, 52-53.
"Plain" error, 121.
Plea bargaining, 243.
Pleading, 12-14, 227.
Polling jury, 96-97.
Post conviction remedies, 244.
Pound, Roscoe, 248, 264.
Precedent, 26, 127-31.
Preclusion, 112-16.
Preference, 64-65.
Prejudicial error, 120.
Prerogative writs, 195-98.
Presumptions, 91-93.
Pretrial conference, 58-60, 62, 228.

Preventive law, 240.
Probate, 216.
Process, 7-9.
Prohibition, 196-97.
Pro se representation, 2.
Public defender, 243, 262.

## Q

Quantum meruit, 191.
Quantum valebat, 192.
Quasi-contract, 192.
Quo warranto, 196.

## R

Real party in interest, 166.
Reception of English law, 221-22.
Record on appeal, 123-24.
Redirect examination, 77.
References, 256.
Reformation, 24, 213-14.
Rejoinder, 201.
Relevancy, 46, 50.
Remedies, 23-25, 104-05, 203, 212-15.
Replevin, 24, 107, 179-80.
Replication, 201.
Rescission, 24, 213-14.
Res judicata, 111-16, 128, 170.
Restraining order, 42-45.
Roth v. Bernhard, 230.

## S

School desegregation, 245.
Self-help, 1.
Settlement, 1, 60, 65, 236, 240.
Severance, 63, 173.
Social problem litigation, 244.
Special verdict, 103.
Specific performance, 24, 211-12.
Speedy trial rules, 242.
Splitting a cause of action, 162.
Stare decisis, 26, 127-31.
Subpoena, 49-50.
Summary judgment, 32, 54-58, 62, 228.

# INDEX

References are to page numbers.